Experiments in Criminology and Law

Experiments in Criminology and Law

A Research Revolution

Edited by
Christine Horne and
Michael J. Lovaglia

ROWMAN & LITTLEFIELD PUBLISHERS, INC.
Lanham • Boulder • New York • Toronto • Plymouth, UK

ROWMAN & LITTLEFIELD PUBLISHERS, INC.

Published in the United States of America
by Rowman & Littlefield Publishers, Inc.
A wholly owned subsidiary of The Rowman & Littlefield Publishing Group, Inc.
4501 Forbes Boulevard, Suite 200, Lanham, Maryland 20706
www.rowmanlittlefield.com

Estover Road
Plymouth PL6 7PY
United Kingdom

British Library Cataloguing in Publication Information Available

Library of Congress Cataloging-in-Publication Data

Experiments in criminology and law : a research revolution / [edited by] Christine Horne
  and Michael J. Lovaglia.—2nd ed.
      p. cm.
  ISBN-13: 978-0-7425-6027-7 (cloth : alk. paper)
  ISBN-10: 0-7425-6027-9 (cloth : alk. paper)
  ISBN-13: 978-0-7425-6028-4 (pbk. : alk. paper)
  ISBN-10: 0-7425-6028-7 (pbk. : alk. paper)
    1. Criminology—Research. 2. Criminology—Experiments. 3. Criminal law—
  Research. I. Horne, Christine. II. Lovaglia, Michael J.
  HV6024.5.E97 2008
  364.072'4—dc22   2007028256

Printed in the United States of America

⊚™ The paper used in this publication meets the minimum requirements of American
National Standard for Information Sciences—Permanence of Paper for Printed Library
Materials, ANSI/NISO Z39.48-1992.

Contents

Foreword

James F. Short, Jr.

*E*xperiments in Criminology and Law: A Research Revolution* is as timely as it is important. Lawrence Sherman (2005) notes that field experimentation has a long but uneven history in criminology. Recently, however, he suggests that with major support from foundations and federal agencies, it has achieved "Warp Speed" (Sherman 2005:127). Acceptance of experimentation in the law enforcement community has been dramatic, thanks to organizations such as the Vera Institute, the pioneering spirit of police chiefs such as Anthony Bouza, and the support of the Police Foundation and the Police Executive Research Forum. Academic and independent research communities embraced field experimentation with enthusiasm, culminating in the establishment of the Academy of Experimental Criminology (AEC) in 1999 and the *Journal of Experimental Criminology*, published soon thereafter.

Virtually all of this experimentation, however, has taken place in various *field situations*, in which treatments are systematically applied to one set of offenders (or probationers or parolees), incidents, such as domestic violence, or other units of analysis, and not in comparison with others. While these have yielded much useful information, despite all-too-frequent "no difference" results, because of the untidiness of individual and social lives, they inevitably raise as many questions as they solve.

Laboratory experiments attempt to eliminate the messiness of our lives by controlling as many variables as possible in order to isolate causal processes. Such experiments have enjoyed success in applications in classrooms and in a few other relatively controlled organizational settings. Whether they can ever be successful in understanding and controlling crime is a very important question. This volume brings laboratory experimentation to bear on several issues of relevance to criminology. Comments by eminent sociologists of crime and law add to the mix. The result is a volume rich in theory, method, and substantive findings that criminologists of many stripes will find provocative, stimulating, and at times entertaining.

REFERENCE

Sherman, Lawrence W. 2005. "The Use and Usefulness of Criminology, 1751–2005: Enlightened Justice and Its Failures." *Annals of the American Academy of Political and Social Science* 600:115–35.

1

Introduction: Why Experiment Now?

Coordinating Research Methods to Accelerate Innovation in Law, Crime, and Deviance

Christine Horne and Michael J. Lovaglia

The answers to three questions can help advance research in criminology, deviance, and law:

1. How can experiments promote research in social science?
2. What are the most effective roles for field experiments and basic laboratory research?
3. Why might now be time to expand the role of experiments in social research programs?

The twenty-first century may become the era of basic research in the social sciences much as the nineteenth century was characterized by advances produced in physics and chemistry, and the twentieth century by the great breakthroughs in the biological sciences. Basic laboratory research played an important role in the rapid advance of physics, chemistry, and biology. It also is an efficient tool for developing and testing *social* theories. Computer and Internet technology have expanded our ability to conduct basic experiments in the social sciences. Thus we may be poised for a period of explosive knowledge growth. The results of research using various methods can complement each other when researchers using them appreciate the knowledge gained by others' work. Basic laboratory experiments, for example, can efficiently develop and test theories that are useful for explaining results found using other methods (Szmatka and Lovaglia 1996).

Suppose that a researcher has the idea that an unseen force acts equally on all matter large and small. He expects, therefore, that all falling objects will have a constant rate of acceleration. He approaches the problem by systematically observing a wide variety of falling objects. He collects videos of airplanes that fall out of the sky and crash; birds falling after being shot by hunters; raindrops, snowflakes, and hailstones falling from clouds; ball bearings of different sizes; and bricks, Ping-Pong balls, and handkerchiefs dropped from the Leaning Tower of Pisa. The rate of acceleration is calculated for the object in each video. All possible data is collected including the mass of the objects, weather conditions, elevation above sea level, and any other convenient information. How likely is it that this researcher could ever confirm that gravity acts with equal effect on the mass of raindrops and snowflakes and bricks and Ping-Pong balls? The likelihood that he would arrive at the correct formula for the rate of acceleration seems even less certain. Yet four hundred years ago, Galileo's simple experiments—rolling metal balls of different sizes, carefully machined to reduce resistance, down ramps—demonstrated convincingly the equal-acceleration effect.

Crime is no easier to understand than gravity. (Many of us would likely agree that it is, in fact, far more complicated.) Is it surprising, then, that research in criminology has difficulty identifying the mechanisms that produce crime? Crime research is methodologically sophisticated. Criminologists are very good at collecting data and analyzing it. But progress in criminological research (and in social science generally) requires more than increasing methodological rigor or conducting additional tests of a particular theory. Sampson (2000) succinctly captures the key problem of knowledge growth in criminology. "[M]ost criminological theory is static in logic and handicapped by a focus on (allegedly) fixed explanatory categories, thereby failing to address the processes and dynamics leading to criminal events. The most important thing about crime that we do not know, in other words, concerns its causal *social processes*" (Sampson 2000:711). Investigating fundamental causal processes is the raison d'etre of laboratory research.

In this chapter we describe the role of laboratory research in developing the understanding of causal processes that is necessary for cumulating social science knowledge. We discuss ways in which laboratory experiments provide a complement to field experiments—an increasingly important tool in criminology. We then present an example illustrating how one might design a laboratory research program to study an issue of interest to criminologists. We conclude by reiterating the potential of laboratory experiments to contribute to increased understanding of fundamental processes in crime, deviance, and law.

CUMULATING SOCIAL SCIENCE KNOWLEDGE

Researchers in law and criminology have a toolbox of methods at their disposal. Coordinated use of these multiple methods could produce substantial benefits. Traditionally, criminologists have relied on data from such sources as surveys, case studies, and official records. Recently, despite a tradition of resistance, they have recognized the usefulness of field experiments for studying crime (Sherman 2005), but they remain skeptical of laboratory experiments. How might laboratory experiments, in conjunction with other methods, increase our understanding of fundamental social processes?

Social science knowledge grows (Wagner and Berger 1985). The philosophy of science explicates this process differently today than it did a century ago. (Philosophical knowledge, it seems, also grows.) Rather than testing the truth value of theories, current research aims to test aspects of a theory in order to improve it. Theory guides empirical research. Research then guides the development of theory. Along the way some aspects may be falsified. Because theories are simplified representations of phenomena, they are all necessarily false. But all good theories also contain a core element of truth. Rather than attempting to falsify theories (as Popper [1965] proposed early in the twentieth century), researchers try to expand a theory's useful core, continuing to promote research that solves practical problems. Kuhn ([1962], 1970) pointed out that scientists doing normal science continued to work comfortably with theories, even as disconfirming evidence accumulated, leading eventually to a paradigm shift. Lakatos (1970) proposed that scientists actually worked in research *programmes.* Loosely confederated researchers (often using different methods) continued to develop a theory as long as it generated good research—research that solved important problems.

The cumulative nature of knowledge, gained through systematic observation of social phenomena and dissemination of results, means that researchers make faster progress in their own work by building on the work of others. No single study, no matter how well-designed, thorough, and rigorous, completely answers any research question. Continuous interplay between theory and empirical research is essential for cumulating knowledge of social phenomena. Research that takes advantage of empirical findings, developing and testing theory accordingly, will produce more knowledge growth.

Laboratory experiments are an important tool in this process because they provide the opportunity to tinker, to quickly test a theoretical idea—thus allowing a researcher to reject the idea or develop it further. Understanding is further increased when researchers rely on standard experimental settings that are part of a research program. That is, when a single experiment is unconnected to any other experimental work, our learning is limited. When research is conducted in standardized settings, results of separate studies can be easily compared. Each experiment can take advantage of knowledge gained from earlier ones. Thus programs of experimental research produce more rapid theoretical development than is possible when individual, unrelated studies take years to complete. Experimental research programs greatly enhance theoretical development because they allow us to vary theoretically important factors quickly and systematically.

Laboratory results do not generalize to the larger population. Rather, they tell us something about the conditions under which the theoretical mechanisms operate and produce the predicted outcomes. They help us understand causal processes. That is, they test a theory, giving us greater confidence in it. Thus, experimental results subtly shift the burden of proof, challenging researchers using other methods to demonstrate that the theoretical processes tested in the lab do not occur in the wild (Roth 1995).

Because of their strengths in contributing to theory development, laboratory experiments are increasingly important for advancing knowledge in social sciences such as political science and sociology. Recent Nobel Prize awards to experimenters Vernon Smith and Daniel Kahneman demonstrate that social scientists recognize the importance of experimental work. Given the role of the laboratory in increasing the pace of theoretical development, adding laboratory experiments to the toolkit of criminological research could be especially beneficial.

Laboratory research is, of course, just one tool. To achieve sustained success, a research program must coordinate research in and out of the lab. Theory that is *only* tested and developed in a laboratory context may or may not be useful. That is, while laboratory experiments are particularly helpful for testing and developing theory, their results only provide evidence that processes and mechanisms operate as theoretically predicted. They contribute to theoretical knowledge. But they do not tell us how useful the theory is in a particular setting. Thus knowledge growth is increased when theories are tested in both laboratory and naturally occurring settings. Such coordination is facilitated when researchers who use laboratory experiments are familiar with the work of those using other methods, and vice versa. Criminology and law journals could publish the results of lab experiments so that they are accessible to criminologists. Researchers working on similar theoretical issues, but with expertise in different methods, might collaborate. In order to maximize knowledge growth, laboratory research should be conducted in conjunction with more traditional approaches such as survey research, case studies, and use of official records, as well as with field experiments—a method that is receiving increasing attention.

COORDINATING LABORATORY AND FIELD EXPERIMENTS: DEVELOPING BASIC KNOWLEDGE AND APPLYING IT TO IMPORTANT SOCIAL PROBLEMS

How might laboratory experiments contribute to field research? Field experiments in the social sciences are analogous to randomized clinical trials in medicine. When criminal cases are randomly assigned to different procedures, with extraneous factors that could influence outcomes carefully controlled, researchers can ascertain the effectiveness of those procedures with some confidence. Replications in different settings that confirm initial findings increase that confidence.

Suppose, for example, that a radically new intervention was developed to control drunk drivers. A field experiment could be conducted in which arrested drunk drivers are randomly assigned to different types of process. Some might spend a weekend in jail, some might be diverted to alcohol abuse awareness classes, and some to the new intervention. All could then be monitored for indicators of drinking and driving during the following year. Suppose further that those who underwent the new intervention showed no signs of drinking and driving during the year, but that the others showed the usual rates. The new intervention could then be implemented on a trial basis in a few communities and would soon diffuse to others as its effectiveness and practicality became widely known.

Field experiments are the only research method that allows us to try out new approaches to difficult social problems (Sherman 2005). Laboratory research has the potential to increase the success of field studies. Descriptions of two experimental research programs follow, one that used field experiments exclusively and another that based its field experiments on a foundation of basic laboratory research.

Arresting Domestic Violence: Experimenting with Police Procedures

In 1981, police in Minneapolis changed the way they responded to reports of domestic violence. Police officers had the discretion to arrest the person who committed the assault, order him to leave the premises for a period of time, or provide brief counseling. There was concern that domestic violence was treated too leniently, resulting in little deterrent effect on future violence. Sherman and Berk (1984) designed a field experiment to test whether making an arrest in domestic violence cases deterred future assaults better than did the other two options (separating the couple or counseling). Whenever police officers responded to a domestic violence call, they were randomly assigned a procedure to follow: arrest, separation, or counseling.

Researchers tracked the behavior of suspects in the study for six months following the domestic violence incident. Results showed a deterrent effect for arrest. That is, suspects who had been arrested were somewhat less likely to commit another assault during the subsequent six months than were those who had been separated or counseled. The beneficial effect of arrest, however, was small.

The study had a dramatic effect on public policy. Arrest in domestic violence cases became the preferred procedure in many police departments. Fifteen states passed mandatory arrest laws.

The experiment also addressed a long-standing dispute between two theoretical traditions in criminology. First, if punishment acts to deter future criminal behavior, then suspects who had been arrested would be *less* likely to commit another assault later than would those who had been separated or counseled. A second theoretical tradition, labeling theory, suggests the opposite result. Labeling theory proposes that when individuals experience arrest, they become labeled as criminals by themselves and others. The criminal label then increases the likelihood of subsequent criminal behavior. If labeling increases future criminal acts, then those arrested for domestic violence would be *more* likely to commit a later assault. The findings provide no support for labeling theory, showing instead that punishment had a deterrent effect.

Debate over implications for social theory and public policy continued, however. Over the next decade, the experiment was replicated in several other police jurisdictions (Sherman et al. 1992; Berk, Campbell, Klap, and Western 1992; Pate and Hamilton 1992). The new results painted a more complicated picture that supported both the deterrent effect of arrest and labeling theory, but for different kinds of suspects. The new studies found that arrest deterred suspects who were employed, perhaps because arrest is more serious for those with more to lose. For the unemployed, arrest had the opposite effect, as predicted by labeling theory. Unemployed men who had been arrested were *more* likely to commit a subsequent assault than were those who had been separated or counseled. The theoretical advance was exciting but it left policy implications unresolved. In practice, we are still unsure of the benefits of arrest to deter domestic violence. What intervention should we try now?

Equalizing Opportunities for Educational Success: Experimenting in the Classroom

Compare the overall progress of field experiments in the context of domestic violence with progress in an area in which basic laboratory research and rapid theory growth were ongoing. We focus here on Elizabeth Cohen's work applying understanding of status processes to education. Cohen demonstrated how fundamental sociological theory, developed in conjunction with laboratory experiments, could be successfully applied in the classroom.

Initial research on status processes was supported by basic laboratory experiments (Wagner and Berger 1985; Berger and Zelditch 1993). *Status characteristics theory* explained how status differences in the larger society shape status hierarchies in small groups. It developed to the point where it could precisely predict the influence that individuals had based on their position in the status hierarchy of a group. More experiments tested those developments and led to related theories that explained aspects of distributive justice and legitimation (Wagner and Berger 1993). The status characteristics (and related expectation states) research program became one of the most successful areas of study in sociology, its research regularly funded by the National Science Foundation and published in top sociology journals.

Despite enormous progress in understanding important social processes, the status characteristics and expectation states research program was vulnerable to the criticism that it was irrelevant. Crucial to its legitimacy was the application of basic theory to address an important social problem.

Elizabeth Cohen's research on the participation and achievement rates of students in grade school through high school is one such application (E. G. Cohen 1993). She began with basic research on race as a status characteristic. In the early 1970s, Cohen and Roper (1972) studied a classroom phenomenon they termed "interracial interaction disability." They proposed that, because race is a status characteristic, African-American students would have less opportunity than European-American students to participate in the classroom in ways that advanced their learning and social status. They then conducted a series of laboratory experiments that not only demonstrated the phenomenon but also showed that with special training, African-American students could overcome problems in interracial interaction, although at some cost to group harmony. That is, while African-American students were able to successfully demonstrate their acquisition of a technical skill in the classroom setting, European-American students resisted giving respect and cooperation to them. Thus the intervention did not fully solve problems in interracial interaction. Application of status characteristics theory to improve outcomes in the classroom remained problematic.

Years of laboratory research on status attainment processes followed, producing important insights. For example, Ridgeway (1982) discovered that competent low-status group members who presented themselves as group-motivated could overcome some of the resistance to increased status commensurate with their ability to contribute to group goals (suggesting a means of reducing the European-American resistance found in Cohen and Roper's [1972] research). Researchers also identified processes through which status characteristics are created and become cultural beliefs (Ridgeway 1991, culminating in Ridgeway, Boyle, Kuipers, and Robinson 1998).

While this laboratory research was being conducted, Cohen was working outside of the laboratory to make systematic interventions in classroom procedure a routine part of program development in the field of education (E. G. Cohen 1993). For example, her students showed that reading ability was an important status characteristic in grade school classrooms (Rosenholtz 1985; Tammivaara 1982). Another piece of the knowledge puzzle grew out of the applied research program in combination with the experience of Elizabeth Cohen's (1993) graduate students who were also teachers. They discovered that emphasizing the importance of multiple abilities reduced some negative effects of status differences in the classroom. In terms of basic theory, the construction of multiple status characteristics mitigated the effects of status differences because most students would be higher on some characteristics and lower on others. Musical ability, for example, could be presented as important along with reading.

Elizabeth Cohen and her students then collaborated with E. DeAvila, a developmental psychologist, to develop a curriculum that emphasized a broad array of important abilities. This curriculum enhanced the academic performance of all students while mitigating the negative effects of status differences for members of diverse ethnic and racial groups (E. G. Cohen and Lotan 1995; E. G. Cohen et al. 1997). It has been successfully instituted at several different grade levels in schools in various regions of the United States and in several countries (E. G. Cohen and Lotan 1997). The final phase of the project involves systematic interventions in teacher training to successfully implement and perpetuate demanding cooperative learning strategies in the classroom (E. G. Cohen et al. 2002, 2004).

Comparable success from field experiments to control domestic violence would have produced at least a few model communities in which domestic violence is dramatically reduced. To date, however, no one response to domestic violence has been demonstrated to be dramatically more effective than other common interventions. Does that mean that nothing works when it comes to crime control? Emphatically not. It means that we have yet to do the coordinated series of laboratory and field experiments needed to discover and implement what works.

Perhaps because Elizabeth Cohen held a position as professor in a school of education rather than in a sociology department, she was ideally suited for the work of interrelating basic research, applied research, and educational program development. She understood and kept abreast with basic theoretical developments in status characteristics theory that she and her colleagues in sociology were rapidly producing. At the same time, she was immersed in the applied problems of effective teaching in the school of education. Thus, she had the necessary knowledge of the laboratory and the field, as well as the autonomy to work through the complexities of a successful application of basic research. Bernard P. Cohen (1989) notes that successful application of basic theory to program development in a complex organization requires (a) basic science that produces and tests new knowledge, (b) applied science that finds new uses for that knowledge, and (c) a complex and sometimes messy process that he terms *engineering* to solve the myriad technical problems required for successful application in a naturally occurring social environment. In the field of education, Elizabeth Cohen managed to do all three.

AN EXAMPLE: IS THERE MORE TO DETERRENCE THAN CERTAINTY, SEVERITY, AND CELERITY?

Are similar successes possible in law and criminology? Understanding of social status processes grew out of a research program that relied on standardized experimental settings. What might a similar laboratory research program in criminology look like? In this chapter, we use deterrence research to provide an example of how one might design a systematic experimental program to contribute to understanding of fundamental social processes in criminology.

Questions of deterrence have been important to the study of crime and punishment since the 1700s when Bentham proposed that effective punishment must be certain, costly relative to the rewards of crime, and swift (Sherman 2005). If we convincingly make the case for deterrence experiments, then the usefulness of laboratory experiments for furthering progress in other areas of criminological theory will be easier to envision. Deterrence is also an unusual research area in criminology having benefited from a few good laboratory experiments.

Recently, Nagin and Pogarsky (2003) conducted an experiment to jointly test the deterrent effects of punishment certainty and severity on cheating. They found, as earlier research had suggested, that certainty has a significant deterrent effect but that the level of severity used in their study did not. The interaction of certainty and severity also had no significant effect. Providing direction for future development of deterrence theory, they also found that cheating was more prevalent among those who preferred delayed penalties and those prone to self serving bias.

This experiment tells us something—but it has limitations. It relied on a sample of college students, no actual crime was involved, and the severity of the punishment was very mild. Because of these limitations, the results would be more informative if the study were part of a sustained experimental research program. We want to know not only how certainty and severity operate under the conditions of this particular experiment—conducted with college students who were given opportunities for fairly mild forms of deviance that had relatively small costs and benefits. We also want to know how these findings might shift if we were to look at a different population, or a different kind of deviance, or a different range of punishment severity. Previous experiments investigating deterrence have not established why certainty, severity, and celerity affect deterrence because they have not been incorporated into a theoretical research program capable of producing rapid knowledge growth.

Given the few basic experiments investigating deterrence, it is not surprising that we know little about the reasons for the deterrent effects of certainty, severity, and celerity of punishment, let alone the complicating factors of individual differences in impulse control or the myriad other factors that could have an effect. Even a relatively small program of laboratory research on deterrence (perhaps only a few hundred studies) might well produce substantial progress—and, perhaps, surprising results.

A Standardized Experimental Setting for Deterrence Research

Here we sketch the outlines of a standardized experimental setting for studying deterrence that could help speed theoretical development. The setting takes the form of a relatively simple computer game that can be played by individuals singly or in groups connected by the Internet. The goal is to create a portable, flexible experimental setting so that diverse participants can complete a variety of experiments. Because the setting is standardized, and changed as little as possible from one experiment to the next, results of experiments can be compared more easily. Each new experiment replicates some aspect of an earlier experiment and tests something new as well.

In our Standardized Deterrence Environment, participants can do routine, even boring, clerical-type tasks to earn money as law-abiding citizens, up to $20 per hour for superior performers. Participants are paid $1 for each piece of work completed with an additional $0.25 going to a bonus pool to be divided by participants who agree to a follow-up session. Because not all participants will return for a second session, the potential bonus might be quite large. Participants see the current size of the pool, several hundred dollars, generated by past participants.

The bonus pool provides the opportunity to deviate from the law-abiding, piecework routine. Participants discover that a "bug" in the system allows them to receive extra pay by typing a particular pattern of keystrokes after submitting each piece of work. When deviant participants time the procedure correctly, the computer will credit between $1 and $10 to their account. This money comes directly out of the bonus pool and diverting it is stealing from participants who contributed it. Participants are shown that past participants have managed to take considerable amounts of money from the bonus pool, one successfully taking $200.

Participants are informed that researchers were unable to fix the bug due to technical and research constraints but have programmed random keystroke monitoring to catch participants who try it. *Certainty of punishment varies* with the percentage of keystrokes monitored, from 1 percent to 100 percent. Participants who are caught forfeit their illicit proceeds for that segment of the experiment. *Severity of punishment varies* as they also incur a fine from $1 to the total value of their account. *Celerity of punishment varies* as the fine is levied either immediately and deducted from their ongoing total, at the end of the session when participants are paid in cash, or from their paycheck that will arrive from a few days to a few weeks hence.

The first series of experiments in the setting would continue until a pattern of deterrence becomes clear. Because of the flexibility in levels of certainty, severity, and celerity, a large number of participants will eventually be required. For example, 10 levels of certainty x 5 levels of severity x 5 levels of celerity produces an experiment with 250 conditions. The rule of thumb that 20 participants are usually required per condition produces an estimated total of 5,000 participants. That large a project would require several years and perhaps $150,000. The advantage of a standardized setting is that results begin coming in immediately from a few initial conditions. For example, comparing three quite different levels of certainty, while holding constant severity and celerity, would be a good place to start because the most consistent evidence exists for the deterrent effect of certainty. Different levels of certainty, severity, and celerity then can be added based on results from initial levels that demonstrate deterrent effects. The results might also point to the theoretical importance of other factors. These additional factors could also be incorporated. Thus, initial experiments will lead to new theoretical development, which will lead in turn to new experiments. The theory will develop in conjunction with a series of empirical studies, each using the standardized experimental setting.

Advantages of the Proposed Standardized Experimental Session

The proposed standardized setting has a number of advantages over the deterrence experiments of the past, each conducted separately in its own unique setting. First, in this setting deviance actually harms others. One major challenge for researchers using laboratory experiments is that they cannot produce or condone actual crimes to study. Instead, experimenters create a situation in which some kind of lesser deviance like cheating can occur. Often this lesser deviance does not actually harm other experimental participants. But a primary reason that we object to many criminal behaviors is that those behaviors cause harm to others. The deviance in the proposed setting comes closer to such crimes in that it actually affects other participants. While not illegal, taking money from the bonus pool causes demonstrable harm to those participants who do not steal and whose financial earnings are reduced by those who do steal.

Second, the setting allows researchers to explore differences in behavior across kinds of people as well as to explicitly investigate the reasons for those differences. A frequent criticism of laboratory experiments is that a sample of college students is unlikely to include many individuals who are or will become serious criminals. While laboratory experiments often produce results in basic agreement with those found by other methods (Bornstein 1999), studies conducted with different kinds of participants could produce substantially different results (Block and Gerety 1995). Such discrepancies occur when the characteristics of individuals interact with the causal factors manipulated in the experiment. For example, there is theoretical reason to think that convicts and college students might differ in their levels of self-control (Gottfredson and Hirschi 1990). If they do (if convicts give less weight to future outcomes than college students), then the speed with which punishment occurs ought to be a more important deterrent factor for convicts than for college students. Using our standardized setting, the interactions between individual level characteristics (like self-control) and external conditions can be investigated systematically. Further, as noted above, experiments using the standardized setting described here could actually be conducted with a variety of participants. Because the experiment relies on laptop computers, it is portable and can be presented to many different kinds of people: browsers in shopping malls and on the Internet, prisoners, conference attendees, and students.

Third, the standardized setting allows researchers to investigate a range of punishment types and severity. Some scholars suggest that the punishments used in experiments are less severe than those used by the criminal justice system. The fact that moving from a low level of punishment to a slightly higher level affects behavior in an experiment does not necessarily mean that moving from a high level of punishment to an even higher level will affect behavior outside the lab (Heckathorn 1985). Others argue that severity of punishment has little or no effect, except possibly when it causes substantial emotional or physical harm (McCarthy and Hagan 2005). That is, humane punishment seems to have no effect. Researchers obviously cannot impose inhumane punishments on experiment participants. But, certainly the kind of punishment imposed could vary. For example, we propose that initial experiments conducted using this standardized setting use financial punishments—if subjects steal, they lose money. But a test of the severity hypothesis should also investigate the possible deterrent effect of various characteristics of incarceration—for example, the loss of time available for engaging in desired activities. The standardized setting can be adapted to accomplish this. Participants could be recruited for studies that last from one to four hours. Then, in the first hour of the experiment, they would discover that those caught cheating could expect a lengthy process that could last from one to three hours. Those not caught cheating could leave early, earning in one hour what they thought they might earn in two, three, or four hours. While not incarceration, the prospect of an hour or more of detention constrains participants in a way that has not been done in other deterrence experiments.

Fourth, the standardized setting can also be adapted to investigate additional questions beyond the straightforward effects of severity, certainty, and celerity. For example, will the various aspects of punishment have an effect on the likelihood that a participant will re-offend after being caught? Using the standardized setting, we can determine the likelihood that a participant caught taking money from the bonus pool during one segment of the study will again take money during a subsequent segment.

A series of experiments conducted using a standard experimental setting has substantial advantages over separate experiments conducted in unique settings. As suggested above, such a research program can address many of the criticisms that might be raised regarding any single experiment—criticisms regarding the characteristics of experimental participants, deviance, and punishment—because variation in these elements can be incorporated and explicitly investigated. While no individual study can examine all of these elements, a series of experiments can.

These ideas about potential studies using the standardized experimental setting are necessarily preliminary suggestions. As researchers begin to conduct experiments and empirical results start to come in, we may have more exciting ideas. These new theoretical ideas can be incorporated and tested with relative ease. As we quickly and systematically test new ideas, our knowledge will grow.

The same process of developing standardized research settings will work for examining other prominent theories in law and criminology—learning theory, strain theory, differential association theory, and others.[1] Experimental settings can be developed to test almost any theory. The development of such settings in the context of ongoing research programs will facilitate the growth of knowledge. Laboratories are knowledge-creation machines.

MOVING FORWARD

Sherman's (2005) history of field experiments in criminology shows that the experiments of crime control researchers have introduced at least a dozen effective new procedures that have been widely implemented. Examples include the invention of a police force paid by the state in 1750s England, sentencing criminals to prison rather than hanging, community organization to prevent crime, and numerous changes in police procedure. Considering the small number of criminology experiments conducted during the last 250 years, field experiments have been remarkably efficient at producing innovations.

Compare the results of crime control researchers to those of medical researchers. Progress in understanding cancer, for example, was slow in the early years when researchers and physicians relied on treatments—trying surgery, chemotherapy, and so forth to see what worked. Understanding increased exponentially following the discovery of DNA. Laboratory research on fundamental processes at the cellular level led to increased knowledge of the mechanisms contributing to cancer. In the medical sciences more generally, researchers have conducted many thousands of laboratory experiments and clinical trials to increase understanding and, in turn, to discover and refine new medicines and procedures. The number of innovations in medicine is, therefore, many times larger than in crime control. The ratio of new crime control procedures to field experiments is high in criminology, but overall progress is painfully slow.[2] And we still do not understand the underlying causal processes that produce crime (Sampson 2000).

Just as attempts at cancer treatment without understanding of the underlying processes led to little advancement, so field experiments without better understanding of social mechanisms may not get us very far. If we do not understand more deeply the processes that produce crime, we are unlikely to discover effective new procedures to try out in a field experiment, and we are not going to understand why an intervention fails or succeeds. Field experiments that compare only procedures currently in use are unlikely to show dramatic results. Further, new procedures based on common sense or untested theory are unlikely to work. A system of field experimentation standing alone may well say little about *why* an intervention works or does not work. It will always be vulnerable to the conclusion that nothing works very well.

Incorporating laboratory experiments in the study of law and crime enhances rather than diminishes the value of other methods. Researchers are touchy about their methods. Most social researchers are comfortable with thinking about research problems from more than one theoretical angle while testily defending the priority of their method against all contenders. Methodological rifts have a long history, from broad approaches like qualitative versus quantitative to more specific areas of contention like closed- or open-ended interview questions. Researchers' attachment to particular methods may stem from the research process—researchers occasionally play with theories to formulate a research design but work and live every day with their method (Szmatka and Lovaglia 1996). Knowledge gained through the systematic collection of data by any method is useful to researchers committed to finding the answers to important questions. The use of multiple methods—each with its own strengths—will advance knowledge more than reliance on any single method alone. Laboratory experiments are one, thus far underutilized, tool.

Suppose that a dozen crime laboratories at top universities each conducted only six good experiments a year trying to find effective new methods to control crime. We might expect a few good prospects to try out in field experiments every year. Perhaps one of those might prove worth implementing. Only one effective new crime control procedure per year, every year. Let's do it.

The chapters in this volume describe work that could represent the beginnings of a network of laboratories researching new ideas related to law, crime, and deviance. Some chapters report the results of experiments that test existing theories in law and criminology. Others propose and test new theories and show how they are relevant for criminological and legal concerns.

Chapters 2 and 3 test theories of self-control and deterrence. Gottfredson and Hirschi's (1990) general theory of crime suggests that people who have low self-control are more likely to commit crimes. Detlef Fetchenauer, Josef Simon, and Felix Fetchenhauer test this theory. Will Kalkhoff and Robb Willer test the implications of self-control for understanding the effects of deterrence. Travis Hirschi's reactions follow.

Chapters 5 and 6 focus on the social environment in which deviance and control of deviance occurs. Christine Horne and John Hoffmann present a theory of norm enforcement and discuss the implications of the theory for understanding the relation between neighborhood characteristics and informal control. Wesley Younts looks at the effect of an individual's relationships on the extent to which that individual comes to accept and transmit justifications of deviant behavior. These chapters are followed with comments by Robert Bursik.

Chapters 8 and 9 focus on law. Jeffrey Lucas, Corina Graif, and Michael Lovaglia look at prosecutorial abuses of discretion. They test a theoretical argument identifying the conditions under which prosecutors behave inappropriately. Richard McAdams and Janice Nadler focus on the effectiveness of the legal system. They argue that law has not only deterrent and legitimacy effects, but also an expressive effect. That is, law draws attention to a particular behavior, thereby affecting the likelihood that people will engage in it. Lisa McIntyre's comments follow.

To conclude the book, the editors provide some summary comments. Then David Farrington and Christopher Uggen respond to the ideas presented regarding the potential of laboratory experiments, in conjunction with field experiments and other methods, to contribute to the growth of knowledge in the fields of law and criminology.

NOTES

1. The chapters in this book describe alternative experimental settings developed to test other theoretical ideas relevant to law and crime.

2. This is not to say there is no progress. Crime has declined over the last several decades. But researchers still debate *why* this is so.

REFERENCES

Berger, Joseph, and Morris Zelditch, Jr., eds. 1993. *Theoretical Research Programs: Studies in the Growth of Theory*. Palo Alto, CA: Stanford University Press.

Berk, Richard A., Alec Campbell, Ruth Klap, and Bruce Western. 1992. "The Deterrent Effect of Arrest in Incidents of Domestic Violence: A Bayesian Analysis of Four Field Experiments." *American Sociological Review* 57:698.

Block, Michael K., and Vernon E. Gerety. 1995. "Some Experimental Evidence on Differences between Student and Prisoner Reactions to Monetary Penalties and Risk." *Journal of Legal Studies* 24:123–38.

Bornstein, Brian H. 1999. "The Ecological Validity of Jury Simulations: Is the Jury Still Out?" *Law and Human Behavior* 23(1): 75–91.

Cohen, Bernard P. 1989. *Developing Sociological Knowledge: Theory and Method*. Chicago: Nelson Hall.

Cohen, Elizabeth G. 1993. "From Theory to Practice: The Development of an Applied Research Program." In *Theoretical Research Programs: Studies in the Growth of Theory*, edited by J. Berger and M. Zelditch, Jr. Palo Alto, CA: Stanford University Press.

Cohen, E. G., J. A. Bianchini, R. Cossey, N. C. Holthuis, C. C. Morphew, and J. A. Whitcomb. 1997. "What Did Students Learn? 1982–1994." In *Working for Equity in Heterogeneous Classrooms: Sociological Theory in Practice*, edited by E. G. Cohen and R. A. Lotan. New York: Teachers College Press.

Cohen, E. G., D. Briggs, N. Filby, E. Chin, M. Male, S. Mata, S. McBride, T. Perez, R. Quntanar-Sarellana, and P. Swanson. 2004. "Teaching Demanding Strategies for Cooperative Learning." In *Teaching Cooperative Learning: The Challenge for Teacher Education*, edited by E. G. Cohen, C. M. Brody, and M. Sapon-Shavin. Albany: State University of New York Press.

Cohen, E. G., and R. A. Lotan. 1995. "Producing Equal-Status Interaction in the Heterogeneous Classroom." *American Educational Research Journal* 32:99–120.

Cohen, E. G., and R. A. Lotan, eds. 1997. *Working for Equity in Heterogeneous Classrooms: Sociological Theory in Practice*. New York: Teachers College Press.

Cohen, E. G., R. A. Lotan, P. L. Abram, B. A. Scarloss, and S. E. Schultz. 2002. "Can Groups Learn?" *Teachers College Record* 104:1045–68.

Cohen, E. G., and S. Roper. 1972. "Modifications of Interracial Interaction Disability: An Application of Status Characteristics Theory." *American Sociological Review* 37:643–57.

Gottfredson, Michael, and Travis Hirschi. 1990. *A General Theory of Crime*. Stanford, CA: Stanford University Press.

Heckathorn, Douglas. 1985. "Why Punishment Does Not Deter." In *The Ambivalent Force*, 3rd ed., edited by A. S. Blumberg. Austin, TX: Holt, Rinehart, and Winston.

Henshel, Richard L. 1980. "Seeking Inoperative Laws: Toward the Deliberate Use of Unnatural Experimentation." In *Theoretical Methods in Sociology: Seven Essays*, edited by L. Freese. Pittsburgh, PA: University of Pittsburgh Press.

Howell, William G., and Paul E. Peterson. 2004. "Uses of Theory in Randomized Field Trials: Lessons from School Voucher Research on Disaggregation, Missing Data, and the Generalization of Findings." *American Behavioral Scientist* 47:634–56.

Kuhn, Thomas S. [1962] 1970. *The Structure of Scientific Revolutions*, 2nd ed. Chicago: University of Chicago Press.

Lakatos, Imre. 1970. "Falsification and the Methodology of Scientific Research Programmes." In *Criticism and the Growth of Knowledge*, edited by I. Lakatos and A. Musgrave. Cambridge, UK: Cambridge University Press.

Lovaglia, Michael J. 2003. "From Summer Camps to Glass Ceilings: The Power of Experiments." *Contexts* 2(4):42–49.

Lucas, Jeffrey W. 2003. "Theory Testing, Generalization, and the Problem of External Validity." *Sociological Theory* 21:236–53.

Martin, Michael W., and Jane Sell. 1979. "The Role of the Experiment in the Social Sciences." *The Sociological Quarterly* 20:581–90.

McCarthy, Bill, and John Hagan. 2005. "Danger and the Decision to Offend." *Social Forces* 83:1065–96.

Mook, Douglas G. 1983. "In Defense of External Invalidity." *American Psychologist* 38:379–87.

Moore, Walter. 1989. *Schrödinger: Life and Thought.* Cambridge, UK: Cambridge University Press.

Nagin, Daniel S., and Greg Pogarsky. 2003. "An Experimental Investigation of Deterrence: Cheating, Self-Serving Bias, and Impulsivity." *Criminology* 41:167–93.

Pate, Anthony M., and Edwin Hamilton. 1992. "Formal and Informal Deterrents to Domestic Violence: The Dade County Spouse Assault Experiment." *American Sociological Review* 57:691–97.

Popper, Karl. 1965. *Conjectures and Refutations: The Growth of Scientific Knowledge*. New York: Harper and Row.

Ridgeway, Cecilia L. 1982. "Status in Groups." *American Sociological Review* 47:76–88.

Ridgeway, C. L. 1991. "The Social Construction of Status Value: Gender and Other Nominal Characteristics." *Social Forces* 70:367–86.

Ridgeway, C. L., E. H. Boyle, K. J. Kuipers, and D. T. Robinson. 1998. "Resources and Interaction in the Development of Status Beliefs." *American Sociological Review* 63: 331–50.

Rosenholtz, S. J. 1985. "Modifying Status Expectations in the Traditional Classroom." In *Status, Rewards, and Influence: How Expectations Organize Behavior*, edited by J. Berger and M. Zelditch. San Francisco: Jossey-Bass.

Roth, Alvin E. 1995. "Introduction to Experimental Economics." In *The Handbook of Experimental Economics*, edited by J. H. Kagel and A. E. Roth. Princeton, NJ: Princeton University Press.

Sampson, Robert J. 2000. "Wither the Sociological Study of Crime." *Annual Review of Sociology* 26:711–14.

Sherman, Lawrence W. 2005. "The Use and Usefulness of Criminology, 1751–2005: Enlightened Justice and Its Failures." *Annals of the American Academy of Political and Social Science* 600:115–35.

Sherman, Lawrence W., and Richard A. Berk. 1984. "The Specific Deterrent Effects of Arrest for Domestic Violence." *American Sociological Review* 49:261–72.

Sherman, Lawrence W., Douglas A. Smith, Jane D. Schmidt, and Dennis P. Rogan. 1992. "Crime, Punishment, and Stake in Conformity: Legal and Informal Control of Domestic Violence." *American Sociological Review* 57:680–90.

Szmatka, Jacek, and Michael J. Lovaglia. 1996. "The Significance of Method." *Sociological Perspectives* 39:123–55.

Tammivaara, J. S. 1982. "The Effects of Task Structure on Beliefs about Competence and Participation in Small Groups." *Sociology of Education* 55:212–22.

Wagner, David G., and Joseph Berger. 1985. "Do Sociological Theories Grow?" *American Journal of Sociology* 90:697–728.

———. 1993. "Status Characteristics Theory: The Growth of a Program." In *Theoretical Research Programs: Studies in the Growth of Theory*, edited by J. Berger and M. Zelditch. Palo Alto, CA: Stanford University Press.

Webster, Murray, and John B. Kervin. 1973. "Artificiality in Experimental Sociology." *Canadian Revue of Anthropology and Sociology* 8:263–72.

Willer, David, and Murray Webster, Jr. 1970. "Theoretical Concepts and Observables." *American Sociological Review* 35:748–57.

Zelditch, Morris, Jr. 1969. "Can You Really Study an Army in the Laboratory?" In *A Sociological Reader on Complex Organizations*, edited by A. Etzioni. Austin, TX: Holt, Rinehart, and Winston.

I

SELF-CONTROL

2

Gottfredson and Hirschi in the Lab: An Experimental Test of the General Theory of Crime

Detlef Fetchenhauer, Josef Simon, and Felix Fetchenhauer

Since its publication in 1990, Gottfredson and Hirschi's general theory of crime has been one of the most influential theories of criminology (Pratt and Cullen 2000). However, despite its huge impact in the field, many criminologists have criticized the theory. The aim of this chapter is twofold. In the first part, we give a short overview of the theory, why it has been criticized, and how people have tried to empirically test its main propositions. In the second part, we report on an experimental study that we conducted to address some of the methodological issues in existing research (Fetchenhauer and Simon 1998).

THE MAIN PROPOSITIONS OF THE GENERAL THEORY OF CRIME

Gottfredson and Hirschi base their theory on a clear distinction between *crime* and *criminality*. With "crime" the authors refer to criminal acts that they define as: "acts of force or fraud undertaken in pursuit of self-interest" (Gottfredson and Hirschi 1990:15). With "criminality" the authors refer to the tendency of a person to behave in a criminal way.

Gottfredson and Hirschi argue that the most important characteristics of criminals can be derived from a proper analysis of crime. We follow this suggestion and summarize how Gottfredson and Hirschi describe typical crimes.

Characteristics of Criminal Acts

According to Gottfredson and Hirschi, the primary characteristic of criminal action is that it brings about immediate rewards and satisfaction. However,

this is accompanied by long-term negative consequences that generally out-
weigh these short-term gains. To give one example, rape can be described as
an act of immediate satisfaction of the rapist's sexual desire with the (potential) negative long-term consequence of a long prison sentence.

Consistent with this description of criminal acts is the fact that they are often committed quite spontaneously. A law-breaker rarely invests much time
or planning in the preparation of his crime (Gottfredson and Hirschi 1990). It
is their trivial and simple nature that distinguishes criminal acts: "The vast
majority of criminal acts are trivial and mundane affairs that result in little
loss and less gain" (1990:16). According to Gottfredson and Hirschi, the
small difference in time between the decision to offend and the actual offence
explains the fact that many crimes are committed within the immediate sur-
roundings of the offender's home.

Due to the lack of planning invested in criminal acts, resulting gains are
generally rather low. Furthermore, the price for which stolen goods can be
sold on the black market is but a fraction of the regular market price. For
these reasons, Gottfredson and Hirschi conclude that the vast majority of
criminals could earn a higher income through regular employment than they
achieve through crime—even if they only earned the minimum wage.

According to Gottfredson and Hirschi, short-term gains of crime reduce
long-term income also in the area of white-collar crime, as perpetrators will
lose their job if their crimes are detected. Interestingly, long before the theory
by Gottfredson and Hirschi was published, Nass (1983) analyzed two thousand cases of white-collar crime and argued that the main characteristic of
perpetrators was a "lack of farsightedness."

This short-sightedness becomes clearer still in cases of violent offences
such as murder, which are often induced by alcohol or drug abuse, and which
offenders often regret immediately after the crime is committed.

Gottfredson and Hirschi do not explicitly mention suicide. However, some
findings of determinants of suicide rates are remarkably consistent with their
description of crimes. As Clarke and Mayhew (1988) showed, suicide rates in
England drastically declined after the introduction of an alternative household
gas, which was no longer suitable for the purpose of suicide. Clarke and Mayhew describe the earlier method of suicide as "readily available and needing
little knowledge or preparation" (p. 24)—a description that is strikingly consistent with Gottfredson's and Hirschi's characterization of criminal acts.

Low Self-Control and Criminal Behavior

According to the general theory of crime, the most important characteristics
of criminals can be derived from the description of crime. Following that de-

scription, criminals can be described as being focused on the positive short-term effects of crime and as failing to consider its long-term negative consequences. By contrast, it is the ability to take negative long-term consequences into consideration that identifies conforming persons that do have the ability to resist the short-term temptations of criminal behavior. Thus, Gottfredson and Hirschi define self-control as the focal personality variable that accounts for diversity in criminal behavior: "A major characteristic of people with low self-control is therefore a tendency to respond to tangible stimuli in the immediate environment, to have a concrete 'here and now' orientation. People with high self-control, in contrast, tend to defer gratification" (Gottfredson and Hirschi 1990:89).

This concept of self-control can be divided into a number of different dimensions:

(1) As criminal actions distinguish themselves by their plainness and simplicity, Gottfredson and Hirschi conclude that persons with low self-control show a preference for plain and simple tasks. "People lacking self-control also tend to lack diligence, tenacity or persistence in a course of action" (Gottfredson and Hirschi 1990:89).

(2) Criminal actions are often linked with excitement, risks, and danger. While persons with high self-control try to avoid such risks and dangers, those with lower self-control tend toward risk and adventure seeking (Gottfredson and Hirschi 1990:89). Grasmick et al. (1993) describe this characteristic of persons with low self-control as "sensation seeking." At this point, we would like to point to a certain logical ambiguity in this argument. It is unclear whether humans with low self-control tend to engage in criminal acts *although* or *because* such risks are involved in the action. The former would simply mean that criminals fail to consider possible risks when making their decisions. The latter, on the other hand, would imply that persons with low self-control are more likely to engage in a certain criminal act when the risk of being discovered is high.

(3) According to Gottfredson and Hirschi the low level of planning involved in criminal actions leads to the conclusion that people with low self-control prefer to pursue physical, as opposed to verbal actions. This characteristic of low self-control corresponds with a preference for simple as opposed to difficult tasks.

(4) Criminal acts are mostly linked with pain or loss on behalf of the victim. It is the indifference and insensitivity toward the emotions of their victims that distinguishes persons with low self-control: "It follows that people with low self-control tend to be self-centered, indifferent or insensitive to the suffering and need of others" (Gottfredson and Hirschi 1990:89). Criminal actions performed as a reaction to injustice, and which are due to a desire for

fairness, are described by the authors as incompatible with the concept of low self-control.

(5) Low tolerance for frustration is an additional trait of low self-control individuals. This low tolerance manifests itself in a tendency to resolve conflicts with force, rather than by discussion (Gottfredson and Hirschi 1990:89).

These characteristics of low self-control are summarized by Gottfredson and Hirschi as follows: "People who lack self-control will tend to be impulsive, insensitive, physical (as opposed to mental), risk-taking, short-sighted and nonverbal and will therefore tend to engage in criminal and analogous acts" (1990:89). Gottfredson and Hirschi argue that criminals (that is, those lacking self-control) will not only engage in crime but will also tend to engage in "analogous" behaviors that have short-term gains and long-term losses. As examples they cite drinking, smoking, drug addiction, not finishing school, often changing one's job or profession, unwanted pregnancies, being involved in all kinds of accidents, or getting divorced. Gottfredson and Hirschi argue that those engaging in crime will show such analogous behaviors more often than noncriminals.

How to Prevent Crime?

Because Gottfredson and Hirschi view criminals as having a short-term orientation, they do not consider legal deterrence to be an effective method for preventing crime. Legal sanctions only take effect at a later time and are thus not taken into consideration when the crime is being committed (1990:256).

The results of a study by Piliavin et al. (1986) can be interpreted as indirect confirmation of this hypothesis. In a longitudinal study of a sample of criminals, the decision to commit a crime was highly influenced by expected gains from such behavior but was independent from anticipated legal sanctions. Similar results were obtained by Carroll (1978) as well as Tunnel (1989). Stewart and Hemsley (1979) report that—based on a comparison between a group of criminal offenders and a control group—criminal offenders turned out to be less influenced by delayed sanctions than noncriminals.

How to Explain Interpersonal Differences in Self-Control?

Why then do people differ in their level of self-control and thus in their tendency to commit crime? The answer given by Gottfedson and Hirschi is straightforward: Adolescents and adults end up with a lack of self-control if they are not educated in a proper way during their (early) childhood. If children engage in reckless and impulsive behavior parents must intervene by punishing such actions. In that way, children learn to control their short-term desires and develop the ability to wait for rewards that lie far away in the future.

However, raising one's children to have sufficient self-control implies a self-control problem itself. In the short run it is often easier for parents to indulge their children (for example, to let them watch television or not control their homework) because demanding that they follow their long-term interests may cause arguments and stress. However, the gains from having self-disciplined children can only be enjoyed at a later time (for example, when being proud that one's children have successfully finished college).

Thus, according to Gottfredson and Hirschi, parents who lack a sufficient level of self-control tend to have children who do the same.

CRITICAL OBJECTIONS TO THE THEORY OF GOTTFREDSON AND HIRSCHI

Although the general theory of crime has stimulated a vast body of empirical research since its publication in 1990, it has been harshly criticized on a number of different dimensions. For space reasons it is not possible to review these discussions in detail. Still, we would at least like to mention some of the critical issues that have been raised most often.

Some scholars have criticized the theory for being tautological (Akers 1991; Geis 2000). Interestingly, Hirschi and Gottfredson (2000) regard this accusation as a compliment, arguing that this tautology mirrors the logical consistency of their theory. We would like to emphasize that one asset of a theory is its potential to stimulate innovative research and to offer new and nontrivial hypotheses. More specifically, we would argue that there are a number of concrete falsifiable hypotheses that can be derived from Gottfredson and Hirschi's main assumptions even if the general statement of their theory might indeed be tautological. The study that we describe in this chapter is one example.

Others have complained that Gottfredson and Hirschi ignore many other theories that highly resemble their own theories (Akers 1991). Such constructs include, for example, the concept of "delay of gratification" developed by Mischel and colleagues (for example, Mischel 1984). Furthermore, Gottfredson and Hirschi ignore to a great extent investigations by Wilson and Herrnstein (1985) and Ainslee (1986, 1992), who intensely analyzed the consequences of hyperbolic discount functions (people's tendency to heavily discount future events) for human behavior.

Because Gottfredson and Hirschi ignore these predecessors, one could say that they discovered the North Pole a second time—this time, however, following a different route. Rather than analyze the typical characteristics of criminal persons, they analyze the typical characteristics of criminal actions.

Gottfredson and Hirschi's neglect of others' work is the more remarkable as Wilson and Herrnstein (1985) offered an elegant way to incorporate the problem of self-control into a broader theory of action that also emphasizes the importance of rewards for the explanation of criminal behavior (see the present study below). Unfortunately, Gottfredson and Hirschi dismiss the work of Wilson and Herrnstein as "psychological positivism" without recognizing its potential.

Other authors have raised the question of whether Gottfredson and Hirschi's characterization of crime is totally appropriate. Indeed, many crimes can be described by short-term gains and (potential) long-term losses, but not all of them. Take for example the case of insurance fraud: a false insurance claim must first be completed and only at a later time the gain from that fraud is received by getting the insurance company's money in one's bank account (the effort that a fraudulent action requires is due a long time before the criminal gains are achieved). Thus, based on the theory of Gottfredson and Hirschi, one should predict that offences like insurance fraud or tax evasion are extremely rare. However, many empirical findings contradict this assumption (Fetchenhauer and Simon 1998). Given these data, the question emerges whether the general theory of crime is as general as it pretends to be. Do we need one theory to explain crimes that result in short-term gains and do we need another theory to explain crimes that do not fit that description? In the study described in this chapter we see that sometimes people engage in fraudulent behavior even if they have to wait to gain the rewards from that behavior.

Another point of critique is that Gottfredson and Hirschi's theory appears to be ideologically biased and mirrors the authors' own conservative (puritan) attitudes. This issue is especially important with regard to the question of whether criminal behavior is indeed always as self-defeating as Gottfredson and Hirschi claim. To the contrary, Daly and Wilson (2001) have argued from an evolutionary perspective that the short time horizon of criminals (their tendency to ignore the long-term consequences of their behavior) might not be a deficit, but a functional adaptation to their local environment. According to these authors it is only reasonable to sacrifice future rewards for one's immediate gains if these long-term rewards are actually likely to occur.

However, when living in an insecure and unstable environment, young males might be well advised to use crimes as one way to attain a social status that might enable them to get access to fertile women and thus be able to transport their own genes into future generations (which is, from an evolutionary perspective, the main function of one's actions) (Fetchenhauer and Rohde 2002).

THE EMPIRICAL STATUS OF
THE GENERAL THEORY OF CRIME

Since its publication in 1990, the general theory of crime has been tested in two ways. On the one hand, some researchers have correlated different indicators of low self-control with each other. On the other hand, some researchers have developed self-report measures of self-control and have correlated these measures either with self-reports on deviant or criminal behaviors or with official records of criminal offences.

Convergence between Different
Behavioral Indicators of Low Self-Control

One way to test the assumptions of the general theory of crime is to investigate the relationship between behaviors that can be regarded as a consequence of low self-control. An early study in that line of research showed that drivers under the influence did not wear safety belts as frequently as those who had consumed no alcohol (Keane et al. 1993). Similarly, it has been shown that risky behavior in traffic and being involved in car accidents is substantially correlated with a driver's criminal record (Junger and Tremblay 1999; Junger, West, and Timman 2001; Sorenson 1994). We would argue that these results both confirm the theory by Gottfredson and Hirschi and contradict the argument that the theory is tautological.

Still, a huge disadvantage of this method is that measurements of behavior are being correlated with measurements of behavior. This approach only partially allows for drawing conclusions based on the underlying personality of the participants. Alternative explanations cannot truly be excluded (Akers 1991). For example, some people might be smoking *and* drinking *and* engage in criminal behavior, respectively, not because they share the personality disposition of low self-control, but because they are socialized into such a behavior by their environment.

Self-Report Studies

Following this line of critique, the dominant way of testing the general theory of crime is not to correlate different behaviors with each other. Much more often, researchers try to test the theory by measuring participants' level of self-control with a self-report questionnaire and relating these self-reports to different dependent variables. These dependent measures are either criminal behaviors or consist of what Gottfredson and Hirschi have called "analogous behaviors" (for example, failure to use a condom to prevent unintended pregnancies and sexually transmitted diseases).

The self-report measure used most often in this regard is a scale by Grasmick et al. (1993) in which participants are asked to indicate their adherence
to twenty-four different items (for example, "I often react spontaneously to a
situation, without thinking about it much"). Their measurement is composed
of six subdimensions: impulsivity, preference for simple tasks, searching for
risks, preference for physical as opposed to mental tasks, self-centeredness,
and impatience.

The scale of Grasmick et al. (1993) has been criticized for its psychometric properties (Marcus 2004) and its questionable one-dimensionality (DeLisi
et al. 2003; Arneklev et al. 1999). Nonetheless, a meta-analysis by Pratt and
Cullen (2000) revealed that the scale was able to predict criminal involvement in a robust way, although the explained variance was rather modest.

Gottfredson and Hirschi are skeptical of measuring self-control with personality scales (Hirschi and Gottfredson 1994). They believe that persons with
low self-control are systematically underrepresented in random surveys—
what should motivate a person with low self-control to participate in such a
study? Therefore, they claim that self-report studies tend to underestimate the
true correlation between deviating behavior and self-control. Furthermore,
they doubt the validity of self-reports, regarding both measures of self-control
and measures of deviant behavior with suspicion. Generally, Gottfredson and
Hirschi see the attempt to measure self-control with personality questionnaires
as a regression into "psychological positivism."

Another problem with most cross-sectional surveys that are based on self-
reports lies in the fact that they do not allow the identification of causal relationships between two (or more) investigated variables (that is, one cannot
exclude the possibility that the influence of intervening variables determines
discovered relationships). For example, it is possible that a correlation between self-control and self-reported delinquency is caused by the extent of
social marginalization of the participant: being unemployed might cause people both to engage in criminal activities *and* to develop a here and now orientation to their life (which might lead to lower values on self-report scales
that measure self-control).

An Alternative Way to Test the General Theory of Crime

From our point of view, both the criticism from Gottfredson and Hirschi toward the use of self-report measures of self-control as well as the criticism of the measurement of self-control by behavior-based indicators is justified. One way out of this dilemma is to follow both lines of research and thus triangulate the empirical results.

However, we would argue that there is still another, and potentially more promising way to test the theory of Gottfredson and Hirschi, namely, the use of controlled experiments both in the laboratory and in the field. If Gottfredson and Hirschi are right, people engage in deviant behavior because they lack a sufficient amount of self-control *and* a given situation promises short-term gains for acting in an antisocial manner. Following Gottfredson and Hirschi, both prerequisites are necessary for the occurrence of deviant behavior.

One way to test this core assumption is to measure participants' levels of self-control via self-reports and to put them in a situation that fits Gottfredson and Hirschi's description of opportunities (that is, give participants the option to gain immediate reward by behaving in an antisocial manner).

The remainder of this chapter reports the outcomes of such a study.

An Experimental Test of the General Theory of Crime

The general setup of our experiment was to put participants into a situation in which they could cheat on the experimenter under a number of conditions. These conditions differed in the immediacy and in the height of the rewards that could be gained by such cheating.

In a local newspaper of Cologne, Germany, we placed a short article that described an opportunity to participate in a wine-tasting session that would deal with different topics derived from consumer psychology. The session set up was as follows: After being welcomed by the experimenter, the participants were asked to fill out a questionnaire for a colleague of the experimenter. This request was justified by the urgent need for more participants in aid of the colleague's research. In this part of the study, participants were asked to fill in the self-control scale by Grasmick et al. (1993).

Thereafter, a "wine market study" took place, in which the participants evaluated the taste of different wines and answered wine-specific questions over a period of approximately seventy minutes.

The actual experiment took place only after the wine tasting and after the participants had already been thanked for taking part in the study. The experimenter informed each participant that he or she now had the chance to win some wine by successfully completing a wine-tasting test. This test involved tasting four different wine samples and relating them to corresponding types of wine listed in a random order.

We explained to each participant that this task was not particularly difficult and merely demanded five minutes of concentration, because of which the participant was now left alone. However, in reality the task was practically impossible to solve and the absence of the experimenter gave the participant the opportunity to "cheat" by turning around the wine bottles and looking at the labels, the names of which they were supposed to guess. During the experiment the participants were observed through a one-way mirror. Those participants that used this opportunity and manipulated the task were classified as "fraudsters."

The setup of this experiment therefore corresponded to a high degree with the characterization of a "criminal situation" defined by Gottfredson and Hirschi: The criminal (in this case fraudulent) action was a reaction to a (coincidentally) offered opportunity, was connected with little inconvenience and effort, and resulted in a comparatively low (fraud-based) gain.

Aside from the self-report measure of self-control, two further independent variables were investigated.

(1) The extent of gain: One half of the participants were informed that one bottle of wine could be won, while the other half were informed that three bottles of wine could be won.

(2) The length of time until the reward: While one half of the participants were told that they would get their wine immediately after the test, the other half of the participants were informed that their wine would be sent to them approximately six weeks after the experiment.

Hypotheses

From the theory of Gottfredson and Hirschi, we deduced the following hypotheses:

Hypothesis 1: In the "immediate reward" condition the frequency of fraud is higher than in the "delayed reward" condition. This hypothesis was derived from the fact that only the "immediate reward condition" was consistent with Gottfredson and Hirschi's description of a typical criminal situation.

Hypothesis 2: The lower the self-control of the participants, the more likely they are to cheat on the test. This hypothesis should apply to participants in all experimental conditions. Those with high self-control should not tend toward fraudulent behavior—independent of the specific experimental condition.

Combining these two hypotheses, the following interaction effect between participants' self-control and experimental conditions was to be expected:

Hypothesis 3: The frequency of cheating will be especially high if a participant has a low level of self-control and the reward for the fraudulent behavior will be gained immediately after the experiment.

We did not deduce a specific hypothesis about how the extent of the reward (gaining one bottle or gaining three bottles) would influence the likelihood of cheating. Yet, it should be obvious that economic and rational choice theories of crime would predict that the participants are more likely to cheat in the "three bottles" condition than in the "one bottle" condition (Niggli 1994; Opp 1989).

Participants

Out of more than one hundred people who responded after having read the newspaper article, eighty-eight participants eventually took part in the experiment. Of these eighty-eight participants, fifty-six were male and thirty-two female. On average, participants were 38.6 years old. Most of our participants were members of the German middle class and their level of formal education was well above the German average, as nearly 60 percent of them held a university degree.

Psychometric Properties of the Self-control Scale

To measure participants' self-control we used the twenty-four-item scale by Grasmick et al. (1993). A factor analysis revealed eight factors with an Eigenvalue > 1. A closer look at the results of that factor analysis revealed that the first six factors closely mirrored the six subdimensions of the scale.

Still, reliability analyses showed that it was justifiable to summarize all items into one scale (Cronbach's alpha = 0.75). Therefore, in the following we only discuss results with respect to the participants' values on the twenty-four-item measure. Further analyses revealed that results were similar when the different subscales were analyzed separately.

Results

Of the eighty-eight participants, a total of thirty-four (39 percent) were classified as "fraudsters." A purposeful action of fraud was only identified when the participants turned around (at least) one bottle of wine and subsequently changed an answer on their question sheet without informing the experimenter.

Before analyzing the influence of participants' self-control on their cheating behavior we discuss the influence of the experimental conditions. Hypothesis 1 stated that participants should cheat more often if they were to get their wine immediately after the experiment as opposed to having to wait for their wine for six weeks. However, this hypothesis could not be confirmed at all. In both conditions, exactly the same percentage of participants cheated. In both the "immediate reward" condition and the "delayed reward" condition, seventeen participants turned around at least one bottle of wine and twenty-seven participants refrained from the temptation to do so.

Interestingly, the number of bottles that were to be gained did influence participants' tendency to cheat. If the reward consisted of three bottles, 47.7 percent cheated. If the reward consisted of only one bottle, only 29.5 percent cheated (Phi = 0.19; $p = 0.07$).

Next, we analyzed the influence of participants' self-control on their cheating behavior. This influence turned out to be only marginally significant and rather small: $r = 0.14$ ($p = 0.10$). Thus, Hypothesis 2 could only partially be confirmed.

Finally, we tested whether there was an interaction effect between participants' self-control and the two different delay conditions. For this purpose we first made a median-split of the self-control scale. Then, we ran a binary logistic regression analysis using cheating behavior as the dependent variable. As independent variables we inserted the dichotomized self-control scale and delay (whether participants had to wait six weeks to get their wine or not). In a second step we added an interaction term of these two variables.

The first step of this analysis revealed that neither delay nor self-control influenced participants' tendency to cheat during the wine quiz ($p > 0.10$). However, in the second step of the analysis, the influence of the interaction term of both independent variables was marginally significant ($p = 0.08$), although only a small fraction of the participants' cheating behavior could be explained (Nagelkerke R square = 0.074).

This result indicates that participants' self-control was more important for their decision to cheat when they got their reward immediately after the experiment, and that participants' self-control was less important for their decision to cheat when they had to wait for their reward for a period of six weeks. To highlight this finding in a less abstract way: In the "delayed reward" condition the correlation between self-control and cheating behavior was only $r = -0.03$ (n.s.), but in the "immediate reward" condition this correlation was $r = 0.28$ ($p < 0.05$).

Discussion

Before we relate the results of our experiment to the theory of Gottfredson and Hirschi, we discuss a few possible critical objections to our experiment. A possible first objection concerns the question whether "cheating" in our experiment is actually a reasonable example of criminal behavior. Gottfredson and Hirschi define "crime" as all "acts of force or fraud in the pursuit of self-interest" and emphatically claim to be able to explain not only capital crimes, but also petty offences with their theory (1990:15).

A further possible point of criticism refers to the sample that we studied. As most of them were members of the German middle class with a high level of education, one might claim that hardly anyone in our sample fits the description of a typical criminal. (Gottfredson and Hirschi would argue that a high level of formal education is usually only attained by people with a sufficient degree of self-control.) We agree with this criticism to some degree, but it raises the question of why such a high percentage of all participants cheated—if indeed such deviant behavior is restricted to people with low self-control.

Additionally one could criticize that no possible (legal) sanctions accompanied the fraudulent behavior in the experiment. Yet, we would argue that it is possible to deduce from Gottfredson and Hirschi's theory that the embarrassment for the participants—if the experimenter was to discover the fraud—should have a larger influence on persons with high self-control than on persons with low self-control.

Thus, we would reason that our experimental setup was well suited to test the core assumption of Gottfredson and Hirschi's general theory of crime, namely, that for a crime to be conducted it takes both a potential perpetrator *and* the perpetrator to expect immediate rewards for his or her deviant behavior.

To summarize our results, the present experiment only partially supports the theory. First, the relationship between participants' self-control and their cheating behavior was weak and only marginally significant. When using the dichotomized self-control scale it turned out that about 45 percent of all those with a low level of self-control cheated, but so did about 32 percent of those with a high level of self-control. This result is in line with many other studies using the scale by Grasmick et al. (1993). Indeed, those with a low level of self-control tend to engage more in criminal and fraudulent behaviors than those with a high level of self-control, but this relationship is often found to be rather modest and not to confirm the proposition that self-control is the main (or even only) determinant of criminal behavior (Pratt and Cullen 2000).

Above, we discussed that Gottfredson and Hirschi generally object to measuring self-control via self-report measures and we assume that they would do the same with regard to our experiment. Yet, even if one shares their reservation toward self-report measures, the question remains why participants' cheating behavior was independent of the length of the period they had to wait for the resulting reward. Following Gottfredson and Hirschi's description of typical crimes and typical "analogous behaviors," it is the immediacy of the rewards that is the essence of these behaviors, and it is this immediacy which is so tempting for people with low self-control.

Interestingly, we were able to confirm our hypothesis that participants with low self-control are especially prone to cheat when they do not have to wait for the reward for such cheating. However, although this result is in line with the general theory of crime, it is difficult to explain why so many participants with a high level of self-control were also cheating—even if they had to wait for their reward for a period of six weeks.

Above, we described that participants' behavior was influenced by the amount of wine that participants got if they were able to pass the wine quiz. This result is very much in line with rational choice theories of crime. Although such a finding does not necessarily contradict the theory of Gottfredson and Hirschi, it seems much more consistent with the theory of Wilson and Herrnstein (1985) that tries to integrate personality dispositions of a potential perpetrator and the rewards that are to be gained from criminal behavior.

Extending the framework of Gottfredson and Hirschi, a further result appears to be noteworthy. The frequency of cheating correlated significantly with the degree to which participants revealed an expertise with regard to wine during the first part of the experiment ($r = 0.30$, $p < 0.05$). A possible explanation for this result might lie in the fact that the more participants knew about wine the more they thought it was convincing to pretend that they were able to solve the wine quiz without cheating. If that interpretation did actually hold, such behavior would imply a lot of Machiavellian reasoning on the part of the participants. However, according to Gottfredson and Hirschi, such sophisticated reasoning is atypical for people who engage in fraudulent behavior.

Still, we do not see our result as a falsification of Gottfredson and Hirschi. To the contrary, we are still impressed by the elegance and appeal of their theory and we are convinced that criminal and deviant behavior can best be described as an interaction of the very situation in which such behaviors take place with the personality dispositions of potential perpetrators.

Thus, we hope that others might follow our suggestion to use experimental methods to test the general theory of crime. Testing the theory experimentally has a number of advantages. One first and important advantage of all experiments lies in the fact that it is possible to manipulate some relevant variables while holding all others constant. This allows conclusions not only about the correlations between variables, but also their causal relations (see Horne and Lovaglia, this volume). For example, in the present study it could be shown that the height of rewards for participants' fraudulent behavior determined their likelihood of cheating.

Another advantage lies in the fact that experiments offer the opportunity to "design" and control a situation in which a certain kind of criminal behavior might take place. For example, Gottfredson and Hirschi claim that opportunities play a major role in stimulating fraudulent and criminal behavior. However, what is perceived as an opportunity might be very dependent on the personality or the lifestyle of a potential perpetrator. In our study it was clear to all participants that by turning the bottles and taking a look at their labels one could solve the quiz and thus win some wine. Therefore, all our participants had the opportunity to cheat, both objectively and subjectively.

A further strength of experiments is their ability to circumvent one of the main disadvantage of self-report studies, namely, their reliance on participants' willingness to honestly report on their past criminal behavior. It is important to note that our dependent variable was not participants' self-reports about whether they cheated or not. Instead, our dependent variable was a real behavioral measure just like Gottfredson and Hirschi recommend (see Kalkhoff and Willer, this volume, for a study that takes a similar approach).

By using our paradigm we were also able to avoid another weakness that is inherent in many self-report studies. As Gottfredson and Hirschi emphasize, self-report studies suffer from a self-selection bias. Only nice and kind people (those with a high level of self-control) participate in such studies that offer no financial gains to their participants. Yet, in our study participants were asked to come to our lab not by asking them to do us a favor, but by offering them some interesting incentives. In the present study these incentives were the opportunity to reveal their knowledge of wine as well as the chance to win some wine at the end of our study. In future research such incentives might simply be the prospect of winning money by solving some rather easy and undemanding tasks (which might make such experiments especially attractive for those with a low level of self-control).

To summarize these methodological reflections, we strongly advocate testing the general theory of crime not only in the ways done in the past, but also with experimental methods. The study presented in this chapter is only a start in that direction and its results should be replicated in other settings and with other samples. We think that the core assumption of Gottfredson and Hirschi's theory, namely, that crime is committed by people with low self-control who expect immediate rewards out of their criminal behavior, is worth testing in a number of different experiments.

Yet, one result of our study remains noteworthy: At least sometimes, antisocial behavior is not influenced by the immediacy of its rewards, but by their height. It seems that antisocial behavior not always is the consequence of a lack of self-control, but sometimes is the consequence of rational decision making.

REFERENCES

Ainslee, G. 1986. "Beyond Microeconomics. Conflict among Interests in a Multiple Self as a Determinant of Value." In *The Multiple Self*, edited by J. Elster. New York: Cambridge University Press.

———. 1992. *Picoeconomics. The Strategic Interaction of Successive Motivational States Within the Person.* New York: Cambridge University Press.

Akers, R. L. 1991. "Self-Control as a General Theory of Crime." *Journal of Quantitative Criminology* 7(2):201–11.

Arneklev, B. J., H. G. Grasmick, and R. J. Bursik. 1999. "Evaluating the Dimensionality and Invariance of 'Low Self-Control.'" *Journal of Quantitative Criminology* 15:307–31.

Carroll, J. S. 1978. "A Psychological Approach to Deterrence: The Evaluation of Crime Opportunities." *Journal of Personality and Social Psychology* 36(12):1512–20.

Clarke, R. V. 1992. *Situational Crime Prevention: Successful Case Studies.* Albany, NY: Harrow and Heston.

Clarke, R. V., and P. Mayhew. 1988. "The British Gas Suicide Story and its Criminological Implications." In *Crime and Justice,* vol. 10, edited by M. Tonry and N. Morris. Chicago: University of Chicago Press.

Daly, M., and M. Wilson. 2001. "Risk-taking, Intrasexual Competition, and Homicide." *Nebraska Symposium on Motivation* 47:1–36.

DeLisi, M., A. Hochstetler, and D. S. Murphy. 2003. "Self-control behind Bars: A Validation Study of the Grasmick et al. Scale." *Justice Quarterly* 20:241–63.

Fetchenhauer, D., and P. Rohde. 2002. "Evolutionary Personality Psychology and Victimology: Sex Differences in Risk Attitudes and Short-Term Orientation and Their Relation to Sex Differences in Victimizations." *Evolution and Human Behavior* 23:233–44.

Fetchenhauer, D., and J. Simon. 1998. "Eine experimentelle Überprüfung der General Theory of Crime von Gottfredson und Hirschi." ["An Experimental Test of the General Theory of Crime by Gottfredson and Hirschi"]. *Monatsschrift für Kriminologie und Strafrechtsreform,* 81:S.301–15

Geis, G. 2000. "On the Absence of Self-Control as the Basis for a General Theory of Crime." *Theoretical Criminology* 4:35–53.

Gottfredson, M. R., and T. Hirschi. 1990. *A General Theory of Crime.* Palo Alto, CA: Stanford University Press.

Grasmick, H. G., C. R. Tittle, R. J. Bursick, and B. J. Arneklev. 1993. "Testing the Core Empirical Implications of Gottfredson and Hirschi´s General Theory of Crime." *Journal of Research in Crime and Delinquency* 30:5–29.

Hirschi, T., and M. Gottfredson. 1993. "Commentary: Testing the General Theory of Crime." *Journal of Research in Crime and Delinquency,* 30:47–54.

———. 1994. *The Generality of Deviance.* London: Transaction Publishers.

———. 2000. "In Defense of Self-Control." *Theoretical Criminology* 4:55–69.

Junger, M., and R. E. Tremblay. 1999. "Self-Control, Accidents, and Crime." *Criminal Justice and Behavior* 4:485–501.

Junger, M., R. West, and R. Timman. 2001. "Crime and Risky Behavior in Traffic: An Example of Cross-Situational Consistency." *Journal of Research in Crime and Delinquency* 38:439–59.

Keane, C., P. Maxim, and J. J. Teevan. 1993. "Drinking and Driving, Self-Control and Gender: Testing a General Theory of Crime." *Journal of Research in Crime and Delinquency* 30:30–46.

Marcus, B. 2004. "Self-Control in the General Theory of Crime: Theoretical Implications of a Measurement Problem." *Theoretical Criminology* 8:33–55.

Mischel, W. 1984. "Convergences and Challenges in the Search for Consistency." *American Psychologist* 39(4):351–64.

Nass, G. 1983. *Wirtschaftskriminalität.* [*White Collar Crimes*]. Akademie für kriminologische Grundlagenforschung.

Niggli, M. A. 1994. "Rational Choice Theory and Crime Prevention." *Studies on Crime and Crime Prevention* 3:83–103.

Opp, K. D. 1989. "The Economics of Crime and the Sociology of Deviant Behaviour. A Theoretical Confrontation of Basic Proposition." *Kyklos,* 42(Facs.3):405–30.

Piliavin, I., C. Thornton, R. Gartner, and R. L. Matsueda. 1986. "Crime, Deterrence and Rational Choice." *American Sociological Review* 51:101–19.

Pratt, T. C., and F. T. Cullen. 2000. "The Empirical Status of Gottfredson and Hirschi's General Theory of Crime: A Meta-Analysis." *Criminology* 38:931–64.

Sorensen, D. W. M. 1994. "Motor Vehicle Accidents." In *The Generality of Deviance*, edited by T. Hirschi and M. Gottfredson. London: Transaction Publishers.

Stewart, C. H., and D. R. Hemsley. 1979. "Risk Perception and Likelihood of Action in Criminal Offenders." *British Journal of Criminology* 19:105–19.

Tunnel, K. 1989. *Doing Crime: An Analysis of Repetitive Property Offenders´ Decision Making.* Doctoral dissertation, University of Michigan, Ann Arbor, MI.

Wilson, J. Q., and R. J. Herrnstein. 1985. *Crime and Human Nature.* New York: Simon and Schuster.

3

Deterring Deviance:
Rationality and Self-Control

Will Kalkhoff and Robb Willer

Grounded in utilitarian philosophy (Beccaria 1775; Bentham 1823), the central idea of general deterrence is that individuals' decisions to commit crime are influenced by the threat of punishment. Specifically, an inverse relationship is expected to hold between crime and the certainty, severity, and celerity of sanctions, although most research has focused on certainty and severity, not celerity, due to practical concerns. These factors may also interact (Anderson, Chiricos, and Waldo 1977; Grasmick and Bryjak 1980; Grasmick and Green 1980; Stafford et al. 1986; Grasmick and Bursik 1990; Nagin and Paternoster 1993).

Theoretical and empirical research on general deterrence has developed along three major lines: interrupted time-series, ecological, and individual-level studies (Nagin 1998). Our focus is on individual-level studies, which examine the relationship between individuals' perceptions of the certainty and severity of sanctions and their reports of illegal involvement. Three types of research designs have been emphasized in this research: cross-sectional, panel, and scenario-based. Although studies of a given sort tend to produce fairly consistent conclusions about the nature and effectiveness of deterrence, these conclusions do not always overlap when findings from the different types of research designs are compared.[1]

Inconsistencies in the findings from deterrence research are due in part to differences among the methodologies that have been used (see, for example, Minor and Harry 1982; Saltzman et al. 1982; Piliavin et al. 1986). This observation is useful because it illustrates the drawbacks of putting confidence in conclusions drawn from studies that tend to rely on a single methodology, a point emphasized by Horne and Lovaglia in Chapter 1 of this volume. Not all methods, however, have gotten their fair share of attention in deterrence research. In spite of their unique ability to disentangle causal processes, laboratory studies have been all but ignored, especially in recent years.[2]

There are also substantive gaps that are just now being addressed. Studies of individual-level deterrence have emphasized the role of situational factors (for example, perceptions of sanction certainty and severity) in persons' decisions about whether to offend. Recently, however, deterrence researchers have started to focus on *both* situational factors and time-stable individual differences in criminal propensity, such as those driven by low self-control. A key issue in the literature is whether low self-control people are more (or less) responsive to situational deterrents. According to Gottfredson and Hirschi (1990), low self-control individuals are, by definition, impulsive and prone to risk-taking. As a consequence, they do not stop to consider the (long-term) costs of crime.

Wright, Caspi, and Moffitt (1999) argue the opposite. According to their model, (1) people who are *high* in self-control are the ones who tend not to even consider committing crime; yet, (2) in order for situational factors to influence decisions to offend, crime must be considered as a behavioral option in the first place. Based on these assumptions, Wright et al. (1999; see also Wright et al. 2000) hypothesize that "the costs of crime should most strongly deter the behavior of individuals with low self-control" (p. 5). They find strong support for this prediction using longitudinal data from the Dunedin Multidisciplinary Health and Development Study (Silva and Stanton 1996).

While Wright et al. (1999) have provided some evidence that appears to contradict Gottfredson and Hirschi's (1990) conceptualization of the ways that low self-control affects crime and deviance, the main goal of our study is to shed further light on this contemporary debate by presenting results from a unique *experimental* test of the effect of punishment certainty on low- and high-self-control subjects.

BACKGROUND THEORY AND RESEARCH

Cross-Sectional Studies

Cross-sectional studies of deterrence examine the relationship between perceived certainty and severity of legal sanctions and self-reports of illegal involvement at a given point in time. Many of these studies find that the certainty but not the severity of sanctions has a negative effect on involvement in illegal behaviors (Waldo and Chiricos 1972; Silberman 1976; Teevan 1976; Jensen, Erickson, and Gibbs 1978). However, a number of cross-sectional studies directly examine and find support for models including an interaction between punishment certainty and severity (Anderson, Chiricos, and Waldo 1977; Grasmick and Bryjak 1980; Grasmick and Green 1980; Grasmick and Bursik 1990). These studies suggest that the effect of punishment severity obtains, but only under conditions of relatively high certainty.

However, cross-sectional perceptual studies of deterrence have some methodological limitations. The most serious issue with cross-sectional studies of deterrence concerns the *temporal ordering* of the data. The deterrence model implies that current perceptions of punishment certainty and severity affect subsequent behavior. In cross-sectional studies of deterrence, this ordering is often reversed: Individuals' perceptions of punishment certainty and severity are examined in relation to self-reports of their past involvement in illegal activities. It is possible, however, that people who have already committed illegal acts feel less threatened by legal sanctions than law-abiding individuals. Thus, results from cross-sectional studies of deterrence may indicate an "experiential effect" (Saltzman et al. 1982) more than a deterrent effect. This would not be the case if people's perceptions of punishment factors remain stable over time. However, a number of studies indicate that this assumption is tenuous. Individuals' perceptions of punishment certainty and severity are not stable (Saltzman et al. 1982; Piliavin et al. 1986; but see also Wright et al. 2000), even over short intervals (Minor and Harry 1982).

A potential remedy is offered by cross-sectional studies that use self-estimates of *future* involvement in criminal behavior as proxies for actual future involvement. In a notable longitudinal study, Murray and Erickson (1987) included both types of measures and achieved the same pattern of results with each. Green (1989) reached the same conclusion and argued in favor of more research to help determine whether cross-sectional studies using estimates of future involvement in crime can be used in place of panel studies, discussed next.

Panel Studies

To address the problem of temporal-ordering in cross-sectional perceptual studies, researchers have employed panel designs. In these, a set of individuals is surveyed about their criminal involvement and sanction perceptions at different points in time, usually one year apart. Four pieces of information are obtained: (1) self-reports of criminal involvement during the year prior to t; (2) perceptions of sanction certainty and severity at t; (3) self-reports of criminal involvement during the period between t and t 1; and (4) perceptions of sanction certainty and severity at t 1. The first two pieces of information can be combined to estimate the experiential effect. The second and third pieces of information can be combined to estimate the "true" deterrent effect, against which the experiential effect estimate can be compared. The second and fourth pieces of information can be combined to estimate the stability of perceptions. Using this method, panel studies of deterrence have consistently produced three conclusions: (1) cross-sectional studies exaggerate the true deterrent effect; (2) the experiential effect is greater than the true deterrent effect; and (3) experiential effect estimates are similar in magnitude to deterrent effect estimates from cross-sectional studies (Saltzman et al. 1982; Paternoster et al. 1982; Paternoster et al. 1983a, 1983b).

The irony, however, is that panel studies of deterrence cannot handle the problem that undermines cross-sectional analyses: the instability of perceptions. Even at intervals as short as three months, perceptions of legal sanctions do not appear to be stable (Minor and Harry 1982). This may render distal measures of perceptions irrelevant to behavior (Piliavin et al. 1986). At the very least, an extended lag between the measurement of perceptions and behavior will result in substantial measurement error, thereby attenuating estimates of the deterrent effect (Nagin 1998). Ideally, then, measurements of perceptions and behavior should be made contemporaneously (Piliavin et al. 1986; Williams and Hawkins 1986; Grasmick and Bursik 1990), yet in the analysis of survey data this leads to difficulties in finding instrumental variables to permit identification of simultaneous effect equations. This is one of the main strengths of experimental approaches to the study of deterrence processes, as we elaborate below: Behavior can be analyzed as a consequence of controlled conditions and individuals' immediate responses to these conditions.

Specification Error in Cross-Sectional and Panel Studies

A serious problem that *both* cross-sectional and panel studies have attempted to address is specification error resulting from excluded causal variables. The problem is very serious when a missing variable would have had a large effect on the outcome or would have been highly correlated with other causal variables: the larger the effect of the unknown regression coefficient, the more serious the bias (Kmenta 1986).

Thus, a central task for deterrence researchers has been to specify a comprehensive deterrence model. Often this has involved inclusion of various operationalizations of social-control factors such as informal sanctions (for example, social disapproval), moral beliefs, and peer involvement in illegal activity. In an extensive review of individual-level research on deterrence, Paternoster (1987) found only two studies (Grasmick and Green 1980; Bishop 1984) where the deterrent effect for *perceived certainty* remained after controls were introduced for social-control factors. However, these two studies included fewer control variables than six other studies that found no effect of perceived certainty in more completely specified multivariate models (Johnson 1979; Jacob 1980; Paternoster et al. 1983a, 1983b; Paternoster and Iovanni 1986; Piliavin et al. 1986). Paternoster (1987) concluded from his review that the effect of *perceived severity* of formal sanctions is inconsequential for deterrence once the nonlegal elements of punishment are taken into account. Specifically, Paternoster (1987) identified six studies where a multivariate test of the perceived severity hypothesis is reported. Among these, four suggest that perceived severity plays no deterrent role when a number of social-control factors are taken into account (Silberman 1976; Meier and Johnson 1977; Jacob 1980; Paternoster and Iovanni 1986). In the two multivariate studies that find support for the severity hypothesis, one did not include exogenous factors besides perceived severity and certainty (Grasmick and Bryjak 1980). The other included only a limited number of controls for nonlegal factors (Grasmick and Green 1980). Thus, when a number of theoretically important causal variables are considered, perceptions of formal sanctions seem to have very little to do with illegal behavior. Nonetheless, the problem of the instability of perceptions (attendant to *both* cross-sectional and panel designs) keeps us from being able to state this conclusion with a high degree of confidence.

Scenario-Based Studies

The scenario-based survey method offers solutions to the problems that confound cross-sectional and panel studies of deterrence. In scenario-based studies, respondents first read short descriptions of events where an illegal act has been or could be committed by an imaginary actor. Respondents are then asked to rate (1) the certainty of detection associated with engaging in the illegal act, (2) the likelihood of more or less severe sanctions conditional on detection, and (3) their intentions to engage in the illegal act.

The scenario-based method offers a number of strengths. First, aspects of scenarios (that is, independent variables) are *randomly varied* across respondents. In other words, the scenario-based method incorporates a quasi-experimental approach in which the researcher manipulates factors of interest. This ensures that the independent variables are essentially orthogonal, which allows for estimation of their uncontaminated effects. In addition, randomizing scenarios across individuals ensures that the expected correlation between scenarios and any excluded exogenous variables is zero. Thus, the problem of omitted variable bias is eliminated. Randomized laboratory experiments also eliminate the unwanted consequences of multicollinearity and omitted variable bias; however, a unique benefit of scenario-based studies is that they allow for manipulation of *large numbers* of independent variables and levels within them. As such, respondents can be provided with detailed descriptions of events, which enhances the correspondence between the experimental realm and the real world (Rossi and Anderson 1982). Finally, a third strength of scenario-based studies is that they facilitate collection of the dependent variable (Nagin and Paternoster 1993). Unlike cross-sectional and panel studies, respondents in scenario-based surveys report their intention to commit an illegal act immediately after being exposed to event descriptions. Thus, results from scenario-based studies are not undermined by the instability of sanction perceptions.

Results from scenario-based studies are mixed, although differences in the measurement of punishment severity make comparison of the varied findings somewhat difficult. For example, Klepper and Nagin (1989) presented a series of scenarios involving tax noncompliance to graduate students in a management program. Besides being asked to "project" their own behavior as if in the imaginary actor's position, respondents were asked to rate (1) the likelihood that the noncompliance would be detected (perceived certainty), and (2) the probability that the noncompliance, if detected, would result in criminal prosecution (perceived severity). In contrast to previous individual-level studies of deterrence, Klepper and Nagin found perceived severity to be a powerful deterrent. However, Klepper and Nagin's measure of perceived severity does not take into account the severity of criminal prosecution *to the respondent* (see Grasmick and Bryjak 1980), and it seems to conflate severity and certainty: perceived severity is measured as the probability that detected noncompliance will result in criminal prosecution. In other words, Klepper and Nagin's measure of severity appears to tap a second level of perceived certainty rather than respondents' feelings about the severity of prosecution for tax noncompliance.

Using a similar measure of perceived severity, Bachman, Paternoster, and Ward (1992) also found an effect of perceived severity on male college students' intentions to commit sexual assault.

However, borrowing from Nagin and Paternoster (1993, 1994), Hillbo and Lovaglia (1995) measured perceived severity in terms of respondents' estimates of how much of a problem various sanctions would pose for them. To measure certainty, respondents rated the likelihood that they would be caught committing a deviant act—cheating in a college class. Measured this way, Hillbo and Lovaglia found a deterrent effect for perceived certainty but no effect for perceived severity of punishment. Nagin and Paternoster (1993) examined and found support for a nonadditive model of deterrence using their revised measure of severity. The interaction effect remained after controls were introduced for respondent differences in self-control.

Finally, in a more recent scenario-based study, Paternoster and Simpson (1996) found that the product of respondents' perceptions of formal sanction certainty and severity did not have a significant effect on intentions to commit corporate crime. However, the interaction of sanction certainty and severity did significantly predict criminal intentions when respondents' perceptions of formal and informal sanctions were considered together. Thus, the weight of the evidence from scenario-based studies of deterrence appears to favor a nonadditive model of deterrence.

Although scenario-based studies of deterrence overcome many of the limitations of cross-sectional and panel designs, they suffer from one serious problem: intentions to engage in behavior are of course not the same thing as actual behavior.

Laboratory Studies

In addition to cross-sectional, panel, and scenario-based designs, sociologists have used laboratory experiments to study individual-level deterrence processes. A main strength of laboratory studies is that behavior can be examined as a result of conditions directly under the investigator's control. Where the objective is testing theory and not the empirical or statistical generalization of findings, experiments are a powerful method for examining social processes (Zelditch 1969; Webster and Kervin 1971; Henshel 1980; Mook 1983).

Stafford and his colleagues (Stafford et al. 1986; see also Ward et al. 1986; Miranne and Gray 1987) have examined deterrence in the laboratory with a particularly clever design involving a computer simulation. The simulation involves a series of trials where for each trial the study participant must choose between two buttons, "1" and "2," showing on a computer console. The participant is told that the computer will also make this choice (in reality a prearranged random ordering of ones and twos). The combination of the participant's choice and the computer's choice determines the participant's payoff. In the initial variant of the simulation created by Stafford et al. (1986), the participant wins fifteen points for each trial where her or his choice matches the computer's choice. The participant loses ten points if the two choices do not match. The outcome is displayed after each of fifty trials. Participants are also told that they can use a "preview" button to see the computer's choice ahead of time. As a way of learning the game, use of the preview button is encouraged during the first ten trials. After that, participants are told that the computer will scan for use of the preview button and that they will be fined for its use if detected.

Table 3.1. Average Frequency of Cheating Across 100 Trials of a Deterrence Simulation (Miranne and Gray 1987)

	Punishment Certainty		
Punishment Severity	*Low*	*High*	
Low	97.4	30.2	63.8
High	55.8	28.6	42.2
	76.6	29.3	Grand Mean = 53

Note: Row and column statistics are the marginal means.

Conditions for the Stafford et al. (1986) experiment constituted a 6 (punishment certainty) by 5 (punishment severity) factorial design. To manipulate certainty, participants were told that the computer would scan for use of the preview button on 10, 20, 30, 40, 50, or 94 percent of the game trials. To manipulate punishment severity, fines of 5, 25, 45, 110, or 200 points were imposed for detected use of the preview button. Participants were randomly assigned to one of the resulting thirty conditions ($n = 5$ in each). Also, participants were told that their earnings for the study would depend on how many points they accumulated during the game. The dependent variable was use of the preview button. Analyses revealed that a nonadditive model of deterrence fit the data substantially better than an additive alternative.

However, using the same experimental paradigm, Miranne and Gray (1987) found that only certainty had a general deterrent effect; the terms for severity and certainty x severity were not significant. Despite the fact that both Stafford et al. and Miranne and Gray implemented the same simulation, their failure to achieve the same results may have resulted from unduly low cell sizes. In each study, there were only five cases per cell.

Because Miranne and Gray used conventional statistical tests (for example, ANOVA), computation of a "power analysis" (Cohen 1988) is straightforward. The cell means, marginal means, and grand mean for their study are shown in Table 3.1.

Using the formulas and power tables in Cohen (1988; see pp. 376–79 for an illustrative example), we calculated the effect sizes for the main effects and the interaction term (certainty x severity), and the power of the associated significance tests. These values are shown in Table 3.2.

Following Cohen (1992), we adopt the convention specifying that a power value less than 0.80 involves too great a risk of a Type II statistical error, β (erroneously failing to reject the null hypothesis), which is equal to $1 - $ power. Using this cutoff, only the test for the effect representing punishment cer-

Table 3.2.   Effect Sizes and Power Values for the Effects Representing Certainty, Severity, and Certainty X Severity in Miranne and Gray (1987)

Effect	Effect Size	Power of F Test
Certainty	0.71	0.99
Severity	0.32	0.49
Certainty x Severity	0.30	0.44

Note: Power values assume an 0.05 alpha level.

tainty is acceptable. And because the interaction, certainty X severity, is a central issue in the research, a power of 0.44 ($\beta = 0.56$) is hardly sufficient. As such, further experimental investigation is needed.

In addition, there is some question as to whether the experimental "impact" (see Aronson 1990, chap. 2) achieved by the simulation described above is sufficient. Even though it is controlled, the simulation can be criticized for its presentation of trivial stimuli. In other words, we question the extent to which participants in Stafford et al.'s (1986) study found the experimental setting meaningful and involving. Even if the empirical realizations of sanction certainty and sanction severity in the study had sufficient impact, we question the correspondence between the operational definitions and their parent concepts. When deterrence researchers use the term *formal sanctions,* they are usually referring to punishments decided on and carried out by occupants of specific statuses in specific bureaucratic organizations. Thus, as it is commonly used, the concept of formal sanctions implies *three* important properties: punishments, occupants of specific statuses, and specific bureaucratic organizations. The second two of these properties are missing from Stafford et al.'s (1986) treatment of sanctions. Fines are imposed in the simulation, but not by occupants of specific statuses in specific bureaucratic organizations. We are not suggesting that this approach is "wrong," but that it does not seem relevant to the concept of formal sanctions in dominant explanations of deterrence.

RATIONALITY AND SELF-CONTROL

Both laboratory and survey studies of individual-level deterrence have emphasized the role of *situational factors* (for example, perceptions of sanction certainty and severity) in persons' decisions whether to offend. In other areas of research, criminologists have emphasized the role of *time-stable individual differences* in criminal propensity. For example, Gottfredson and

Hirschi (1990) argue that negligent parenting causes children to develop low self-control, which is evident in people who show signs of being impulsive, self-centered, incautious, short-tempered, drawn to simple tasks, and physically rather than cognitively oriented (Grasmick et al. 1993). People who are low in self-control are attracted to the thrill and immediate gratification that crime and deviance may provide. Much research confirms that low self-control is positively related to involvement in crime and analogous deviant behaviors such as smoking, drinking, and gambling (Arneklev et al. 1993; Brownfield and Sorenson 1993; Keane, Maxim, and Teevan 1993; Wood, Pfefferbaum, and Arneklev 1993; Polakowski 1994; Sorenson and Brownfield 1995; Longshore, Turner, and Stein 1996; Evans et al. 1997; Longshore 1998).

Recently, deterrence researchers have come to focus on *both* situational factors and time-stable individual differences in criminal propensity. For example, Nagin and Paternoster (1993) collected scenario-based data from college students and found that both perceived costs and benefits (situational factors) and lack of self-control (criminal propensity) predicted decisions to commit three offenses: drunk driving, theft, and sexual assault. Hillbo and Lovaglia (1995) replicated this finding in their scenario-based study of academic cheating. In a recent laboratory study, Nagin and Pogarsky (2003) found that cheating behavior occurred (1) less frequently when the certainty of detection was relatively high, and (2) more frequently among subjects with stronger "present-orientation" or with greater "self-serving bias." Severity had no effect, nor did severity interact with certainty. Furthermore, Nagin and Pogarsky did not look for interaction effects between their situational (certainty and severity) and individual-difference variables (present-orientation and self-serving bias).

Wright, Caspi, and Moffitt (1999; see also Wright et al. 2000) have offered an integrated model of rational choice and self-control theories focusing on the nonadditive effects of situational and individual-level factors on criminal behavior. The logic of the model is as follows. People who are high in self-control differ from low self-control individuals in one important respect: they tend not to even consider committing crime. However, in order for situational factors to influence decisions to offend, crime must be considered as a behavioral option in the first place. It is individuals low in self-control who consider crime as a behavioral option. Those with high self-control ignore situational inducements because such people are not prone to crime to begin with. Based on these assumptions, Wright et al. (1999) hypothesize that "the costs of crime should most strongly deter the behavior of individuals with low self control" (p. 5). They find strong support for this prediction using longitudinal data from the Dunedin Multidisciplinary Health and Development Study

(Silva and Stanton 1996). This study included measures of low self-control, perceived certainty of detection and perceived severity of informal sanctions associated with various crimes, and self-reported involvement in forty-eight different types of crimes. Wright et al. (1999) created four interaction terms using these measures: (1) low self-control in childhood x high perceived certainty; (2) low self-control in adolescence x high perceived certainty; (3) low self-control in childhood x high perceived informal costs; and (4) low self-control in adolescence x high perceived informal costs. All of the product terms were negative and statistically significant in regression equations predicting criminal behavior at age twenty-one (the final wave).

There is actually some disagreement in the deviance literature, however, as to whether low self-control people are *more* responsive to situational deterrents. According to Gottfredson and Hirschi (1990), positing connections among punishment factors, criminal propensity, and the likelihood of criminal behavior "misconstrues the nature of self-control" (pp. 255–56). Because low self-control individuals are impulsive and prone to risk-taking, they do not even stop to consider the (long-term) costs of crime. Such individuals thwart danger and feel immune to the potential costs of engaging in crime (Caspi et al. 1994).

Thus, while Wright et al. (1999) have provided some evidence that seems to go against Gottfredson and Hirschi's (1990) conceptualization of how low self-control affects crime and deviance, our study will help to shed further light on this important debate. The main goal of our research is to test the effect of certainty of punishment on low and high self-control subjects using a unique laboratory experiment that counterbalances the limitations of traditional survey approaches (susceptible to specification error) and newer scenario-based approaches, which examine *imagined* behavior only.

METHOD

Subjects and Procedures

College students were recruited from classes at a large Midwestern university to participate in an experimental study for pay. Male students who agreed to participate were scheduled for an experimental session.[3] All were Caucasian and between the ages of eighteen and twenty. Upon arriving at our facility, each participant was asked to fill out an anonymous questionnaire for an apparently unrelated "Lifestyles" study. No one refused to complete the survey. In reality, items from the survey were used to construct an index of low self-control (described below).

After the participant completed the survey, an assistant escorted him to a private room furnished with a cubicle, a chair, a computer terminal, a closed-circuit camera, and a TV monitor. At this point, the participant received instructions for the study from the assistant.

During the instructions, the assistant described and demonstrated a task that the participant would be asked to complete: a one-pattern Contrast Sensitivity task. In this task, participants view a series of pictures containing black and white rectangles (see, for example, Moore 1965, 1968; Berger, Cohen, and Zelditch 1972). They are instructed to decide whether each picture contains a greater amount of white area or black area. In reality, each picture contains the same amount of black and white area (that is, there are no "correct" answers), although this fact is highly ambiguous to naïve participants.

Each participant in our study was informed that he would be completing twenty-five Contrast Sensitivity problems, and that he would be paid $.80 for each "correct" answer. Each participant was also informed that he would be prompted by the computer to view the correct answer after each trial by pressing the control key on the computer keyboard. In demonstrating several practice problems, however, the assistant "accidentally" pressed the control key *before* entering an answer on one of the problems. When doing so, the "correct" answer appeared prematurely, supposedly to the assistant's surprise. With this modification of the software for the Contrast Sensitivity task (Troyer 2000), each participant was shown a method of obtaining answers to the task problems without having to rely on ability. In pointing out his "mistake," the assistant instructed the participant not to repeat it, thereby establishing a rule to be broken if the participant would choose to do so. Furthermore, an example results screen at the end of the tutorial showed that the assistant's mistake had gone undetected by the computer. That is, the assistant was given credit for having input an answer that he obtained prior to entering it. The assistant emphasized once more that the participant should not use the control key to view answers before entering them.[4]

Following the demonstration, the assistant explained that after the participant completed all of the Contrast Sensitivity problems, his task results would be sent over a local area computer network to the sociology main office. The assistant then presented the participant with a coupon indicating a personal identification number and instructed the participant to go to the sociology main office after the task and exchange the coupon for pay (supposedly up to twenty dollars, depending on performance). Finally, just before exiting the room, the assistant instructed the participant to click a button on his computer console labeled "Begin Contrast Sensitivity Task."

When the participant exited the lab room after completing the task, the assistant approached the participant and said that he needed to read a "debriefing statement." In the debriefing session, the participant was informed about the true nature of the study, and his questions about the study, if any, were addressed. Finally, all participants were paid twenty dollars in cash for their involvement in the study.

Independent Variables

Punishment Certainty

To examine deviance in the setting described above, we initially assigned thirty participants at random to one of two experimental conditions.[5] In a *low certainty of formal sanctions* condition ($n = 14$), a surveillance camera in the participant's room was placed in a position that clearly could not reveal the participant's illegitimate use of the control key to solve Contrast Sensitivity problems. In a *high certainty of formal sanctions* condition ($n = 16$), the surveillance camera was placed directly behind the participant such that the assistant could monitor the participant's performance on task problems closely. For the purposes of this initial study, we held the severity of formal sanctions constant at a high absolute level, particularly because most research seems to show that the certainty of punishment (as opposed to its severity) is what matters most for deterrence (Nagin and Pogarsky 2003). Accordingly, all participants were told during the task instructions that students caught engaging in laboratory misbehavior (for example, harassment of others, vandalism, and cheating) would have their academic advisors contacted, a disciplinary file created, and could be dismissed from the university pending a case review.

Low Self-Control

We measured the "risk-seeking" dimension of low self-control (see Grasmick et al. 1993) with three items in the pre-questionnaire delivered to participants at the outset of the study. Participants used a six-point Likert-type scale (1–Strongly Disagree; 6–Strongly Agree) to respond to the following statements: (1) "I enjoy new and exciting experiences in life even if they are frightening"; (2) "Excitement and adventure in life are more important to me than security"; and, (3) "In life, you have to take chances." We focused on the risk-seeking dimension of low self-control for three reasons. First, embedding all twenty-three of the items from the Grasmick et al. (1993) low self-control scale in our mock "Lifestyles" survey would have resulted in a lengthy instrument, one too time-consuming in the context of the entire experimental session. Second, we were concerned that a number of items from the original scale (for example, those representing "temper" and "self-centeredness") would serve to alert most participants to the true purposes of the study. Finally, empirical research suggests that the risk-seeking dimension of low self-control is the most important one. Studies have shown that subscales representing risk-seeking are as valuable in predicting crime as the full twenty-three-item scale (Longshore, Turner, and Stein 1996; Piquero and Rosay 1998) and sometimes more valuable (Arneklev et al. 1993). As such, Longshore et al. (1996) argue that it might be best to focus theory development on risk-seeking alone because it appears to be the "most efficient form" of low self-control (p. 223).

In addition to our cognitive measure of low self-control, we included several behavioral measures. Specifically, we asked participants to use a six-point Likert-type scale to rate *how often* (1=never; 6=every day) they had smoked cigarettes and drunk alcohol in the past thirty days. We also asked participants to estimate *how many* cigarettes and alcoholic beverages, on average, they had consumed per day in the past thirty days. We multiplied the two measures (how often X how many) to produce a single measure of incidence for each behavior, smoking and drinking.[6] Hirschi and Gottfredson (1993) argue in favor of using behavioral items to assess low self-control as long as the dependent variable can be measured independently. For adults, they recommend using difficulties in interpersonal relations, employment instability, automobile accidents, drinking, and smoking as important indicators. We focus on smoking and drinking because these two behaviors went nicely with our mock "Lifestyles" survey and because they are salient events in the population of college students that served as our research participants. Importantly, our study is the first that we know of to include both cognitive and behavioral measures of low self-control.

Dependent Variable

The dependent variable in our study was whether or not the participant used the control key at least once to view the "correct" answer before submitting a solution. As mentioned above, the computer software that we developed for the study privately recorded this information for each trial.

RESULTS

Consistent with much experimental and nonexperimental research on deterrence, analyses of our data revealed a strong effect of our certainty manipulation. None of the participants in the *high certainty* condition ($n = 14$) used the control key to see correct answers to task problems before submitting their own solutions. However, 50 percent of the participants in the *low certainty* condition ($n = 16$) used the control key for illegitimate purposes, even

Table 3.3. Results from a Logistic Regression Predicting Illegitimate Use of the Control Key (Cheating) from Low Self-Control in the Low Certainty of Detection Setting (*n* = 34)

Variable	*b*	(*S.E.*)
Low self-control	1.00*	0.38
Intercept	−0.58	0.42
Likelihood ratio χ^2	36.78	
(d.f. = 32)		

*$p < 0.01$ (two-tailed)

though the severity of the penalty for detection was ostensibly serious (that is, dismissal from the university). This difference is not attributable to chance ($\chi^2 = 9.00$, d.f. $= 1, p < 0.01$). In the setting we employed, then, the certainty of formal sanctions was a powerful deterrent of a deviant behavior, cheating on a difficult task to earn more money. This result is consistent with a rational choice model of deterrence.

More importantly, we wanted to know if low self-control discriminated between the cheaters and noncheaters in the low certainty condition. To assure our ability to detect any difference, we assigned eighteen additional participants to this condition.[7] In the end, fourteen (41 percent) out of the thirty-four participants in the low certainty condition used the control key to see correct answers to task problems before submitting their own solutions. To examine the relationship between cheating and low self-control, we estimated a logistic regression equation with illegitimate use of the control key as the dependent variable and our measure of low self-control as the independent variable. Table 3.3 summarizes the logistic regression results.

Indeed, low self-control had a significant, positive effect on illegitimate use of the control key in the low certainty condition ($b = 1.00$, two-tailed $p < 0.01$). Specifically, the odds of cheating in the low certainty condition were increased by a factor of $e^{1.00} = 2.72$ for a unit change in low self-control. This finding in conjunction with the finding that no one in our study cheated under conditions of high certainty is consistent with Wright et al.'s (1999) argument that *low* self-control individuals are particularly sensitive to changes in crime-relevant situational factors such as the certainty and severity of formal sanctions.[8]

DISCUSSION

We conducted a laboratory experiment and found support for Wright et al.'s (1999) integration of rational choice and self-control theories, which predicts that only individuals who are low in self-control are responsive to changes in the certainty or severity of punishments. Importantly, this finding provides additional evidence calling into question Gottfredson and Hirschi's (1990) claim that crime and deviance (broadly speaking) cannot be deterred effectively among individuals with low levels of self-control. In our study, no one cheated on the task when the risk of getting caught was relatively high. However, when the risk of getting caught was relatively low, fourteen out of thirty-four participants (41 percent) cheated. This finding is strikingly similar to the prevalence of "fraud" (39 percent) reported in Fetchenhauer and colleagues' experimental test of Gottfredson and Hirschi's (1990) general theory of crime (this volume). While Fetchenhauer et al. did not manipulate the certainty of detection in their study, it was arguably "low" and comparable to the low certainty condition in our study. Despite other study differences, what makes the similarity of our results and theirs particularly striking is the fact that we examined deviance among college students recruited from classes at one large Midwestern university, whereas Fetchenhauer and his colleagues examined deviance across the ocean in Cologne (Germany) among individuals recruited by means of a local newspaper ad.

Our study is unique, however, in that we examined the *interaction* of punishment certainty and a critical dimension of self-control (risk-seeking) in a laboratory setting. When the risk of getting caught was relatively low, the odds of a participant cheating on the task for personal gain were increased almost threefold for each unit increase in our measure of low self-control. But again, no one cheated in the high certainty condition. Thus, with increasing levels of self-control, participants in our study were less likely to cheat, *under any conditions*. At lower levels of self-control, participants in our study tended to explore illegitimate means, but only when the chances were good that they could get away with it. Thus, Wright et al. (1999) may be correct in assuming that low self-control individuals, while crime *prone*, are still mindful of, and responsive to, the attractiveness of criminal opportunities.

While these findings are notable, our study has some limitations that should be addressed in subsequent research. First, we did not manipulate the severity of formal sanctions (we held it constant at a high absolute level); thus, we were not able to examine the simultaneous effects of formal sanction certainty and severity on the probability of deviance as others have (see, for example, Nagin and Pogarsky 2003). Second, we believe that other experimental manipulations of formal sanction certainty (and formal sanction severity) should be examined. The first issue can be addressed easily in future experimental studies. Addressing the second will require more ingenuity and is arguably the most important. Because there is never a one-to-one correspondence between a concept and its empirical realization, investigating different operationalizations of independent variables through systematic replication is invaluable for understanding social processes (Aronson 1990). Our results suggest that this task is worth pursuing.

Much work remains to be done in the area of reconciling our work and that of Wright and his colleagues (1999) with the general theory of crime (Gottfredson and Hirschi 1990). At this point, we suspect that *both* Gottfredson and Hirschi (1990) and Wright and his colleagues (1999) may turn out to be correct, but that each is likely to be correct under specialized conditions. On the one hand, Wright and colleagues' integration of rational choice and self-control theories may apply best to more instrumental types of both violent and nonviolent offenses, such as *premeditated* murder and fraud/cheating, respectively. On the other hand, Gottfredson and Hirschi's arguments may apply best to more expressive varieties of offending, such as those now often associated with "intermittent explosive disorder" (Olvera 2002). With respect to expressive offenses, biological studies have focused on the link between dysfunction in the frontal lobes of the brain (the seat of impulse control) and impulsive violence in particular (Raine and Liu 1998). For one thing, individuals presenting frontal dysfunction appear to be less able to hold back violent impulses during high emotional arousal (for example, when they are angry), regardless of the consequences (Scarpa and Raine 2000). However, during periods of relatively low emotional arousal, it may be that individuals lacking impulse control are quite able to discriminate among more and less attractive instrumental-criminal opportunities, as determined by situational factors (certainty and severity). By contrast, individuals who exhibit higher levels of impulse control much more rarely participate in *any* kind of antisocial activity because they can continuously draw on their abundant control "reserves" as a resource for conformity even in emotionally upsetting situations (see Muraven, Tice, and Baumeister 1998). In short, both Gottfredson and Hirschi and Wright et al. would agree that high self-control people tend to avoid crime. However, whether individuals who exhibit *low* self-control pay any attention to situational factors such as punishment certainty and severity may depend upon the level of emotional arousal, which we believe is relevant to a discussion of different types of offenses (instrumental versus expressive).

Indirectly, the points we raise here also bear on a question raised by Fetchenhauer and his colleagues in chapter 2: Do low self-control persons engage in crime *because* it is risky, or *although* it is risky? Here again, we suspect that the answer to this question might be "both," depending on the type of crime. On the one hand, to the extent that thrill-seeking is part of what it means to be low self-control, then the thrillingness of a criminal act (for example, the "rush" of breaking and entering) may indeed serve as part of the "reward" for engaging in the act, particularly in the case of instrumental crimes. That is, individuals characterized by low self-control engage in instrumental crimes in part *because* they are exciting and risky to pull off. On the other hand, when enraged by someone, individuals who lack self-control might precipitously disregard the fact that most homicides are quickly solved ("cleared") by the police (relatively high certainty). In other words, individuals characterized by low self-control may engage in expressive crimes like violent aggression *although* risks are involved in such action. They cannot help it. For example, individuals with impaired frontal cortical functioning lack the ability to attenuate (or constrain) powerful signals emanating from the brain's emotional centers (that is, the limbic system), and, as a consequence, they are more likely to lash out with aggression, sometimes with deadly consequences. In statistical terms, we are suggesting that self-control will interact with situational factors *only for instrumental crimes*. For expressive crimes, we would expect to find a main effect of self-control, but no interaction effect of self-control and situational factors.

Given these insights, and in light of the unique ability of laboratory studies to disentangle causal processes, our goal is to continue a program of experimental research that will lead to the further development of a rigorous set of procedures for testing and improving theories of deviance. The rationale for this goal and some possible means of attaining it are described by Horne and Lovaglia in chapter 1 of this volume. In sharing their viewpoint, we are hopeful that increased communication among experimentalists and researchers using other kinds of methodologies and theoretical perspectives will greatly improve our understanding of crime and deviance. Eventually, this collaborative strategy should facilitate the implementation of more effective strategies of crime control.

NOTES

1. For two excellent overviews of the literature on deterrence, see Paternoster (1987) and Nagin (1998).

2. A notable exception is Nagin and Pogarsky (2003).

3. Men are more likely to commit illegal acts than women, "always and everywhere" (Gottfredson and Hirschi 1990:145). Our concern was that participants, whether male or female, might be unlikely to exhibit deviance in the laboratory under *any* conditions. Thus, to maximize variation in the dependent variable, we used only male participants in our first study. If successful, future laboratory research can build on existing survey research (for example, Burton et al. 1998; LaGrange and Silverman 1999) and use low self-control and rationality to explore gender differences in deviant behavior.

4. To determine whether the participant did end up using the control key to cheat despite the assistant's warning, the computer software privately recorded the points at which the participant pressed the key in the sequence of task problems.

5. Four of the original thirty participants were replaced because they were suspicious that the goal of the experiment was to study deviant behavior.

6. A factor analysis with principal axis factoring suggested that the risk-seeking and behavioral items (all standardized) were bidimensional. However, this solution might reflect differences in shared error variance between the cognitive and behavioral items. There are also theoretical reasons for treating the items as unidimensional (Nagin and Paternoster 1993). Thus, to construct our measure of low self-control, we summed the factor scores from a two-factor solution obtained with quartimax rotation.

7. Two of the original eighteen participants were replaced because they were suspicious that the goal of the experiment was to study deviant behavior. Three others were replaced for failing to understand how to use the control key for illegitimate purposes. In the entire study, then, data from 16 percent of the participants was replaced. Higher rates (20–25 percent) are typical for sociological experiments (Lovaglia 1995).

8. Differences in the distribution of low self-control between our two study conditions cannot account for the observed difference in illegitimate use of the control key. Between the two conditions, the means for our measure of low self-control do not differ significantly (mean diff. = 0.51; $t = 1.23$, df = 46, $p = 0.23$), and the variances are equal (Levene's test: F (1,46) = 0.03, $p = 0.86$).

REFERENCES

Anderson, Linda S., Theodore G. Chiricos, and Gordon P. Waldo. 1977. "Formal and Informal Sanctions: A Comparison of Deterrent Effects." *Social Problems* 25:103–14

Arneklev, Bruce J., Harold G. Grasmick, Charles R. Tittle, and Robert J. Bursik. 1993. "Low Self-Control and Imprudent Behavior." *Journal of Quantitative Criminology* 9:225–47.

Aronson, Elliot. 1990. *Methods of Research in Social Psychology,* 2nd ed. New York: McGraw-Hill.

Bachman, Ronet, Raymond Paternoster, and Sally Ward. 1992. "The Rationality of Sexual Offending: Testing a Deterrence/Rational Choice Conception of Sexual Assault." *Law and Society Review* 26:343–72.

Beccaria, Cesare. 1775. *An Essay on Crimes and Punishments*, 4th ed. London: F. Newberry.

Bentham, Jeremy. 1823. *An Introduction to the Principles of Morals and Legislation.* London: W. Pickering.

Berger, Joseph, Bernard P. Cohen, and Morris Zelditch, Jr. 1972. "Status Characteristics and Social Interaction." *American Sociological Review* 37:241–55.

Bishop, Donna M. 1984. "Legal and Extralegal Barriers to Delinquency: A Panel Analysis." *Criminology* 22:403–19.

Brownfield, David, and Ann Marie Sorenson. 1993. "Self-Control and Juvenile Delinquency: Theoretical Issues and an Empirical Assessment of Selected Elements of a General Theory of Crime." *Deviant Behavior: An Interdisciplinary Journal* 14:243–64.

Burton, Velmer S., Jr., Francis T. Cullen, T. David Evans, Leanne Fiftal Alarid, and R. Gregory Dunaway. 1998. "Gender, Self-Control, and Crime." *Journal of Research in Crime and Delinquency* 35:123–47.

Caspi, Avshalom, Terrie E. Moffitt, Phil A. Silva, Magda Stouthamer-Loeber, Robert F. Krueger, and Pamela S. Schmutte. 1994. "Are Some People Crime-Prone? Replications of the Personality-Crime Relationship across Countries, Genders, Races, and Methods." *Criminology* 37:163–95.

Cohen, Jacob. 1988. *Statistical Power Analysis for the Behavioral Sciences*, 2nd ed. Hillsdale, NJ: Erlbaum.

———. 1992. "A Power Primer." *Psychological Bulletin* 112:155–59.

Evans, David T., Francis T. Cullen, Velmer S. Burton, Jr., R. Gregory Dunaway, and Michael L. Benson. 1997. "The Social Consequences of Self-Control: Testing the General Theory of Crime." *Criminology* 35:475–504.

Gottfredson, Michael R., and Travis Hirschi. 1990. *A General Theory of Crime*. Palo Alto, CA: Stanford University Press.

Grasmick, Harold G., and George J. Bryjak. 1980. "The Deterrent Effect of Perceived Severity of Punishment." *Social Forces* 59:471–91.

Grasmick, Harold G., and Robert J. Bursik. 1990. "Conscience, Significant Others, and Rational Choice: Extending the Deterrence Model." *Law and Society Review* 24:837–61.

Grasmick, Harold G., and Donald E. Green. 1980. "Legal Punishment, Social Disapproval and Internalization as Inhibitors of Illegal Behavior." *Journal of Criminal Law and Criminology* 71:325–35.

Grasmick, Harold G., Charles R. Tittle, Robert J. Bursik, Jr., and Bruce J. Arneklev. 1993. "Testing the Core Empirical Implications of Gottfredson and Hirschi's General Theory of Crime." *Journal of Research in Crime and Delinquency* 30:5–29.

Green, Donald E. 1989. "Measure of Illegal Behavior in Individual-Level Deterrence Research." *Journal of Research in Crime and Delinquency* 26:253–75.

Henshel, Richard L. 1980. "The Purpose of Laboratory Experimentation and the Virtues of Deliberate Artificiality." *Journal of Experimental Social Psychology* 16:466–78.

Hillbo, Alec, and Michael J. Lovaglia. 1995. "Cheating in College: A Test of Rational Choice and Control Theories." Paper presented at the annual meeting of the American Sociological Association, August, Washington, D.C.

Hirschi, Travis, and Michael Gottfredson. 1993. "Commentary: Testing the General Theory of Crime." *Journal of Research in Crime and Delinquency* 30:47–54.

Jacob, Herbert. 1980. "The Deterrent Effects of Formal and Informal Sanctions." *Law and Policy Quarterly* 2:61–70.

Jensen, Gary F., Maynard L. Erickson, and Jack P. Gibbs. 1978. "Perceived Risk of Punishment and Self-Reported Delinquency." *Social Forces* 57:57–78.

Johnson, Richard E. 1979. *Juvenile Delinquency and Its Origins: An Integrated Theoretical Approach*. Cambridge, UK: Cambridge University Press.

Keane, Carl, Paul S. Maxim, and James J. Teevan. 1993. "Drinking and Driving: Self-Control and Gender: Testing a General Theory of Crime." *Journal of Research in Crime and Delinquency* 30:30–46.

Klepper, Steven, and Daniel Nagin. 1989. "The Deterrent Effect of Perceived Certainty and Severity of Punishment Revisited." *Criminology* 27:721–46.

Kmenta, Jan. 1986. *Elements of Econometrics*, 2nd ed. New York: Macmillan.

LaGrange, Teresa C., and Robert A. Silverman. 1999. "Low Self-Control and Opportunity: Testing the General Theory of Crime as an Explanation for Gender Differences in Delinquency." *Criminology* 37:41–72.

Longshore, Douglas. 1998. "Self-Control and Criminal Opportunity: A Prospective Test of the General Theory of Crime." *Social Problems* 45:102–13.

Longshore, Douglas, Susan Turner, and Judith A. Stein. 1996. "Self-Control in a Criminal Sample: An Examination of Construct Validity." *Criminology* 34:209–28.

Lovaglia, Michael. 1995. "Power and Status: Exchange, Attribution and Expectation States." *Small Group Research* 26:400–26.

Meier, Robert F., and Weldon T. Johnson. 1977. "Deterrence as Social Control: The Legal and Extra-legal Production of Conformity." *American Sociological Review* 42:292–304.

Minor, William W., and Joseph Harry. 1982. "Deterrent and Experiential Effects in Perceptual Deterrence Research: A Replication and Extension." *Journal of Research in Crime and Delinquency* 19:190–203.

Miranne, Alfred C., and Louis N. Gray. 1987. "Deterrence: A Laboratory Experiment." *Deviant Behavior* 8:191–203.

Mook, Douglas G. 1983. "In Defense of External Invalidity." *American Psychologist* 38:379–87.

Moore, James C., Jr. 1965. "Development of the Spatial Judgment Experimental Task." Technical report no. 15. Laboratory for Social Research, Stanford University, Palo Alto, CA.

———. 1968. "Status and Influence in Small Group Interactions." *Sociometry* 37:47–63.

Muraven, Mark, Dianne M. Tice, and Roy F. Baumeister. 1998. "Self-Control as Limited Resource: Regulatory Depletion Patterns. *Journal of Personality and Social Psychology* 74:774–89.

Murray, Glenn F., and Patricia G. Erickson. 1987. "Cross-Sectional Versus Longitudinal Research: An Empirical Comparison of Projected and Subsequent Criminality." *Social Science Research* 16:107–18.

Nagin, Daniel S. 1998. "Criminal Deterrence Research at the Outset of the Twenty-First Century." In *Crime and Justice: A Review of Research*, edited by M. Tonry. Vol. 23:1–24. Chicago: University of Chicago Press.

Nagin, Daniel S., and Raymond Paternoster. 1993. "Enduring Individual Differences and Rational Choice Theories of Crime." *Law and Society Review* 27:467–96.

———. 1994. "Personal Capital and Social Control: The Deterrence Implications of Individual Differences in Criminal Offending." *Criminology* 32:581–606.

Nagin, Daniel S., and Greg Pogarsky. 2003. "An Experimental Investigation of Deterrence: Cheating, Self-Serving Bias, and Impulsivity." *Criminology* 41:167–93.

Olvera, Rene S. 2002. "Intermittent Explosive Disorder: Epidemiology, Diagnosis and Management." *CNS Drugs* 16:517–26.

Paternoster, Raymond. 1987. "The Deterrent Effect of the Perceived Certainty and Severity of Punishment: A Review of Evidence and Issues." *Justice Quarterly* 4:173–217.

Paternoster, Raymond, and Leeann Iovanni. 1986. "The Deterrent Effect of Perceived Severity: A Reexamination." *Social Forces* 64:751–77.

Paternoster, Raymond, Linda E. Saltzman, Theodore G. Chiricos, and Gordon P. Waldo. 1982. "Perceived Risk and Deterrence: Methodological Artifacts in Perceptual Deterrence Research." *Journal of Criminal Law and Criminology* 73:1238–58.

Paternoster, Raymond, Linda E. Saltzman, Gordon P. Waldo, and Theodore G. Chiricos. 1983a. "Perceived Risk and Social Control: Do Sanctions Really Deter?" *Law and Society Review* 17:457–79.

———. 1983b. "Estimating Perceptual Stability and Deterrence Effects: The Role of Perceived Legal Punishment in the Inhibition of Criminal Involvement." *Journal of Criminal Law and Criminology* 74:270–97.

Paternoster, Raymond, and Sally Simpson. 1996. "Sanction Threats and Appeals to Morality: Testing a Rational Choice Model of Corporate Crime." *Law and Society Review* 30:549–83.

Piliavin, Irving, Craig Thornton, Rosemary Gartner, and Ross L. Matsueda. 1986. "Crime, Deterrence, and Rational Choice." *American Sociological Review* 51:101–19.

Piquero, Alex R., and Andre B. Rosay. 1998. "The Reliability of Grasmick et al.'s Self-Control Scale: A Comment on Longshore et al." *Criminology* 36:157–73.

Polakowski, Michael. 1994. "Linking Self- and Social-Control Deviance: Illuminating the Structure Underlying a General Theory of Crime and Its Relation to Deviant Activity." *Journal of Quantitative Criminology* 10:41–78.

Raine, Adrian, and Jiang-Hong Liu. 1998. "Biological Predispositions to Violence and Their Implications for Biosocial Treatment and Prevention." *Psychology, Crime and Law* 4:107–25.

Rossi, Peter H., and Andy B. Anderson. 1982. *Measuring Social Judgments: The Factorial Survey Approach.* Beverly Hills, CA: Sage Publications.

Saltzman, Linda, Raymond Paternoster, Gordon P. Waldo, and Theodore G. Chiricos. 1982. "Deterrent and Experiential Effects: The Problem of Causal Order in Perceptual Deterrence Research." *Journal of Research in Crime and Delinquency* 19:172–83.

Scarpa, Angela S., and Adrian Raine. 2000. "Violence Associated with Anger and Impulsivity." In *The Neuropsychology of Emotion*, edited by J. Borod, 320–39. New York: Oxford University Press.

Silberman, Matthew. 1976. "Toward a Theory of Criminal Deterrence." *American Sociological Review* 41:442–61.

Silva, Phil A., and Warren R. Stanton. 1996. *From Child to Adult: The Dunedin Multidisciplinary Health and Development Study.* Auckland: Oxford University Press.

Sorenson, Ann Marie, and David Brownfield. 1995. "Adolescent Drug Use and a General Theory of Crime: An Analysis of a Theoretical Integration." *Canadian Journal of Criminology* 37:19–37.

Stafford, Mark C., Louis N. Gray, Ben A. Menke, and David A. Ward. 1986. "Modeling the Deterrent Effects of Punishment." *Social Psychology Quarterly* 49:338–47.

Teevan, James J., Jr. 1976. "Subjective Perception of Deterrence (Continued)." *Journal of Research in Crime and Delinquency* 13:155–64.

Troyer, Lisa. 2000. MacSES. Unpublished software manual.

Waldo, Gordon P., and Theodore G. Chiricos. 1972. "Perceived Penal Sanctions and Self-Reported Criminality: A Neglected Approach to Deterrence Research." *Social Problems* 19:522–40.

Ward, David A., Ben A. Menke, Louis N. Gray, and Mark C. Stafford. 1986. "Sanctions, Modeling, and Deviant Behavior." *Journal of Criminal Justice* 14:501–8.

Webster, Murray, and John B. Kervin. 1971. "Artificiality in Experimental Sociology." *Canadian Review of Sociology and Anthropology* 8:263–72.

Williams, Kirk R., and Richard Hawkins. 1986. "Perceptual Research on General Deterrence: A Critical Overview." *Law and Society Review* 20:545–72.

Wood, Peter B., Betty Pfefferbaum, and Bruce J. Arneklev. 1993. "Risk-Taking and Self-Control: Social Psychological Correlates of Delinquency." *Journal of Crime and Justice* 16:111–30.

Wright, Bradley R. Enter, Avshalom Caspi, and Terrie E. Moffitt. 1999. "Integrating Rational Choice and Criminal Propensity Theories of Crime: The Variable Effects of the Costs of Crime." Paper presented at the annual meeting of the American Sociological Association, August, Chicago, IL.

Wright, Bradley R. E., Avshalom Caspi, Terrie E. Moffitt, and Ray Paternoster. 2000. "Does the Perceived Threat of Punishment Deter Criminally-Prone Individuals?" Unpublished manuscript.

Zelditch, Morris, Jr. 1969. "Can You Really Study an Army in the Laboratory?" In *A Sociological Reader in Complex Organizations*, edited by A. Etzioni. New York: Holt, Reinhart, and Winston.

4

Comment: Self-Control in the Lab

Travis Hirschi

A colleague of mine lined up a half-dozen bottles of wine in brown paper bags. The wines ranged in price from \$2 (Two-Buck Chuck [\$3 in Arizona]) to \$65 (probably a gift). His guests, academics not ashamed of their discriminating tastes, were invited to sample these offerings and rate their goodness. The results, which my colleague has relayed to me and I am sure to many others more than once, were clear. The \$2 wine was rated best of the bunch.

As described, the tasters did not know which wine they were tasting, and my colleague did not know which wine they had tasted when he recorded their responses. So, using a classic double-blind experiment, my colleague's theory, *snobs are frauds*—or, *price and taste are orthogonal*—was confirmed.

This little story, true to the best of my recollection, may be taken as a synopsis of the history and current condition of experimental social psychology. An experiment confirms an experimenter's theory. The results are widely and often reported, but the experiment itself is not repeated—at least, as far as we know.[1] The incentives to report findings contrary to one's own much-admired story are presumably limited.

The consequences of these perhaps natural tendencies are not pretty, as Augustine Brannigan has amply and persuasively demonstrated. The tendency of experimenters to corroborate and publish "interesting and important" theories has given us the famous and embarrassing Hawthorne and Pygmalion effects (2004:63–90). And the easily demonstrated tendency to remain silent about critical evaluations and failed replications has allowed many such results to attain the status of urban legends.

A science machine with this kind of record obviously needs—at the very least—tweaking of some sort. Brannigan suggests that social psychology might follow physics and divide the duties of theoreticians and experimentalists. The

63

resulting "triple-blind" experiments would reduce the tendency to corroborate rather than falsify theories, increase the likelihood of rigorous replication, and encourage the publication of negative findings (2004:164–65). Properly conducted, I might add, such experiments would provide no cause for "comment" by those whose ideas they are designed to test.

In triple-blind mode, my colleague would be forced to state his theory with sufficient clarity that it could be tested without his involvement. I doubt that he would find this requirement congenial. In all likelihood, he did not have an articulated theory before he conducted his experiment. Come to think of it, the theories I have ascribed to him are mine, not his. He is content to let the facts speak for themselves. But there is a more serious problem with requiring the theorist to go first. Theorists facing controlled experiments are not free to go wherever their logic and observation may take them. If social psychologists, they would be required to fashion ideas appropriately tested in situation mode, by "short term, emotionally innocuous, low-impact designs calculated to have very little lasting effect on the subjects" (Brannigan 2004:26). Most theorists, I would guess, would prefer other arrangements. And many would be reluctant to trust their ideas to specialists in the execution of such designs.

But if the triple-blind design puts theorists in an uncomfortable position, it may be worse for experimenters. In physics, chemistry, and biology, experimentalists often have unique skills, knowledge, and equipment, and well-staffed ongoing research programs. No stigma attaches to involvement in the testing of theories, whatever their source. In social psychology, combinations of unique skills, knowledge, and equipment are at best rare. And ongoing research programs with well-defined goals are found largely (only?) in plans for the future (Horne and Lovaglia, this volume). In this situation, we might predict uneasy acceptance of the experimenter's role as the tester of ideas supplied by others.

So, in my characterization, we have a method with problems and a remedy that seems to have problems of its own. Not incidentally, my comment and the papers by Fetchenhauer, Simon, and Fetchenhauer and by Kalkhoff and Willer should provide a test of the adequacy of this characterization.

I begin by looking at one of the problems Brannigan would have experimenters fix, the tendency of the laboratory experiment to corroborate theory. Leon Festinger famously observed:

> Negative results from a laboratory experiment can mean very little indeed. If we obtain positive results—that is, demonstrably significant differences among conditions—we can be relatively certain concerning our interpretation and conclusion from the experiment. If, however, no differences emerge, we can generally reach no definitive conclusion. (1954:142, quoted by Brannigan 2004:20)

If it is true, as Horne and Lovaglia state in chapter 1, that "theories are all necessarily false," what are we to make of a method tilted in favor of confirming them, or at least tilted in favor of finding the "core element of truth" in *good* ones? How might this unhappy bias be countered or neutralized? Brannigan's solution removes the tilt by taking the theorist out of the picture, by leaving questions of truth and falsity to disinterested experimenters. The two tests of self-control theory in this volume should shed light on the adequacy of this solution—since neither Gottfredson nor I was consulted on any matter pertaining to their design and execution.

What do they conclude? Are their findings negative or positive? As I read the Fetchenhauer, Simon, and Fetchenhauer account, the results of their experiment are essentially negative. Nothing predicted by our theory seems to work. Fetchenhauer, Simon, and Fetchenhauer report not seeing their results as a falsification of self-control theory, but the theory framework they endorse (an interaction of situation and personality) bears little resemblance to our position. As I read the Kalkhoff and Willer account, their results are even more clearly negative. They report positive results favoring rational choice theory, a theory they say contradicts self-control theory. We think our theory is a rational choice theory. Kalkhoff and Willer would limit application of self-control theory to expressive crimes, a use of the theory we consider strictly contrary to its logic.

So, Brannigan's remedy appears to work. We would not see the evidence contrary to our theory. When we are taken out of the picture, independent laboratory research is able to produce evidence contrary to the theory that prompted it. With triple-blind designs, it might be concluded, the bias toward corroborating theory may be effectively controlled.

An alternative interpretation is that these experiments are not triple-blind designs at all, but are in fact further evidence of the tendency of the laboratory experiment to produce results consistent with the *experimenter's* theory.

Fetchenhauer and his colleagues appear to make self-control theory the exclusive focus of their attention, devoting much of their space to a summary of its propositions and the results of research bearing on them. Their criticisms and interpretations of the theory, however, raise questions about the value and possible implications of laboratory tests of it. If, as they say, it "discovers the North Pole a second time," its falsification would seem to require rethinking the accuracy of the reports of previous expeditions.[2] If it has been established that our theory is ideologically slanted to reflect our "puritan" beliefs, why not simply report the unslanted truth and be done with it?

But I should not make too much of their criticisms of the theory. They merely repeat criticisms advanced by others and accept most but not all of them.[3] The problem is that the theory Fetchenhauer and his colleagues actually test is not self-control theory, but a "research" version of the theory that bears little resemblance to the borrowed original. Our self-control theory does not concern itself with the rewards or benefits of crimes, or with the motives behind them. Our self-control theory is not an opportunity theory unless opportunity is seen as another word for self--control (Gottfredson and Hirschi 1990:25–44; Hirschi and Gottfredson forthcoming). Self-control theory is a rational choice theory where actors differ in the significance they place on the long-term costs of criminal behavior.

Kalkhoff and Willer see the problems of criminology as essentially methodological and pin their hopes for solution of these problems on the controlled laboratory experiment, where "the objective is *testing theory*" (p. 45, emphasis in original) I will try to avoid large methodological issues and concentrate instead on their substantive or theoretical conclusions. For this purpose, I find it useful to identify and focus on four overlapping segments of their report.

The first is their summary of two deterrence experiments embodying "a particularly clever design" (p. 45–46). Their discussion turns out to be a particularly nice illustration of what we might call the "Festinger" problem. The initial experiment "revealed that a non-additive model of deterrence fit the data substantially better than an additive alternative." The replication, however, found that "only certainty had a general deterrent effect; the terms for severity and certainty x severity were not significant" (p. 46). Kalkhoff and Willer use "power analysis" to show that only the common positive finding is safe from the risk of Type II error ("erroneously failing to reject the null hypothesis"). As if "further research is needed" were not enough to save for the time being the whole of deterrence theory, Kalkhoff and Willer go on to question the validity and relevance of the design they have previously described as particularly clever. The net result is that their idea of deterrence theory is unlikely to be threatened by replications of the experiment in question whatever results they produce.

The second is their summary of research comparing the effects of "time-stable individual differences" (self-control) and "situational factors" (perceptions of sanction certainty and severity). The issue Kalkhoff and Willer appear to be addressing is whether or how self-control bears on the actor's responsiveness to situational constraints. Apparently, research shows that those high on self-control may be set aside because they "tend not to even consider committing crime" (p. 49). This shifts the focus to persons low on self-control. They consider crime, and therefore consider its costs. This conclusion, supported by research, appears to contradict our view, according to which "low self-control individuals are impulsive and prone to risk-taking [and therefore] do not even stop to consider the (long-term) costs of crime" (p. 49).[4]

The third encounter between rational choice and self-control theory takes place in the context of Kalkhoff and Willer's experiments.

When sixteen students were threatened with possible dismissal from the university and a camera was positioned to record their every move over a presumably very short (but unreported) period of time, none of them cheated on the impossible little task before them. This result is said to be "consistent with a rational choice model of deterrence" (p. 53).[5]

When the camera was for all intents and purposes removed, fourteen of thirty-four students cheated—that is, they at least once in twenty-five opportunities pressed a key to see a phony "correct" answer before answering it themselves. In this "low certainty" condition, the experimenters' measure of self-control was significantly negatively related to cheating. This result too is reported as consistent with a rational choice modification of self-control theory. Taken together, the two experiments show that low self-control individuals are "particularly sensitive to changes in crime-relevant situational factors such as the certainty and severity of formal sanctions" (p. 54).

The fourth and final confrontation of rational choice and self-control theory comes as a summary of what has gone before. Interestingly, the evidence against self-control theory appears to grow stronger. The Kalkhoff-Willer experiment is said to have produced "additional evidence" calling into question our claim that crime and deviance "cannot be deterred effectively among individuals with low levels of self-control" (p. 54). Here, as the bloggers say, is the money quote:

> Our study is unique . . . in that we examined the interaction of punishment certainty and a critical dimension of self-control (risk-seeking) in a laboratory setting. When the risk of getting caught was relatively low, the odds of a participant cheating on the task for personal gain were increased almost three-fold for each unit increase in our measure of low self-control. But again, no one cheated in the high certainty condition. Thus, with increasing levels of self-control, participants in our study were less likely to cheat, *under any conditions*. At lower levels of self-control, participants in our study tended to explore illegitimate means, but only when the chances were good that they could get away with it. Thus, Wright et al. ([unpublished]1999) may be correct in assuming that low self-control individuals, while crime-*prone*, are still mindful of, and responsive to, the attractiveness of criminal opportunities. (pp. 54–55, emphases in original)

Kalkhoff and Willer go on to paint a picture of people with low levels of self-control. According to them, such people:

- are irrational
- do not consider the long- or short-term costs of crime

- cannot help themselves
- are, perhaps intermittently, impervious to sanctions
- have interludes of pure impulse
- tend to specialize in crimes involving explosive violence
- may well suffer from "dysfunction in the frontal lobes of the brain" and
- may on occasion be drawn to instrumental crimes *because* they are risky and therefore exciting

I have spent so much space quoting and summarizing Kalkhoff and Willer's argument about the connections between rational choice and self-control theory—an argument presumably perfectly familiar to the reader—because I have been trying to convince myself that they mean what they say. Their constancy is remarkable. I am convinced. I therefore conclude that in all essential respects their version of self-control theory is essentially opposite to that found in *A General Theory of Crime.*

We have put the theory in our own words many times. It seems appropriate in this context to rely on independent explications of the theory based on pretty much all that has been written about it. Thus Stefan Schulz (2006):

> The authors of the general theory deem the agency of the actor untouched by differential levels of self-control, since self-control as a variable is located inside the actor (internal control) and does, therefore, not determine (heteronomously) the actor's choice. . . .
>
> At the time of decision-making, Gottfredson and Hirschi's actor exerts his or her private choice to do what he or she wants to do, according to his or her predilection. (p. 41) . . .
>
> Gottfredson and Hirschi reject the conception of crime as a rehearsal of a pre-determined behavioral program. Actors act, they don't behave in response to external stimuli! Thus, Gottfredson and Hirschi presuppose a theory of action, a principled selection of action. . . .
>
> Self-control is, then the non-technical re-definition of a phenomenon otherwise known as myopia/akrasia, which denotes the fact that human beings are attracted in respect of their goals and attention by proximate aspects of the situation and have only limited power to withstand temptation, even if non-action or other action probably yield long-term advantages. (p. 42)

Thus Erich Goode (forthcoming):

> The lack of self-control . . . does not require crime and can be counteracted by situational conditions. This makes [self-control] theory very different from the "kinds of people" theories that argue that because criminals are different from the rest of us, the commit crime. Whether or not they commit crime . . . depends on the circumstances in which they are implicated. (p. 12)

I suspect that Kalkhoff and Willer guessed their version of our theory from a measure of self-control widely used in tests of it (Grasmick et al. 1993; cf. Hirschi 2004). But there must be other sources as well. The Grasmick et al. measure cannot be responsible for suggestions of brain dysfunction or the assertion that "negligent parenting causes children to develop low self control" (p. 48). This statement too reverses our position. In our view, self-control is acquired; neglect tends to leave the child in a "natural" state (Gottfredson and Hirschi 1990:94–107).

Whatever its sources, and whatever the implications of multiple failures to detect it, the Kalkhoff-Willer interpretation of self-control theory is unfortunate because it replaces a rational choice alternative to "deterrence theory" with an alternative falsified by the everyday observation that potential offenders are influenced by the nature of the choices available to them.

In self-control theory, as we understand it, we are all potential offenders and *everyone* is influenced by the nature of the choices available to them. But some are more short-sighted than others, and some are more likely than others to assume that luck is on their side. Such people are less likely to attend to the long-term natural consequences of crime. Their choices are therefore unlikely to be altered by changes in the certainty or severity of legal sanctions.

Differences across individuals in their *perceptions* of the certainty and severity of legal sanctions are related to the likelihood that they will engage in criminal acts *because* these estimates are a function of (are evidence of) differences in their levels of self-control. These differences and their effects are not altered by changes in the *actual* certainty and severity of punishment. It is therefore a mistake to treat their perceptions as evidence in favor of "deterrence theory" as it is ordinarily understood.

As far as I can see, which may not be very far, the Festinger/Brannigan problem remains unsolved. Rational choice theory, and one of its variants, self-control theory, have survived laboratory experiments unscathed. Self-control theory, properly understood, actually gains support from experiments ostensibly tilted against it. (College students who take chances and smoke and drink are more likely to cheat on a "test.") I do not have a solution to this problem. I do have a tautology to offer. The problem will not be solved until it is recognized by those designing and executing laboratory experiments.

NOTES

1. Many experiments of course cannot be replicated in any meaningful sense of the term. Wines presumably vary in quality from year to year. So, too, may the tastes of

wine consumers. Thus, experimental results on such matters are more history than science. Some (for example, von Mises 1996:30–32) argue that social science is best understood as history in the sense that it is incapable of verifying or falsifying general propositions.

2. Strictly speaking, the "old wine in new bottles" putdown—and its many variants—say nothing about the truth of a theory. Those raising the issue of originality, it seems to me, have an obligation to spell out the implications of their findings for the theories they allege to be sources of the unoriginal theory they have, for unknown reasons, chosen to test.

3. Fetchenhauer et al. rightly understand that were our theory tautological in the derogatory sense of the term there would be no point in attempting to test it. We continue to accept the idea that theories of human action should be tautological in the sense that their conclusions follow logically from their premises. Whether they should be falsifiable is another question (see von Mises 1996:30–71).

4. Kalkhoff and Willer do not themselves appear to distinguish between short- and long-term costs. This is the only occasion I can find where either of these terms is employed. The distinction is central to self-control theory, as Fetchenhauer and his colleagues recognize.

5. The students were told not to cheat by the assistant who showed them how they could do so. It is likely, in my judgment, that this instruction, in the situation of certain detection, would be sufficient to deter cheating, and that it was in fact the operative "penalty" in the situation of unlikely detection. Put another way, it is far from clear that severity was "held constant at a high level" by warnings of clearly disproportionate penalties contrary to everyday experience in a permissive university.

REFERENCES

Brannigan, Augustine. 2004. *The Rise and Fall of Social Psychology: The Use and Misuse of the Experimental Method.* New York: Aldine de Gruyter.

Festinger, Leon. 1954. "Laboratory Experiment." In *Research Methods in the Behavioral Science*, edited by L. Festinger and D. Katz. London: Staples.

Goode, Erich. Forthcoming. "Introduction: Theoretical Implications of Self-Control Theory." In *Crime and Criminality: Assessing the General Theory of Crime*, edited by E. Goode. Palo Alto, CA: Stanford University Press.

Gottfredson, Michael R. and Travis Hirschi. 1990. *A General Theory of Crime.* Palo Alto, CA: Stanford University Press.

Grasmick, Harold G., Charles R. Tittle, Robert J. Bursik, Jr., and Bruce J. Arneklev. 1993. "Testing the Core Empirical Implications of Gottfredson and Hirschi's General Theory of Crime." *Journal of Research in Crime and Delinquency* 30:5–29.

Hirschi, Travis. 2004. "Self-Control and Crime." In *Handbook of Self-Regulation*, edited by R. F. Baumeister and K. D. Vohs. New York: Guilford Press.

Hirschi, Travis, and Michael R. Gottfredson. Forthcoming. "Critiquing the Critics: A Reply." In *Crime and Criminality: Assessing the General Theory of Crime*, edited by E. Goode. Palo Alto, CA: Stanford University Press.

Schulz, Stefan. 2006. *Beyond Self-Control: Analysis and Critique of Gottfredson and Hirschi's General Theory of Crime (1990)*. Berlin: Duncker and Humblot.

von Mises, Ludwig. [1949] 1996. *Human Action*. San Francisco: Fox and Wilkes.

II

SOCIAL INFLUENCE

5

Norms and Neighborhoods: Explaining Variation in Informal Control

Christine Horne and John Hoffmann

> Social control refers generally to the capacity of a group to regulate its
> members according to desired principles—to realize collective . . . goals.
> One central goal is the desire of community residents to live in safe and
> orderly environments that are free of predatory crime, especially interper-
> sonal violence.

(Sampson, Raudenbush, and Earls 1997:918)

In the tradition of Shaw and McKay ([1942], 1969), many criminologists seek
to explain why some communities appear to be better than others at realizing
their goal of safety and security (see, for example, Bursik and Grasmik 1993;
Kornhauser 1978; Lowencamp, Cullen, and Pratt 2003; Sampson and Groves
1989). Recent studies have reinvigorated an interest in macro- and micro-level
factors that affect criminal and delinquent conduct within and across communities. While criminologists have sought to understand variation in levels of informal control across neighborhoods, social scientists who study norms are engaged in a similar endeavor (Hechter and Opp 2001). They explain why
groups enforce social norms—that is, why people punish deviance. Conceptu-
ally, it seems obvious that these two sets of researchers ought to have much to
say to each other. They each are interested in the conditions and mechanisms
that affect the exercise of control and, in turn, various kinds of behavior.

Among crime researchers, social disorganization theory is the dominant
approach to explaining variation in crime rates (Agnew 1999; Akers and Sellers 2004). Criminologists have identified a number of neighborhood-level
characteristics (residential mobility, concentration of poverty, and so forth)
that are statistically associated with crime. Some suggest that neighborhoods
with these characteristics have different levels of formal and informal control,

and that this variation in control across communities accounts for variation in rates of crime and delinquency. Thus, neighborhood-level social control is thought to be important in explaining crime. After decades of research, however, we still do not know why particular community characteristics are linked to social control (and, in turn, to crime). Perhaps the most prominent advocate for a social control explanation, Robert J. Sampson, admits, "over the twentieth century we have been repeatedly confronted with structural correlates . . . associated with crime-rate variation. . . . By contrast, the social mechanisms hypothesized to account for the effects of neighborhood and community-level structural characteristics remain relatively unknown" (Sampson 2000a:712).

In this chapter, we provide a brief overview of social disorganization explanations for crime rate variation across neighborhoods. We then describe a theory of norm enforcement, identifying two key causal factors and the mechanisms linking those factors to sanctioning. Next, we describe a series of laboratory experiments that test the theoretical predictions. Finally, we discuss the implications of the theory of norm enforcement and experimental findings for understanding the relation between neighborhood characteristics, informal control, and crime. We explore ways in which norm enforcement theory provides an explanation for the link between neighborhood characteristics and informal control, thus filling part of the gap in knowledge noted by Sampson. And we suggest that insights from norms research provide a useful complement to existing social disorganization research.

FROM CRIMINOLOGY:
COMMUNITY CRIME AND CONTROL

Macro-level studies of crime were originally motivated by the question of why some urban neighborhoods experienced more crime than others. It was obvious to observers of urban life in nineteenth-century London and early twentieth-century Chicago that poor neighborhoods suffered from a disproportionate number of criminal and deviant activities. Shaw and McKay ([1942] 1969) offered the first systematic interpretation of crime and delinquency patterns in Chicago. They observed that the highest crime rates occurred in communities that had high population turnover, many immigrant residents, and substantial poverty. Relying on Thomas and Znaniecki's research on Polish immigrants and Burgess's concentric zone model of urban growth, they argued that social disorganization explained variation in crime rates. That is, disorganized communities were unable "to realize the common values of their residents or solve commonly experienced problems" (Bursik 1988:521). A decade or so after their seminal study, Shaw (1951:24) wrote that in disorganized areas "the effectiveness of the neighborhood as a unit of social control and as a medium of the transmission of the moral standards of society is greatly diminished."

As implied by Shaw's statement, social disorganization was originally seen as related to variations in both social control and the transmission of values. Areas with high population turnover, ethnic heterogeneity, or a lack of investment in the community experienced a lack of social control and inconsistent values concerning conventional behaviors. Recent criminological research focuses primarily on social control (rather than values) as the mechanism that mediates the association between demographic factors and crime rates. Scholars argue that residents of highly disorganized areas are unable to monitor and control the behavior of adolescents and adults (Sampson 2000b).

In a compelling and influential series of articles, Robert J. Sampson and colleagues (1997, 2002) refine this argument. Based on extensive research conducted in Chicago, they propose that informal social control and social integration together explain the association between demographic conditions and crime. In their model, the joint effect of informal social control and social integration is termed "collective efficacy"—the linkage of mutual trust and shared willingness to intervene for the public good (Sampson et al. 1997). Empirically, collective efficacy is a combination of items measuring trust (or cohesion) and respondents' perceptions that people in the neighborhood exercise informal social control. These items load together and are combined to form a latent variable. Research indicates that demographic measures of concentrated disadvantage, immigrant concentration, and residential stability are, as expected, associated with collective efficacy. Further, the association between these demographic measures and crime is partially mediated by collective efficacy.

The notion of collective efficacy is consistent with and extends research on social disorganization theory. It fits neatly as an intervening variable into statistical models. It avoids the problem of trying to look at actual control efforts on crime—a difficult thing to do because crime rates also affect control efforts. And it is highly predictive (see, for example, Almgren 2005; Browning, Feinberg, and Dietz et al. 2004; Sampson et al. 1997; Sampson, Morenoff, and Gannon-Rowley 2002). Thus, it is an attractive macro-level social control theory of crime.

FROM NORMS RESEARCH:
A THEORY OF NORM ENFORCEMENT

Like social disorganization researchers, norms scholars are interested in understanding social control. Norms are rules, about which there is some degree of consensus, that are socially enforced (Horne 2001a). Enforcement is an essential component of norms.

Explaining Norm Enforcement

Norms theory identifies two important causes of enforcement: (1) the direct costs and benefits associated with sanctioning, and (2) the reactions of group members to individual sanctioning efforts. Of course, social reactions may also be seen as a kind of cost and benefit. To avoid confusion, we use the terms "costs" and "benefits" when describing the direct consequences of sanctioning (time and effort, potential retaliation, change in the deviant behavior, and so forth) and talk about social reactions when discussing how people respond to sanctioners. Below we describe these factors and the mechanisms linking them to enforcement.

Norm enforcement produces a variety of benefits—including reduction in deviant behavior. People prefer that those around them behave in prosocial rather than antisocial ways. If they are negatively affected by another's deviant behavior, they have an interest in discouraging that behavior (Coleman 1990; Heckathorn 1988, 1989). This interest motivates them to punish deviance. Accordingly, one reason that individuals punish antisocial behavior is anticipated improvement in their own well-being. The greater the benefit associated with sanctioning, the stronger the interest. Larger sanctioning benefits therefore produce higher rates of norm enforcement.

Just as individuals take into account the potential benefits of punishing a behavior, they also consider the costs of doing so. Sanctioning can take time, energy, and money, as well as create the risk of physical injury. The larger these costs, the less willing people will be to impose a punishment. As costs increase, therefore, the likelihood that people will sanction deviance declines.

But people are social creatures. They take into account not only the immediate costs and benefits of addressing a deviant act, but also the likely reactions of others to their sanctioning efforts. Such reactions are called metanorms. Metanorms are a particular kind of norm that regulates sanctioning (Axelrod 1986, 1997; Coleman 1990). They work because people want others to think well of them. People want to show that they are a "good type" worth interacting with (Posner 2000). And they want others to respond to their behavior positively rather than negatively (Horne 2001b). In other words, when individuals are making a decision about sanctioning, they will consider the likely responses of others. Expectations of positive reactions encourage sanctioning. And the stronger and more favorable the reactions to sanctioning, the more likely people are to punish deviance. Thus, when people expect support for their sanctioning efforts they are more likely to enforce norms.

Explaining Social Support for Norm Enforcers

Why do people reward sanctioning efforts?[1] We might be happy to see others bear the risk of punishing deviance, but why do we make the effort to support them?

Research suggests that the key factor motivating support for sanctioners is concern with social relations. If an individual is in a relationship with another person, and that person bears the costs of sanctioning deviance, then the individual will give support to that person. The higher the costs, the more support will be given. This is because, if people want to maintain a relationship over the long run, they cannot just be fair-weather friends. When people with whom they interact experience costs, they need to be appropriately supportive. The larger the cost, the more support the individual will give. Accordingly, when sanctioners experience greater costs, we would expect them to receive larger rewards from others. That is, metanorms favoring sanctioning will be stronger.

Metanorms are also stronger in groups in which people are dependent on each other. Dependence refers to the value that people place on their relationships with others and the goods they receive through those relationships (Emerson 1962, 1972). If an individual is dependent on another, then they care what that person thinks of them and how they might react to them. So, if a group member is dependent on a sanctioner, and they care about maintaining a relationship with that person, then they will provide support to the sanctioner. In turn, this support (metanorms) leads to increased norm enforcement.

Note that dependence refers to relations between those who are affected by deviant behavior, not to relations between the *deviant* and potential sanctioners. Individuals who are dependent on those who engage in deviant behavior would be less likely to sanction, not more (see, for example, Patillo 1998).

In summary, theoretical work on norm enforcement predicts that rates of informal control will increase when the benefits of sanctioning are high, the costs are low, and people expect and obtain support from others for their sanctioning efforts. Such support is stronger in groups in which people are dependent on each other.

THE STANDARDIZED EXPERIMENTAL SETTING

These theoretical predictions have been tested in a series of laboratory experiments using a standardized norms game (Horne 2001b, 2004, 2007; Horne and Cutlip 2002).

Subjects and Procedures

All the experiments were conducted at a large university. Participants were recruited from undergraduate classes on the basis of wanting to make money. They were telephoned the night before the experiment to schedule their participation and were asked to come to the sociology laboratory. Subjects participated in the experiment in groups of four (W, X, Y, and Z). When they arrived at the lab they were individually escorted to separate rooms, each equipped with a computer connected to the lab network. Thus subjects never saw each other face to face; their only interaction occurred over the computer network.

Subjects read instructions on their computer screens and participated in practice trials. They were able to ask questions of the experimenter over an intercom. Once the five practice trials were completed, the experiment began. Subjects did not know the exact number of rounds beforehand. At the end of the experiment they were paid the money they had earned. Earnings varied depending on the conditions to which subjects were randomly assigned, as well as on their decisions and those of other participants in their experimental group. After receiving their earnings, participants were individually escorted from the lab. They thus had no contact with each other either before or after the experiment.

The Experimental Setting

Subjects were told that they were participating in an experiment on social interaction. Each group had five members—V, W, X, Y, and Z. Members W, X, Y, and Z could exchange points with each other. The fifth member, V, could steal points from any of the other four. (In actuality, V was a computer-simulated actor.) If V decided to steal from someone, that person was able to punish. Participants were given information about the gains that could be made from exchange as well as the consequences of punishing the thief. They knew that their earnings would be affected by the decisions that they and other group members made regarding exchange and punishment.

Income

At the beginning of each round, every subject received thirty points of income. These points were placed in the Personal Income box on their computer screen. All participants received the same number of points.

Deviance

Next, the computer-simulated actor (V) had the opportunity to steal ten points from one of the participants. V's behavior thus harmed group members. On any particular round, V could steal from one person, or nobody. The decision was randomly generated by the computer. After V acted, everyone was told what it had done.

Norm Enforcement

After the theft, the victim was able to decide how to respond. She could decide to punish the thief or to do nothing. If the victim decided to punish the thief, it cost her a certain number of points. All group members were told what the victim's decision was. In addition, if the victim punished, each person in the group received a benefit in the form of points added to their personal incomes. This operationalization reflects the idea that everyone in a community benefits when deviance is sanctioned.

Metanorm Enforcement

After everyone had been told about the victim's decision and received the appropriate number of benefit points, all subjects (including the victim) were able to engage in exchange. Subjects could give any number of points from their personal income to any other person, and they could keep any number of points that they wished. The only rule was that the number of points that people gave away and kept for themselves could not be greater than what they had in their personal income. Of course, when deciding how many points to give, one thing people could consider was whether or not an individual had sanctioned the thief. Thus the decision to react to a sanctioner was made in conjunction with choices about giving to other participants and about keeping points. Everyone made their decisions at the same time. After each participant made their decision and entered it, they learned how many points each other person had given to them. The points they gave away were taken from their personal incomes; the points they received were added.

End of Round

All the points in each subject's personal incomes were moved into their Total Savings box on their computer screen and thirty points were added to their Personal Income. The points in savings could not be used. They accumulated throughout the experiment. Subjects' earnings were determined by the number of points they had in their savings at the end of the experiment.

Manipulation of the Experimental Conditions

Dependence is defined as the value of relations and the goods people can receive from those relations. Different levels of this variable were created by altering the value of points that subjects received from others relative to the value of their own points. In the high dependence condition, points from others were worth three times one's own points. Accordingly, in this condition, if X gave Y ten points, Y would receive thirty points. If X and Y each gave each other ten points, then both would make a profit of twenty. People were highly dependent on each other in this condition.

In the low dependence condition, points received from others were worth the same amount as one's own. If X gave Y ten points, Y would receive ten points. If X and Y each gave each other ten points, then they would both break even. Each of them would do just as well if they did not interact. Subjects were not dependent on each other.

Sanctioning benefit was manipulated by varying the number of points that each group member received if the thief was punished. The idea here is that everyone benefits when a norm is enforced—that is, everyone has an interest in whether antisocial behavior occurs or is discouraged. In the experiments, this benefit took the form of points.

Note that sanctioning benefit was not operationalized as variation in rates of deviance. Such an approach would build into the experiment the same problems that arise in natural settings. Sociologists have lots of data from such settings—where it is difficult if not impossible to disentangle the relations between sanctioning and deviance. Sanctioning affects deviance, but levels of deviance in turn presumably affect sanctioning rates. By holding rates of deviance constant, the standardized norms game avoids the problem of disentangling causal relations that arise in studies of informal control outside the laboratory.

Sanctioning cost was manipulated by varying the number of points that the victims lost if they decided to punish the thief. When people sanction, they experience a variety of costs—time, emotional distress, the threat of retaliation, and so forth. In the standardized norms game, costs are operationalized in terms of points lost.

Measurement of the Dependent Variables

Norm enforcement was measured by counting the number of times in each experimental group that people punished, and dividing that sum by the number of times that the thief stole. This calculation produced a sanctioning rate for each experimental group. Sanctioning is very difficult to measure in natural settings, but the norms game produces a clear behavioral indicator.

Metanorm enforcement was measured by determining the mean difference between the number of points people gave to victims who punished and the number they gave to victims who did not punish. The larger the gap between points given to victims who punished and those who did not, the greater the metanorm enforcement. This approach produced a measure of mean metanorm enforcement for each experimental group. Importantly, these calculations were based on the number of points that people *gave* to the sanctioner rather than the number of points the sanctioner actually received. In other words, suppose the metanorm for a group was 5. In order to determine how many points sanctioners in that group would receive in the high interdependence condition, we would have to multiply 5 (the mean metanorm) x 3 (the number of people who could reward the sanctioner) x 3 (the exchange ratio in the high interdependence condition). In the low interdependence condition, we would need to multiply 5 x 3 (the number of people) x 1 (the exchange ratio in that condition). Thus the metanorm measure reflects how people react to sanctioners. Metanorm enforcement is even more difficult to identify and measure than norm enforcement. But again, the norms game provides a clear behavioral indicator.

EXPERIMENTAL FINDINGS AND IMPLICATIONS

This series of laboratory experiments produced the following findings:

1. Sanctioning benefits increase and sanctioning costs reduce norm enforcement. These results imply that the more that people think their actions will actually have an effect, the more likely they will be to sanction deviance. Further, the more afraid they are of retaliation, the less likely they are to enforce norms.

2. The effects of sanctioning benefits and costs on norm enforcement vary depending on the social relations between group members. While sanctioning costs and benefits affect norm enforcement, these effects differ depending on the interdependence of group members. When group members are highly dependent on each other, they may be able to overcome high sanctioning costs. Similarly, even when the benefits are low, close-knit groups may be able to produce sanctioning.

3. Metanorms are positively correlated with norm enforcement. People care about their social relations and they care about how others react to their sanctioning decisions. When people get more positive responses for sanc-

tioning and more negative responses when they fail to do so, they take those responses into account. Thus, metanorms are important for explaining sanctioning.

4. Metanorms are driven by a concern with social relations. Specifically, dependence and sanctioning costs both strengthen metanorm enforcement. These findings are consistent with the theoretical argument that people give support to norm enforcers because they care about maintaining their relationships with them.

What are the implications of these experimental findings for explaining variation in informal control across neighborhoods? The research identifies two group-level causal factors—sanctioning costs and benefits, and dependence. These two factors affect norm enforcement—both directly, and indirectly through their effect on metanorms.

Neighborhood Characteristics

One way to think about the implications of this research is to consider the connections between the abstract causal factors identified by the theory and the empirical factors commonly used in social disorganization research. According to the theory, we should expect neighborhood characteristics to affect informal control if they capture something about sanctioning costs and benefits. They may. For example, police may be less likely to respond to calls for help from some neighborhoods than from others (Klinger 1997; Kubrin and Weitzer 2003). In neighborhoods where calling 911 produces no response, the benefits of acting are low. Therefore we would expect residents in such neighborhoods to make fewer control efforts.

We can make logical inferences about the costs and benefits of sanctioning in different kinds of neighborhoods. But people living in these neighborhoods ought to be able to tell us something as well. We could ask them about their perceptions of the costs and benefits of sanctioning. In terms of benefits: Do people think their efforts will have any effect? Do they believe that rates of deviant or criminal behavior will change as a result of their action? In terms of costs: Do people think that if they sanction deviance that the target or the target's allies will retaliate? If responses correspond to neighborhood characteristics like racial composition, socioeconomic status, and so forth, then we can have greater confidence that neighborhood characteristics capture sanctioning costs and benefits. In turn, we would expect those perceptions of costs and benefits to affect control efforts.

While sanctioning costs and benefits directly affect sanctioning, interdependence is important for informal control, in part, because it affects the support that people give to sanctioners. Measures traditionally used by social disorganization researchers appear to capture interdependence. Residential stability, for example, is likely, at least in part, an indicator of interdependence.[2] This is because when a neighborhood is transient, people do not know each other as well, and they are therefore less likely to value and rely on each other.

Neighborhood homogeneity measures may also capture interdependence. There is reason to believe that people value relations with people who are like them. So, it is possible that people in homogeneous neighborhoods value their relations with neighbors more than those in heterogeneous neighborhoods—that there are higher levels of interdependence in these neighborhoods. For example, in some contexts, religious homogeneity may be associated with higher levels of dependence (for a related discussion see Regnerus 2003). In Quebec, we might expect French-English heterogeneity to matter. If people value certain kinds of homogeneity, levels of dependence will be higher, and we would expect to see more support for sanctioning efforts.

To the extent that neighborhood characteristics are indicators of sanctioning costs, sanctioning benefits, and interdependence, they will affect informal control. Norms theory suggests that we ought to identify the characteristics of communities that provide indicators of the theoretical concepts, and also ask people about their perceptions of sanctioning costs and benefits and the value they place on their relationships with community members.

Collective Efficacy and Metanorms

According to the theory, community level characteristics affect enforcement both directly and indirectly through their effect on metanorms. Thus metanorms are important for explaining sanctioning. In the lab, we can measure how much support people give to sanctioners; we can measure actual metanorm enforcement. Outside the lab, we are more likely to be able to get information about how people *expect* others to respond. That is, what does the individual think others are likely to do if she sanctions deviance?

Data on collective efficacy provide partial information regarding such expectations. The trust component of collective efficacy measures residents' perceptions regarding whether their neighbors are prosocial (are willing to help neighbors, can be trusted, generally get along, share the same values, and so forth). The control component primarily measures residents' expectations that neighbors would intervene if they saw deviant behavior (such as skipping school, spray-painting graffiti, showing disrespect to an adult, or fighting). Thus, empirically, collective efficacy captures some of the respondent expectations that are relevant for sanctioning decisions. Collective efficacy research tells us that in neighborhoods with particular characteristics (poor, unstable, and so forth) residents view their neighbors as less prosocial and less likely to respond to deviance. Norm enforcement theory tells us that these perceptions affect individuals' sanctioning behavior. When residents feel that their neighbors are not prosocial and not concerned with deviance, they will expect less support for their own sanctioning efforts. These expectations of the social consequences in turn affect individual control activity.

Because the concept of collective efficacy captures at least some relevant expectations, findings on community level characteristics, collective efficacy, and crime are relevant for norm enforcement theory. The results of such studies are consistent with the experimental results reported here.

In order to fully test the metanorms argument outside the lab, however, researchers would need to look more carefully at the characteristics of neighborhoods and the perceptions of people living in those neighborhoods. That is, how do people think others in the neighborhood will respond to their sanctioning action? Do they expect that if they intervene to chastise neighborhood teenagers that they will be viewed positively by other neighborhood residents? Do they think that others will not care and they will be left to act on their own without support? The theory predicts that answers to these questions will be correlated with individuals' actual sanctioning activity.

In addition to getting answers to these questions using survey methods, we could use lab experiments to explicitly examine not just the effects of abstract factors like costs and benefits, but the effects of particular concrete neighborhood characteristics. Consider race. Social psychological research on status characteristics and race suggests that people (both black and white) view African Americans as less competent and less prosocial than European Americans (Ayres 1991; Ridgeway 1982; Webster and Driskell; for a related argument see Sampson and Raudenbush 2004). If this is the case, then people in black neighborhoods would be more likely than those in white neighborhoods to fear retaliation for sanctioning. They would also be less likely to think that their neighbors would support sanctioning efforts. Thus neighborhood racial composition may affect control because it affects how residents perceive the costs of sanctioning and the likely reactions of others.

There are established experimental protocols for studying status characteristics. These standardized settings could be used to obtain behavioral indicators of the extent to which blacks and whites view blacks as less competent and prosocial. We could then have people participate in the standardized experiments described in this chapter—but also give participants information about the race of their fellow participants. If status characteristics theory and norms theory are right, we would expect participants (both black and white) to expect less support for sanctioning efforts from other black participants, and in turn, to engage in less sanctioning activity. We could investigate socioeconomic status and a variety of other characteristics in the same way. These ideas could be tested in the lab using college student participants. We could also take laptop computers out in the field to see if the same mechanisms operate for people living in the neighborhoods in which we are interested. Such data, in conjunction with survey and ethnographic data, could enhance our understanding of the factors and mechanisms contributing to informal control.

Norms Theory and Crime

The theory presented here explains informal control. It does not explicitly address the relation between group-level characteristics and crime. It is relatively simple to extend the argument, however, given the generally accepted assumption that higher levels of informal control decrease crime rates. For instance, people contemplating a criminal or deviant act will consider the likely consequences of their action. Their expectations of these consequences will be affected by neighborhood characteristics and the level of control in the neighborhood. If they expect that people will respond negatively to their action, they are less likely to engage in deviance. In turn, we would expect to see lower rates of deviance and crime. And, of course, to the extent that deviance actually is sanctioned, people will be less likely to engage in deviant activities. Extending the argument in this way suggests mechanisms mediating not only the relation between neighborhood characteristics and informal control, but also between neighborhood characteristics and crime.

Applying Norms Theory to Neighborhoods

Importantly, neighborhood characteristics will matter for informal control to the extent that they are indicators of the theoretical constructs (sanctioning benefit, sanctioning cost, or interdependence) or affect individual perceptions of the likely consequences of sanctioning. We should not expect particular neighborhood characteristics to have the same effects across all times and places. The same characteristic may be an indicator of a particular theoretical concept in one setting, but not in another.[3]

Similarly, neighborhood characteristics may affect expectations regarding the consequences of sanctioning differently in different contexts. Poverty rates in urban neighborhoods may produce different perceptions than poverty rates in rural areas. The correlation between poverty and crime therefore may be different in urban and rural areas or across cultures. Racial composition may affect individual perceptions in some settings but not others. Religion is salient in some communities. In others, it is not. Thus, instead of assuming that factors like race or poverty are necessarily important and produce the same consequences everywhere, norms theory suggests that we should focus on the key theoretical concepts and identify indicators of those concepts that are appropriate in a particular setting. We need to be very careful in thinking about the kinds of characteristics that might provide appropriate indicators of sanctioning costs and benefits and interdependence, and the kinds of characteristics that might affect individuals' perceptions of sanctioning consequences in specific situations.

In other words, we expect the predictions suggested by the theory of norm enforcement to hold across a variety of contexts. But the precise indicators of these abstract factors will vary. Increased sanctioning benefits, decreased costs, and increased interdependence should always lead to increased norm enforcement (all else being equal), but the empirical indicators of these factors will vary across time and place. Similarly, people's perceptions of sanctioning consequences will reflect sanctioning costs, sanctioning benefits, and interdependence, but effects of particular group-level empirical indicators on perceptions may differ across cultures and societies. In the United States, we often focus on factors like race and socioeconomic status. In other countries and cultures, other empirical indicators might be more appropriate.

CONCLUSION

Social disorganization approaches, and the concept of collective efficacy in particular, have clear links with norms research. The neighborhood level factors studied by social disorganization researchers over many decades coincide with the abstractly defined causal factors identified by norms scholars. The concept of collective efficacy is consistent with norms scholars' emphasis on the importance of social relations in affecting norm enforcement. In particular, the individual perceptions and expectations that are the empirical basis for the concept are central in explanations of norm enforcement.

Norm enforcement theory and research complement social disorganization approaches to explaining variation in crime rates, suggesting directions for further empirical work. The theory identifies abstract group-level causal factors. Accordingly, we can seek to identify corresponding group-level empirical indicators—moving beyond the oft studied neighborhood level characteristics that are so frequently relevant in American society. Because the theory is stated abstractly, we can easily apply it to different cultures and settings. For example, we can use it in cross-national research or we can move outside the neighborhood context to explain control of deviance in other settings such as organizations and informal associations.

The theory also points to the importance of particular kinds of individual level data. It identifies questions that could be easily incorporated into traditional survey instruments—questions that could illuminate the relation between neighborhood characteristics and control. In particular, as discussed above, researchers should ask respondents about the consequences of sanctioning deviance. How do they think others will respond? What are the risks of retaliation? Do they think their actions will have any effect? According to norms theory, this kind of information is crucial to efforts to understand the mechanisms linking neighborhood characteristics and informal control, yet these questions have not, as far as we know, been systematically asked or answered.

Finally, this chapter suggests some ways in which experimental methods could be used in conjunction with traditional methods to learn more about why people sanction and why they sanction differently in different neighborhoods. Survey methods could be coordinated with further experimental work—including taking the standardized experimental settings into neighborhoods. Such use of multiple methods has the potential to contribute to our understanding of an important issue in criminology—why informal control and crime vary across neighborhoods.

NOTES

1. The term *sanctioning* typically refers to both positive and negative reactions to a behavior. Here we use sanctioning in the context of norm enforcement. Throughout the paper, sanctioning is synonymous with punishment. We use *rewarding* in the context of metanorm enforcement.

2. In situations of extreme poverty, however, stability may not indicate interdependence because neighborhood residents may not be in a position to provide much assistance to each other. If this is the case, then stability does not coincide with interdependence and would not produce increased sanctioning.

3. Further, predictions regarding the effects of neighborhood characteristics will vary depending on which theoretical concept they are thought to indicate. For example, in settings where race is associated with social status, we would expect the proportion of black residents to produce negative expectations, and in turn, less sanctioning. But under conditions in which racial homogeneity is an indicator of interdependence, then high proportions of black residents ought to produce more interdependence, and therefore, more sanctioning.

REFERENCES

Agnew, Robert. 1999. "A General Strain Theory of Community Differences in Crime Rates." *Journal of Research in Crime and Delinquency* 36:123-55.

Almgren, Gunnar. 2005. "The Ecological Context of Interpersonal Violence: From Culture to Collective Efficacy." *Journal of Interpersonal Violence* 20:218–24.

Akers, Ronald L., and Christine S. Sellers. 2004. *Criminological Theories: Introduction, Evaluation and Application.* Los Angeles, CA: Roxbury Press.

Axelrod, Robert. 1986. "An Evolutionary Approach to Norms." *American Political Science Review* 80:1095–111.

———. 1997. *The Complexity of Cooperation: Agent-Based Models of Competition and Collaboration.* Princeton, NJ: Princeton University Press.

Ayres, Ian. 1991. "Fair Driving: Gender and Race Discrimination in Retail Car Negotiations." *Harvard Law Review* 104:817–72.

Browning, Christopher. R., Seth Feinberg, and Robert. D. Dietz. 2004. "The Paradox of Social Organization: Networks, Collective Efficacy, and Violent Crime in Urban Neighborhoods." *Social Forces* 83:503–34.

Bursik, Robert. J., Jr. 1988. "Social Disorganization and Theories of Crime: Problems and Prospects." *Criminology* 26:519–51.

Bursik, Robert J., Jr., and Harold. G. Grasmick. 1993. *Neighborhoods and Crime.* New York: Lexington.

Coleman, James S. 1990. *Foundations of Social Theory.* Cambridge, MA: Harvard University Press.

Emerson, Richard M. 1962. "Power-Dependence Relations." *American Sociological Review* 27:31–41.

———. 1972. "Exchange Theory, Part II: Exchange Relations and Networks." In *Sociological Theories in Progress*, vol. 2, edited by J. Berger, M. Zelditch Jr., and B. Anderson. Boston, MA: Houghton Mifflin.

Hechter, Michael, and Karl-Dieter Opp, eds. 2001. *Social Norms.* New York: Russell Sage.

Heckathorn, Douglas D. 1988. "Collective Sanctions and the Creation of Prisoner's Dilemma Norms." *American Journal of Sociology* 94:535–62.

———. 1989. "Collective Action and the Second Order Free Rider Problem." *Rationality and Society* 1:78–100.

Horne, Christine. 2001a. "Sociological Perspectives on the Emergence of Norms." In *Social Norms*, edited by M. Hechter and K. Opp. New York: Russell Sage.

———. 2001b. "The Enforcement of Norms: Group Cohesion and Meta-norms." *Social Psychology Quarterly* 53:253–66.

———. 2004. "Collective Benefits, Exchange Interests, and Norm Enforcement." *Social Forces* 82(3):1037-62.

———. 2007. "Explaining Norm Enforcement." *Rationality and Society* 19:139-70.

Horne, Christine, and Anna Cutlip. 2002. "Sanctioning Costs and Norm Enforcement: An Experimental Test." *Rationality and Society* 14:285–307.

Klinger, David. 1997. "Negotiating Order in Police Work: An Ecological Theory of Police Response to Deviance." *Criminology* 35:277–306.

Kornhauser, Ruth Rosner. 1978. *The Social Sources of Delinquency: An Appraisal of Analytic Models.* Chicago: University of Chicago Press.

Kubrin, Charis E., and Ronald Weitzer. 2003. "Retaliatory Homicide: Concentrated Disadvantage and Neighborhood Culture." *Social Problems* 50:157–80.

Lowenkamp, Christopher T., Francis T. Cullen, and Travis C. Pratt. 2003. "Replicating Sampson and Groves's Test of Social Disorganization Theory: Revisiting a Criminological Classic." *Journal of Research in Crime and Delinquency* 40:351–73.

Patillo, Mary. 1998. "Sweet Mothers and Gangbangers: Managing Crime in a Middle-Class Black Neighborhood." *Social Forces* 76:747–74.

Posner, Eric A. 2000. *Law and Social Norms*. Cambridge, MA: Harvard University Press.

Regnerus, Mark D. 2003. "Moral Communities and Adolescent Delinquency: Religious Contexts and Community Social Control." *Sociological Quarterly* 44:523–54.

Ridgeway, Cecilia. 1982. "Status in Groups: The Importance of Motivation." *American Sociological Review* 47:76–88.

Sampson, Robert J. 2000a. "Whither the Sociological Study of Crime?" *Annual Review of Sociology* 26:711–14.

———. 2000b. "A Neighborhood-Level Perspective on Social Change and the Social Control of Adolescent Delinquency." In *Negotiating Adolescence in Times of Social Change*, edited by L. Crockett and R. Silbereisen. New York: Cambridge University Press.

Sampson, Robert J., and W. Byron Groves. 1989. "Community Structure and Crime: Testing Social Disorganization Theory." *American Journal of Sociology* 94:774–802.

Sampson, Robert J., Jeffrey D. Morenoff, and Thomas Gannon-Rowley. 2002. "Assessing Neighborhood Effects: Social Processes and New Directions in Research." *Annual Review of Sociology* 28:443–78.

Sampson, Robert J., and Stephen W. Raudenbush. 2004. "Seeing Disorder: Neighborhood Stigma and the Social Construction of 'Broken Windows.'" *Social Psychology Quarterly* 67:319–42.

Sampson, Robert J., Stephen W. Raudenbush, and Felton Earls. 1997. "Neighborhoods and Violent Crime: A Multilevel Study of Collective Efficacy." *Science* 277:918–24.

Shaw, Clifford R. 1951. *The Natural History of a Delinquent Career*. Philadelphia, PA: Albert Saifer.

Shaw, Clifford R., and Henry D. McKay. [1942] 1969. *Juvenile Delinquency and Urban Areas*. Chicago: University of Chicago Press.

Webster, Murray, Jr., and James E. Driskell, Jr.1978. "Status Generalization: A Review and Some New Data." *American Sociological Review* 43:220–36.

6

The Effects of Status and Peer Support on the Justifications and Approval of Deviance

C. Wesley Younts

In the 1950s and 1960s, criminology was dominated by subcultural perspectives that focused on small groups as the social context within which deviance was constructed and legitimated. These perspectives drew heavily from the classic statements of differential association theory and social disorganization theory. While these theories emphasized different levels of analysis and different causal processes, they shared an interest in the transmission of norms that support deviance and crime. According to these perspectives, deviance occurs more frequently in groups that have subcultures justifying deviance. Such subcultures exist when group members come to define a deviant behavior as appropriate in a given situation, even though that behavior violates societal norms.

Despite the original central role of deviant subcultures in the differential association and social disorganization traditions, in later work the processes through which justifications of deviance are transmitted and maintained across generations of group members have been theoretically and empirically neglected. As Horne and Hoffmann (this volume) note, for example, social disorganization scholars now focus primarily on the social control component of peer influence, rather than on the ways in which groups define particular behaviors as deviant or acceptable. Recently, however, interest in the effects of group processes on deviant conduct has been revived with the incorporation of symbolic interactionist ideas into classic culture conflict theories (for example, Heimer and Matsueda 1994) and the increasing emphasis on the role of deviant peers (for example, Matsueda and Anderson 1998; Warr 2002).

In this chapter, I draw on theoretical insights from culture conflict theories of deviance and social psychological explanations of justifications to explore the conditions under which a justification offered for deviant behavior will be internalized by actors and subsequently transmitted to other actors as part of a subcultural normative system. Specifically, I investigate two research questions: (a) How does the relative social status of the person justifying a deviant behavior affect the extent to which others internalize and transmit the justification? (b) How does endorsement of the behavior by peers affect the extent to which individuals internalize and transmit the justification?

STATUS, ENDORSEMENT, AND
THE JUSTIFICATION OF DEVIANCE

Norms are rules defining appropriate behavior that are generally shared by members of a society, and thus they "exist" outside of particular individuals and situations (Becker 1963; Berger and Luckmann 1966; Heimer and Matsueda 1994). Deviant behavior violates norms and thus is socially unacceptable. Under some conditions, however, individuals may learn to define deviance as legitimate by justifying it (Akers 1998; Heimer 1997; Matsueda 1988; Mills 1940; Scott and Lyman 1968; Sykes and Matza 1957). When individuals internalize these justifications and transmit them to other group members, deviant subcultures may emerge. What factors and processes contribute to the internalization and transmission of justifications of deviance?

Status and the Internalization of Justifications

All individuals are exposed to definitions that are both favorable to and unfavorable to violating societal norms (Matsueda 1988). According to culture conflict theories, the multitude of conflicting norms to which individuals are exposed do not have equal effects. Those encountered in more important relationships carry more weight. For instance, Sutherland (1947) suggests that qualities of social relationships, including their frequency, duration, priority, and intensity, determine the effect of a given definition regarding deviance on an individual's overall view of the behavior. Similarly, Heimer and Matsueda claim that whether an individual is affected by others depends in part on the prestige, influence, and power of those others (Heimer and Matsueda 1994; see also Webster and Sobieszek 1974).

Like work in criminology, social psychological research also points to the importance of social status. Because the primary purpose of a justification is to legitimate deviant behavior in the eyes of others, the effectiveness of a justification depends partly on the credibility of the individual offering the justification (Massey et al. 1997; Zelditch 2001; Zelditch and Floyd 1998). Research in social psychology demonstrates that people with higher status are seen as more credible, competent, and capable of defining a situation. This is particularly true in novel or problematic situations, as is arguably the case when an individual advocates deviant behavior (for example, Chaiken et al. 1989; Chaiken and Maheswaran 1994; Petty and Cacioppo 1986). An extensive body of social conformity research demonstrates that social status produces such informational influence (Deutsch and Gerard 1955). Across a variety of settings, high status actors change others' opinions and attitudes (see Allen 1965 and 1975; Petty, Wegener, and Fabrigar 1997; Turner 1991; Zimbardo and Lieppe 1991; and Cialdini and Trost 1998 for reviews of this research).

Research in both criminology and social psychology therefore point to the importance of status. I hypothesize that the status of the person offering a justification for deviance affects the extent to which others internalize that justification.

> Hypothesis 1: An individual will be more likely to approve of deviance if the person justifying the deviance is higher status rather than lower status.

Endorsement and the Internalization of Justifications

Early criminological research emphasized the importance of the collective support of deviance (for example, Cohen 1955; Short and Strodtbeck 1965). The most relevant findings demonstrate that the number of deviant peers affects the internalization of attitudes favorable to deviance (see Warr 2002 for a comprehensive review of deviant peer effects).

A long tradition in social psychology similarly shows that individuals, when faced with an ambiguous situation, look to the consensus of the group to define the situation (Festinger 1950). The classic conformity studies of Sherif (1936) and Asch (1955, 1956) demonstrate that individuals actually internalize group norms—particularly when all of the other group members agree. Individuals conform with a unanimous group even when they give their opinion anonymously and there is, therefore, no risk of social sanction (Deutsch and Gerard 1955). Further, individuals who make perceptual judgments within a group continue to make similar judgments when alone—even as much as a year later (Sherif 1936; Rohrer et al. 1954). In fact, several participants in the Asch experiments reported that they perceived the judgments of the unanimous majority to be more correct than their own (Asch 1956; Deutsch and Gerard 1955). More recent research suggests that group consensus may lead to internalization when the situation is ambiguous, but only to outward conformity (without internalization) when the situation is objectively unambiguous (Nail 1986).

The *validity* of a justification refers to the extent to which it is treated as legitimate by others and affects whether an individual will personally accept that justification (Zelditch and Floyd 1998). A key source of validity is endorsement, defined as support from one's peers (Zelditch and Walker 1984). Given that deviance occurs in relatively novel situations in which there is a conflict between the deviant behavior and the norms of the larger culture, explicit endorsement by one's peers should lead to internalization of justifications supporting deviance, and thus to greater personal approval of the behavior.

> Hypothesis 2: An individual will be more likely to approve of the deviance the carrier justifies if it is endorsed.

Status and the Transmission of Justifications

The cultural transmission of deviance to subsequent generations of group members has been a critical element of differential association theory (Sutherland 1947) and social disorganization theory (Shaw and McKay 1942). According to culture conflict theories, groups in heterogeneous societies not only differ in the norms, values, and interests they espouse, but also in their degree of organization in favor of or in opposition to deviance (Matsueda 1988). Belying criticisms from control theorists (for example, Hirschi 1969; Kornhauser 1978), culture conflict theories argue that not all such groups are equally effective at socializing their members. Rather, the efficacy of any group, whether generally deviant or conventional, in guiding the conduct of its members is affected by the strength of its organization in favor of or in opposition to specified conduct (Sutherland 1947; Matsueda 1988). Since individuals give more weight to definitions learned through associations with important others, membership in peer groups that are strongly organized in favor of deviant behavior invokes the conditions necessary for the intergenerational transmission of prodeviance justifications.

Similarly, Shaw and McKay (1942) proposed that the cultural transmission of deviance across generations is a critical process for understanding the stability of high rates of crime and deviance in lower-class neighborhoods. Specifically, physical deterioration, high rates of residential mobility, and the preponderance of foreign-born immigrants in poor neighborhoods prevent the formation of strong bonds among community members and institutions. Such social disorganization, including cultural conflict regarding values and norms, prevents community members from working together to achieve their collective interests (Bursik 1988). Assuming, as Shaw and McKay did, that most communities have an interest in preventing crime, social disorganization leads to high rates of crime and deviance because it hinders the supervision and control of residents' behavior, especially the behavior of potentially deviant youths.

Although the connection between ecological conditions and social disorganization explains differences in rates of crime and deviance across communities, Shaw and McKay (1942) recognized that social disorganization alone could not explain two of their findings: (a) the specific types of deviance characterizing specific communities and (b) the persistence of deviance rates despite drastic changes in the ethnic and racial makeup of the communities over the three decades for which they had data. Based on their analysis of extensive life histories (for example, Shaw 1966), they suggest that youth behavior is organized around informal groups, and when coupled with social disorganization and an age-graded hierarchy of offenders in a community, these groups become contexts for the cultural transmission of deviant values (Shaw and McKay 1942). High deviance areas are "characterized by a wide diversity in norms and standards of behavior. The moral values range from those that are strictly conventional to those in direct opposition to conventionality. . . . Thus within the same community, theft may be defined as right and proper in some groups, and as immoral, improper and undesirable in others" (Shaw and McKay 1942:171). Over generations within a neighborhood, deviant traditions and the groups carrying them may therefore become institutionalized.

Shaw and McKay provide more specific arguments than Sutherland regarding the aspects of community structure that facilitate the cultural transmission of deviant behavior. By their focus on the importance of an age-graded structure of relations between experienced and inexperienced criminals, Shaw and McKay imply that the social status of the carrier of deviance is a critical factor for explaining the cultural transmission of deviance—higher status (for example, older, more experienced) deviants are better able to socialize new generations of youths to engage in "traditional" forms of deviance. For Shaw and McKay, then, the persistence of deviance across generations, at least in part, is the result of the formation and transmission of prodeviance norms (as the term *traditions* implies) from older, more experienced deviants to younger, less experienced youths.

On the one hand, individuals are more likely to transmit the carrier's justification to new group members if the initial carrier is higher status because they are more likely to agree with and internalize it. On the other hand, if the carrier is lower status, individuals are likely to feel a strong need to justify the deviance to new group members because they are less likely to personally approve of it or to believe that others will naturally support it. Simultaneously, they are unlikely to transmit the same justification because of the

lower credibility of the low status source, and thus individuals in such a situation should construct new justifications from the elements of the culture in
order to bring local behavior in line with global norms. These arguments
suggest the third hypothesis.

> Hypothesis 3: An individual will be more likely to transmit the carrier's justifi-
> cation if the carrier is higher status than if she or he is lower status. An individ-
> ual will be more likely to create and transmit a new justification if the carrier is
> lower status than if she or he is higher status.

Endorsement and the Transmission of Justifications

Theories that focus on the process of generating and disseminating definitions
favoring deviance within adolescent groups (for example, Cohen 1955; Short
and Strodtbeck 1965; Warr 2002) suggest that the collective support of peers
for deviance is also critical in transforming individualistic motivations to deviate into enduring norms that generate subcultural deviance. According to
Cohen (1955), deviant subcultures develop as youths engage in a conversa-
tion of gestures, sharing their frustrations and supporting the deviant solutions offered by others in the group. This process of endorsement (what Cohen refers to as "mutual conversion") results in the formation of an alternative
status structure based on characteristics attainable within the group, such as
toughness.

According to social psychological theories, endorsement of a justification
has two effects on the transmission of deviance. First, individuals are more
likely to transmit valid justifications because others are more likely to support
them, and endorsement is a powerful source of validity within a situation
(Zelditch and Floyd 1998). Second, when group members endorse a behavior,
individuals expect that others will treat the behavior as legitimate—as the way
things are typically done in such situations and therefore as the way things
ought to be done in this situation (Walker, Thomas and Zelditch 1986; Zelditch
and Walker 1984). Once a behavior is seen as legitimate, it is more likely to
become part of the culture that is taken for granted and unquestioned (Berger
and Luckmann 1966; Zucker 1977). Thus when a justification is endorsed, deviance becomes legitimate. Once legitimate, deviance no longer represents an
untoward act requiring justification, but rather becomes expected. These ideas
are incorporated into the fourth hypothesis.

> Hypothesis 4: An individual will be more likely to either transmit the carrier's
> justification or to provide no justification at all if the carrier's justification is en-
> dorsed.

METHODS AND RESULTS

I conducted a laboratory experiment to test these hypotheses. The experiment creates a situation in which participants realize that cheating is possible, although it explicitly violates university rules. A confederate provides a justification for cheating, and I vary the status of the confederate relative to participants. I also vary whether peers support cheating in the situation. Participants are given an opportunity to cheat at the task and then to teach a new group of participants to cheat at the same task.

Data come from one hundred four male freshman and sophomore students between the ages of eighteen and twenty who participated in a study of "remote-site job training" at a large Midwestern university. Participants were randomly assigned to one of four conditions ($n = 26$ for each condition) representing two levels of status and two levels of endorsement in a simple random design. Table 6.1 describes the experimental conditions created for the study.

Task Instructions, Manipulations, and Dependent Variables

All instructions were conveyed to participants via a software instruction program that is a modification of a standardized experimental setting used by expectation states researchers called MacSES (Troyer 2000). An external norm was created by telling participants that university rules prohibiting assault, theft, and academic misconduct in the form of cheating have been explicitly extended to this research setting.[1]

During the introductory section of the instructions, participants were told that the purpose of the study was to investigate job training methods utilizing a new computerized video-conferencing system. The study would involve three phases.

In part one of the study, participants completed an individual test of perceptual ability called "Meaning Insight" (Berger et al. 1977; Moore 1968) and were told this test provides an excellent measure of general perceptual ability and is highly correlated with success at similar perceptual tasks. In reality, participants completed a fictitious computerized word matching test that had no correct or incorrect responses. At the conclusion of the test, participants in

Table 6.1. Experimental Design

Trainer's status	Higher than participant	Condition 1
	Lower than participant	Condition 2
Endorsement	Endorsed	Condition 3
	Not endorsed	Condition 4

all conditions were told that they had average perceptual ability. I used this information to manipulate the relative status of the carrier (discussed below).

In part two of the study, participants were told that they and two other students constituted a workgroup that would receive strategy training from a previous participant and would then complete a different perceptual task called "Contrast Sensitivity." Before receiving strategy training and beginning the task, participants were asked to introduce themselves to the trainer of their workgroup via a computerized video-conferencing system by stating their first name, age, year in school, and their score on the Meaning Insight test (average for all participants). After introducing themselves, participants saw an ostensibly live video feed from the trainer on their computer screen. The trainer was actually a video-recorded confederate of the experimenter.

I manipulated the status of the confederate by providing information to subjects regarding his age, year in school, and perceptual ability. In higher status condition 1, the trainer introduced himself as "Mark, a twenty-four-year-old graduate student who scored above average on the Meaning Insight Test." In lower status condition 2, the trainer introduced himself as "Mark, a sixteen-year-old high school student who scored below average on the Meaning Insight Test." Based on these introductions, conditions 1 and 2 provided participants with information on three salient and consistently evaluated status characteristics—age, education, and meaning insight ability (see Berger et al. 1977).

After meeting the trainer, participants read instructions for completing the Contrast Sensitivity task. During the task, participants viewed a series of pictures, each containing a rectangle composed of smaller black and white shapes (Berger et al. 1977; Moore 1968). Participants were asked to determine whether each of the pictures contained more black area or more white area. In reality, the pictures contained approximately equal amounts of black and white, and therefore participants believed there was an unambiguously correct answer when, in fact, there was not. Moreover, participants were told that the amount of pay they would earn for taking part in the study depended on the number of problems they answered correctly, ensuring that they took the task seriously.

Participants were told that they would have approximately ten seconds to view each picture, select either "b" (if they think there is more black area) or "w" (if they think there is more white area), and submit their choice to the computer. Participants were also told that, after they submitted their answer to each problem, they should press the control key on their keyboard, and the software would indicate the correct answer to the problem. The instructions indicated, however, that they were not allowed to change their answers after submitting them and checking the correct answer. Coupled with the statement against cheating presented at the beginning of the study, premature use of the control key was unambiguously defined as deviant within the research setting, and participants' responses to several questionnaire items and during debrief interviews suggest that they recognized this fact.

After completing a practice contrast sensitivity problem, the participants were shown another ostensibly live video feed from the trainer ("Mark") who was supposed to communicate strategies for completing the task. In reality, Mark was a prerecorded confederate and he suggested to research participants a way of cheating at the experimental task, a strategy that clearly violated the norm defining cheating as deviant. Mark justified cheating based on an equity principle that suggested that participants deserved the full amount of pay for assisting the researchers with the study, which involved a difficult task. This justification was held constant across the four conditions of the study, as the focus was on the effects of status and endorsement, not the qualities of the particular justification itself. Specifically, he acted out the following script:

> One of the things they told me to try to do when I took this test was to count the number of white and black blocks in the picture, and the only problem with that was there's really not enough time to count all of the blocks. At least I couldn't count all of the blocks in ten seconds. So, another thing you can do is. . . . You know how they tell you to use the control key to check your answers after you've submitted them? Well . . . they don't know this, but you can use the control key *before* you submit your answer and that way you can make sure you always get the correct answer. You can try to figure it out on your own, but before you submit it you should definitely use the control key, because that way you make sure you make some money for helping them with this study.

After the training session and prior to the work period, participants completed a short computerized questionnaire that contained a question asking them to rate the extent to which the trainer for their group was an expert (on a one-hundred-point scale from "not at all" to "completely"). Table 6.2 provides

Table 6.2. Descriptive Statistics for Continuous Variables in the Analysis (*n* = 100)

Condition	Expert		Support		Approval Ratings	
	Mean	Std. Dev.	Mean	Std. Dev.	Mean	Std. Dev.
1. High status	57.5	24.5	59.4	22.6	58.7[a]	40.7
2. Low status	44.3	27.2	50.8	29.6	35.4[a]	41.8
3. Endorsed	51.2	25.1	81.3	18.6	77.7	31.8
4. Not endorsed	51.9	25.6	63.3	24.3	49.8[b]	36.9
Total	51.2	25.7	63.7	26.2	55.7	40.5

Notes: *n* = 26 for all means except as noted.
[a]*n* = 25.
[b]*n* = 24.

the means and standard deviations for this item across the four conditions of the study. Because only conditions 1 and 2 invoked information regarding the status of the trainer, only these conditions significantly differed on this item, such that participants in higher status conditions rated Mark as more expert than those in lower status conditions ($t_{50} = 1.84$, one-tailed $p = 0.036$), confirming the validity of the status manipulation. This questionnaire also asked participants to rate the appropriateness of the strategies suggested by the trainer on a similar one-hundred-point scale.

Following the work of Massey et al. (1997) and Walker et al. (1986), I manipulated endorsement by presenting evidence of consensus among group members regarding the appropriateness of the cheating strategy. Workgroup members were actually computer simulated actors. Specifically, after completing the questionnaire, the software presented participants in endorsement condition 3 with a table summarizing their own and the other group members' evaluations of the appropriateness of the trainer's strategies. This summary revealed that the other workgroup members gave uniformly high appropriateness ratings, indicating that they supported using the control key prematurely to always get the correct answer.

In contrast, participants in nonendorsement condition 4 did not receive any information regarding other workgroup members' ratings of the appropriateness of the cheating strategy. Instead, participants in the two status conditions (1 and 2) and in nonendorsement condition 4 saw a summary table indicating their own and the other workgroup members' ratings of the "difficulty" of the trainer's strategies, feedback that is irrelevant to their support for cheating. In order to detect the effect of endorsement unclouded by status processes, participants were not given any information regarding the status of the trainer in condition 3 or 4. Moreover, participants were not provided with any information regarding the characteristics of the other workgroup members in any conditions. As a result, conditions 1 and 2 manipulate only status, while conditions 3 and 4 manipulate only endorsement of the justification.

Immediately following the endorsement manipulation, participants completed fifteen Contrast Sensitivity problems with no further contact with the experimenter, trainer, or other members of their workgroup. The computer software unobtrusively recorded whether participants cheated at the task by pressing the control key prematurely to determine the correct answer before submitting it to the computer (Kalkoff and Willer, this volume; Troyer 2000). This procedure provides a convenient measure of participants' deviance that does not rely on self-reports or records maintained by official agencies. Analyses of these behavioral data reported elsewhere indicate that participants were more likely to cheat in conditions in which deviance was suggested by a higher status trainer and when it was endorsed by group members (Younts forthcoming).

After completing the task, participants completed a second computerized questionnaire, in which they rated the degree to which they believed other group members support the trainer's strategies (on a one-hundred-point scale from "not at all" to "completely") to assess the endorsement manipulation. The means and standard deviations for this item are reported in Table 6.2, and participants in condition 3 rated the group's support for cheating higher than those in condition 4 ($t_{50} = 2.99$, one-tailed $p = 0.002$), confirming the validity of this manipulation. The difference between conditions 1 and 2, which varied in status but not endorsement, is not significant.

In the third part of the study, participants were asked to provide strategy suggestions to a new group of participants by using the same computerized videoconferencing system as before. Participants were only told that these new group members had not previously completed the task but were not given any other information about the members of the new group (who were, in fact, fictitious) and were not introduced to them prior to communicating strategies. In reality, participants' communications with the workgroup were videotaped and were content-analyzed to assess the degree to which they had internalized the trainer's justification for cheating and subsequently transmitted it to the new participants. After participants communicated their strategies, the research assistant returned to the room, conducted the debrief interview, answered any questions raised by participants, and then paid each participant a flat rate of $15.

Content Analysis of Transmission Videos

Three independent coders analyzed the recordings according to a coding scheme established at the outset of the study. I used the video recordings from approximately forty paid volunteers who participated in a pre-test of the study to train the coders and assess the coding scheme. Because these coders also served as research assistants on the project (and therefore might recognize participants from the sessions and debrief interviews they conducted), I randomly assigned approximately two-thirds of the recordings to each coder such that each recording was analyzed by two coders and no coder analyzed recordings from sessions in which he was involved or otherwise recognized the participant. In the end, the coders analyzed video recordings from one hundred of the one hundred four participants included in the analyses, while the recordings for the other four participants were lost due to equipment failure.

Table 6.3.   ANOVA for Approval Ratings (*n* = 100)

Source	Sum of Squares	df	Mean Square	F Statistic	p value
Condition	24024.7	3	8008.2	5.56	0.001
Error	138313.7	96	1440.8		
Total	162338.4	99			

Internalization of Justifications for Deviance

Among other measurements, the independent coders rated the recordings in terms of the extent to which the participant appeared to personally approve of the cheating strategy (on a 100-point scale from "not at all" to "completely"), indicating he had internalized the trainer's justification for cheating in the situation. Two coders made ratings for each participant, and these ratings were averaged to form a composite index indicating the extent to which the participant had internalized definitions favorable to the cheating strategy. This index had an average inter-rater correlation of 0.90. The means and standard deviations are presented in Table 6.2 and results of the analysis of variance are presented in Table 6.3.

The results of the ANOVA and preplanned *t*-tests support Hypotheses 1 and 2. Consistent with Hypothesis 1, participants for whom deviance was justified by a higher status trainer (condition 1) more strongly approved of cheating than those for whom deviance was justified by a lower status trainer (t_{48} = 1.998, one-tailed p = 0.026). Consistent with Hypothesis 2, participants for whom deviance was endorsed by other group members more strongly approved of cheating than those for whom deviance was not endorsed (t_{48} = 2.87, one-tailed p = 0.003).

Transmission of Justifications for Deviance

I performed a content analysis of each of the videos, blind to experimental conditions, recording whether each participant told the new workgroup how to cheat and the primary justification each participant provided. Specifically, I assigned each participant to one of the following four nominal categories developed from pre-test videos, indicating whether the participant (a) did not say how to cheat, (b) said how to cheat but did not provide any justification for the behavior, (c) provided a justification similar to the trainer's equitable pay justification, or (d) provided a new justification that was not provided by the trainer (for example, denial of injury, denial of victim, condemning the condemners). Table 6.4 provides the observed frequencies and probabilities for the cross classification of condition-by-justification, along with 90 percent Wald confidence intervals estimated through a multinomial logistic regression analysis.[2]

Table 6.4. Observed Frequencies and Probabilities for Conditions by Justification (90% Wald Confidence Intervals in Parentheses)

	Justification				
Condition	Didn't Say How	Without Justification	Mark's Justification	New Justification	Total
1. Count	7	3	12	3	25
Probability	0.28	0.12	0.48	0.12	1.0
	(0.13, 0.43)	(0.01, 0.23)	(0.32, 0.64)	(0.01, 0.23)	
2. Count	10	6	3	6	25
Probability	0.40	0.24	0.12	0.24	1.0
	(0.24, 0.56)	(0.10, 0.38)	(0.01, 0.23)	(0.10, 0.38)	
3. Count	0	11	11	4	26
Probability	0.00	0.42	0.42	0.15	1.0
	(0.00, 0.00)[a]	(0.26, 0.58)	(0.26, 0.58)	(0.04, 0.27)	
4. Count	5	6	8	5	24
Probability	0.21	0.25	0.33	0.21	1.0
	(0.07, 0.35)	(0.11, 0.40)	(0.18, 0.49)	(0.07, 0.35)	

[a]The Wald confidence intervals are infinitesimally small for zero probabilities.

The likelihood ratio chi-squared statistic provides strong evidence that the conditions and justification categories are not independent ($G^2_{df=9}$ 27.17, $p = 0.001$).[3] The pattern of probabilities generally suggests that (a) when a higher status carrier justifies deviance, individuals tend to stick with that justification; (b) when a lower status carrier justifies deviance, individuals are less likely to even say how to engage in deviance, and if they do, they tend to provide either no justification or create their own; (c) when deviance is endorsed by peers, individuals tend to either pass along that justification or provide none; and (d) when deviance is not endorsed, individuals seem to be nearly equally likely to fall into any of the justification categories, possibly reflecting the ambiguity of the situation.

More precise tests of Hypotheses 3 and 4 are provided by comparing the relevant probabilities and confidence intervals in Table 6.4, and by constructing odds ratios for comparisons of interest. Consistent with Hypothesis 3, 48 percent of participants who were told to cheat by a higher status trainer communicated his justification to the new group, while only 12 percent of those in the lower status condition did so, and their confidence intervals do not overlap. Further, compared to condition 2, those in condition 1 were 5.7 (90% CI = [1.5, 21.7]) times more likely to pass on Mark's equity justification than to not say how to cheat and 8.0 (90% CI = [1.7, 38.6]) times more likely to pass on Mark's equity justification than to say how without providing any justification. Consistent with the second part of Hypothesis 3, 24

percent of participants in the lower status condition created new justifications while only 12 percent of higher status participants did so. Relative to
condition 1, participants in condition 2 were 8.0 (90% CI = [1.7, 38.6]) times
more likely to create a new justification than to pass on Mark's equity justification.

Providing some evidence for Hypothesis 4, 42 percent of participants for
whom cheating was endorsed (condition 3) passed on Mark's equity justification, while only 33 percent did so in condition 4, although their confidence
intervals overlap somewhat. Similarly, 42 percent of participants in condition
3 told the new group how to cheat but provided no justification for doing so,
compared to only 25 percent of participants in condition 4, although again
this difference is not statistically significant. In terms of odds ratios, relative
to condition 4, participants in the endorsement condition were 1.7 (90% CI =
[0.45, 6.58]) times more likely to pass on Mark's justification rather than create their own, a result that is again potentially due to chance.

DISCUSSION

The results are generally consistent with the hypotheses. Status and endorsement have the predicted positive effect on the internalization of justifications.
Further, the findings suggest that individuals are more likely to transmit a justification for deviance if it is offered by higher status carriers or if it has been
endorsed by one's peers, that they are more likely to create new justifications
when it is initially suggested by a lower status carrier, and that endorsement
may validate the behavior to the extent that no justification is deemed necessary when transmitting it to new group members.

The results of this study offer insight into the process through which deviant
peers affect deviant behavior. According to culture conflict theories, the relative
status of a person who suggests, promotes, or engages in deviance affects the
extent to which others will internalize justifications for deviance. Moreover,
these theories suggest that deviance can become normative when endorsed
by peers. The results presented here augment analyses presented elsewhere
(Younts forthcoming) that clearly demonstrate that the status of the carrier of
deviance and endorsement by peers affect cheating *behavior*, to further suggest
that part of the effects of these variables on behavior may be through the internalization of justifications that cheating is legitimate in the situation.

Perhaps more important than the results presented here regarding internalization and transmission of justifications for deviance, however, is the potential this study and the others discussed in this volume demonstrate for investigating deviance and crime through laboratory experiments. The experimental

protocol developed for this study modified Kalkhoff and Willer's (this volume) design, most notably by introducing a greater degree of social interaction. Specifically, video and audio equipment created a realistic communication situation in which participants were able to introduce themselves to others and receive training from a person who had supposedly completed the study before. Although participants believed that these communications were occurring in "real-time," they were actually pre-recorded videos used to manipulate the theoretically relevant variables and to strictly control variation in extraneous factors (for example, speech style, number and type of justifications offered). The potential for using video-based communications to create realistic social situations as a means for studying the effects of group processes on deviance is clear. In fact, a follow-up study is in progress that increases the amount of communication between participants and their simulated workgroup, such that their endorsement of deviance is communicated visually and verbally. The amount and type of communication that is allowed between confederates and study participants is nearly unlimited and should be systematically varied in future research.

The protocol also has the advantage of providing complete surveillance of participants' behavior, including their communications with one another. There is no "undetected" deviance in such a situation, since all task-related behavior is recorded unobtrusively through computer software. Additionally, the setting unobtrusively records participants' communications with other group members (both audio and video), allowing a rich and detailed investigation of both qualitative and quantitative aspects of the transmission of deviant behavior among group members. Future research should capitalize on these features to provide further investigations into the processes through which deviance is justified, when those justifications will be internalized, and the conditions under which they eventually diffuse through a population.

This setting also has the unique advantage of allowing participants the opportunity to engage in deviance that is real and defined as it is in most observational designs. Unlike prior laboratory studies that defined "deviant" behavior in terms of variation from either the *local* group norm (for example, other people's expressed attitudes or judgments in the situation) or an assumed objective reality (for example, the obvious relative length of two lines), this study gave participants the opportunity to violate rules established and potentially sanctioned by authorities (the university) in order to ostensibly make more money. Although the rule and the consequences for violating it were, in fact, never enforced, participants did not know this during the study. In fact, the legitimacy and enforcement of the rule itself are potentially interesting topics of future investigation (for example, Kalkhoff and Willer, this volume). Most importantly, this allows the study of deviance without

confounding its definition with group support/behavior and/or individual beliefs about the behavior, as in most prior lab studies.

A key issue in applying the setting to study deviance, however, is that there
clearly are causal processes (for example, historical processes, individual
processes that occur over long periods of time) and types of deviance (for example, violence against persons) that are not amenable to laboratory experiments (for examples emphasizing situational approaches to deviance research
see Briar and Piliavin 1965; Hagan and Palloni 1988; Heimer and Matsueda
1994; Matsueda 1992; McCarthy, Hagan, and Cohen 1998; Short and Strodtbeck 1965). One may be tempted to ask, then, can a laboratory experiment re-
alistically tell us anything about why individuals engage in deviance? Em-
bedded in this question is the implicit position that laboratory experiments,
with their intentional artificiality and extensive controls, are inherently limited in terms of external validity (for example, Borgatta and Bohrnstedt 1974;
Campbell and Stanley 1963; Cartwright and Zander 1968; Drabek and Haas
1967; Harre and Secord 1972). Deviant behavior in natural settings, and especially criminal deviance (for example, illicit drug use, theft, violent crime),
involves a variety of factors not necessarily implicated in the deviant behavior investigated in the present experiment, not least of which are the degree
of consensus in society regarding the norm being violated and the severity of
punishment for transgressions (for example, Stafford et al. 1986). Moreover,
the social groups in which deviance occurs naturally have a degree of history,
future, and structure (for example, status hierarchies, mechanisms of informal
social control) that are unlikely in ad hoc experimental groups (for example,
Warr 2002; Zelditch 1969).

To the extent that external validity refers to the ability of the researcher to
directly extrapolate findings from the experiment to other concrete, natural
settings (for example, Campbell and Stanley 1963; Harre and Secord 1972),
there is little doubt that experimental investigations of deviance are weak in
terms of external validity. By this criterion, in fact, all scientific research pos-
sesses a questionable degree of external validity (Lucas 2003; Martin and Sell
1979; Webster and Kervin 1974; Zelditch 1969). The issue of external validity, when framed in terms of the similarities between the concrete features of
multiple empirical settings, however, is of questionable significance. Is it
more desirable that a theory be supported by results from multiple empirical
settings with approximately identical concrete features or that it be supported
by results from diverse concrete settings that meet the abstract conditions set
forth by the theory (for example, Cohen 1989)? A more scientifically fertile
criterion of external validity refers to the degree to which a theory is applica-
ble to and supported in a broad range of empirical contexts, which cannot be
determined by comparing the particular features of any concrete settings,

whether "natural" or "artificial" (Lucas 2003; see also Martin and Sell 1979; Webster and Kervin 1974; Zelditch 1969).

The question of external validity, therefore, is not whether a laboratory experiment itself can tell us why a given individual or group in a temporally and culturally specific instance (that is, a natural setting) commits deviance, but rather whether the abstract claims generated by a theory of deviance are supported by empirical instances in a wide range of settings, including those "artificially" constructed in the laboratory and those "naturally" occurring in the course of human history. As such, the present laboratory experiment can only provide one piece of evidence as to the empirical viability of theories of deviance, while external validity can only be determined by future replication in a wide range of both natural and laboratory settings. The research reported in this chapter and in this volume provides an important step in the development of meaningful laboratory experiments in the study of deviance that complement the extensive body of research on crime, delinquency, and deviance obtained using field observations, self-report surveys, and official records.

NOTES

1. I would like to thank Will Kalkhoff and Robb Willer, who generously allowed me to use an adaptation of the norm statement and task setting they employed in their study of the effectiveness of punishment certainty for deterring deviance (Kalkhoff and Willer, this volume).

2. Specifically, I estimated a baseline category logit model (see Agresti 2002 for details) that estimates the effects of the nominal condition categories on the logits representing the log-odds that a participant in condition X_i relative to condition X_j provided justification Y_k rather than justification Y_l, comparing each condition 1-3 to condition 4. Because Hypotheses 3 and 4 make predictions comparing the *probabilities* of justification categories within conditions, I do not report the parameter estimates for the models, but rather the Wald confidence intervals for the estimated probabilities in Table 6.4. Model details and estimates are available upon request.

3. Fisher's exact test, which provides a better estimate for small samples and sparse tables (Agresti 2002), produces the same substantive result (Fisher's P = 3.53E-11, p = .003).

REFERENCES

Agresti, Alan. 2002. *Categorical Data Analysis*, 2nd ed. Hoboken, NJ: Wiley.
Akers, Ronald L. 1998. *Social Learning and Social Structure*. Boston: Northeastern University Press.

Allen, V. L. 1965. "Situational Factors in Conformity." In *Advances in Experimental Social Psychology,* vol. 2, edited by L. Berkowitz. San Diego, CA: Academic.

———. 1975. "Social Support for Nonconformity." In *Advances in Experimental Social Psychology,* vol. 8, edited by L. Berkowitz. New York: Academic.

Asch, Solomon E. 1955. "Opinions and Social Pressure." *Scientific American* 193(5):31–35.

———. 1956. "Studies of Independence and Conformity: I. A Minority of One Against a Unanimous Majority." *Psychological Monographs*, 70(9).

Becker, Howard S. 1963. *Outsiders: Studies in the Sociology of Deviance*. Glencoe: The Free Press.

Berger, Joseph, M. Hamit Fiflek, Robert Z. Norman, and Morris Zelditch, Jr. 1977. *Status Characteristics and Social Interaction: An Expectation States Approach*. New York: Elsevier.

Berger, Peter L., and Thomas Luckmann. 1966. *The Social Construction of Reality*. New York: Doubleday.

Borgatta, Edgar R., and George W. Bohrnstedt. 1974. "Some Limitations of Generalizability from Social Psychological Experiments." *Sociological Methods and Research* 3:111–20.

Briar, Scott, and Irving Piliavin. 1965. "Delinquency, Situational Inducements, and Commitment to Conformity." *Social Problems* 13:35–45.

Bursik, Robert J., Jr. 1988. "Social Disorganization and Theories of Crime and Delinquency: Problems and Prospects." *Criminology* 26(4):519–52.

Campbell, Donald T., and Julian C. Stanley. 1963. *Experimental and Quasi-Experimental Designs for Research*. Chicago: Rand McNally.

Cartwright, Dorwin, and A. Zander. 1968. *Group Dynamics*. New York: Harper and Row.

Chaiken, Shelly, Akiva Liberman, and Alice H. Eagly. 1989. "Heuristic and Systematic Information Processing within and beyond the Persuasion Context." In *Unintended Thought*, edited by J. S. Uleman and J. A. Bargh. New York: The Guilford Press.

Chaiken, Shelly, and Durairaj Maheswaran. 1994. "Heuristic Processing Can Bias Systematic Processing: Effects of Source Credibility, Argument Ambiguity, and Task Importance on Attitude Judgment." *Journal of Personality & Social Psychology* 66(3):460–73.

Cialdini, Robert B., and Melanie R. Trost. 1998. "Social Influence: Social Norms, Conformity, and Compliance." In *The Handbook of Social Psychology,* vol. 2 (4th ed.), edited by D. T. Gilbert and S. Fiske. New York: McGraw-Hill.

Cohen, Albert K. 1955. *Delinquent Boys: The Culture of the Gang*. New York: The Free Press.

Cohen, Bernhard P. 1989. *Developing Sociological Knowledge: Theory and Method*. Chicago: Nelson-Hall.

Deutsch, Morton, and H. B. Gerard. 1955. "A Study of Normative and Informational Social Influences upon Individual Judgment." *Journal of Abnormal and Social Psychology* 51:629–36.

Drabek, Thomas E., and J. Eugene Haas. 1967. "Realism in Laboratory Simulation: Myth or Method?" *Social Forces* 45:337–46.

Festinger, Leon. 1950. "Informal Social Communication." *Psychological Review* 57:271–82.

Hagan, John, and Alberto Palloni. 1988. "Crimes as Social Events in the Life Course: Reconceiving a Criminological Controversy." *Criminology* 26(1):87–100.

Harre, R., and P. F. Secord. 1972. *The Explanation of Social Behavior*. Oxford: Blackwell.

Heimer, Karen. 1997. "Socioeconomic Status, Subcultural Definitions, and Violent Delinquency." *Social Forces* 75(3):799–833.

Heimer, Karen, and Ross L. Matsueda. 1994. "Role-Taking, Role Commitment, and Delinquency: A Theory of Differential Social Control." *American Sociological Review* 59:365–90.

Hirschi, Travis. 1969. *Causes of Delinquency*. Berkeley, CA: Free Press.

Kornhauser, Ruth. 1978. *Social Sources of Delinquency*. Chicago: University of Chicago Press.

Lucas, Jeffrey W. 2003. "Theory-Testing, Generalization, and the Problem of External Validity." *Sociological Theory* 21(3):236–53.

Martin, Michael W., and Jane Sell. 1979. "The Role of the Experiment in the Social Sciences." *The Sociological Quarterly* 20:581–90.

Massey, Kelly, Sabrina Freeman, and Morris Zelditch, Jr. 1997. "Status, Power, and Accounts." *Social Psychology Quarterly* 60:238–51.

Matsueda, Ross L. 1988. "The Current State of Differential Association Theory." *The Journal of Research in Crime and Delinquency* 34:277–306.

———. 1992. "Reflected Appraisals, Parental Labeling, and Delinquency: Specifying a Symbolic Interactionist Theory." *American Journal of Sociology* 97:1577–611.

Matsueda, Ross L., and Kathleen Anderson. 1998. "The Dynamics of Delinquent Peers and Delinquent Behavior." *Criminology* 36(2):269–308.

McCarthy, Bill, John Hagan, and Lawrence E. Cohen. 1998. "Uncertainty, Cooperation and Crime: Understanding the Decision to Co-offend." *Social Forces* 77:155–84.

Mills, C. Wright. 1940. "Situated Actions and Vocabularies of Motive." *American Sociological Review* 5:904–13.

Moore, James C. 1968. "Status and Influence in Small Group Interaction." *Sociometry* 31:47–63.

Nail, Paul R. 1986. "Toward an Integration of Some Models and Theories of Social Response." *Psychological Bulletin* 100(2):190–206.

Petty, Richard E., and John T. Cacioppo. 1986. *Communication and Persuasion: Central and Peripheral Routes to Attitude Change*. New York: Springer-Verlag.

Petty, Richard E., Duane T. Wegener, and Leandre R. Fabrigar. 1997. "Attitudes and Attitude Change." *Annual Review of Psychology* 48:609–47.

Rohrer, J. H., S. H. Baron, E. L. Hoffman, and D. V. Swander. 1954. "The Stability of Autokenetic Judgments." *Journal of Abnormal and Social Psychology* 49:595–97.

Scott, Marvin B., and Stanford M. Lyman. 1968. "Accounts." *American Sociological Review* 33:46–62.

Shaw, Clifford. 1966. *The Jack-roller: A Delinquent Boy's Own Story*. Chicago: University of Chicago Press.

Shaw, Clifford, and Henry McKay. 1942. *Juvenile Delinquency and Urban Areas*. Chicago: University of Chicago Press.

Sherif, Muzafer. 1936. *The Psychology of Social Norms*. New York: Harper.

Short, James F., and Fred T. Strodtbeck. 1965. *Group Processes and Gang Delinquency*. Chicago: University of Chicago Press.

Stafford, Mark C., Louis N. Gray, Ben E. Menke, and David A. Ward. 1986. "Modeling the Deterrent Effects of Punishment." *Social Psychology Quarterly* 49:338–47.

Sutherland, Edwin H. 1947. *Principles of Criminology*. Chicago: Lippincott.

Sykes, Gresham M., and David Matza. 1957. "Techniques of Neutralization: A Theory of Delinquency." *American Sociological Review* 22:664–70.

Troyer, Lisa. 2000. "MacSES." Unpublished software manual.

Turner, John C. 1991. *Social Influence*. Pacific Grove, CA: Brooks/Cole.

Walker, Henry A., George M. Thomas, and Morris Zelditch, Jr. 1986. "Legitimation, Endorsement, and Stability." *Social Forces* 64(3):620–43.

Warr, Mark. 2002. *Companions in Crime*. Cambridge, UK: Cambridge University Press.

Webster, Murray A., Jr., and John B. Kervin. 1974. "Artificiality in Experimental Sociology." *Canadian Review of Sociology and Anthropology* 8:263–72.

Webster, Murray A., Jr., and Barbara I. Sobieszek. 1974. "Sources of Evaluations and Expectation States." In *Expectation States Theory: A Theoretical Research Program*, edited by. J. Berger, T. L. Conner, and M. H. Fiflek. Cambridge, MA: Winthrop.

Younts, C. Wesley. Forthcoming. "Status, Endorsement and the Legitimacy of Deviance." *Social Forces.*

Zelditch, Morris, Jr. 1969. "Can You Really Study an Army in the Laboratory?" In *Sociological Reader on Complex Organizations*, edited by A. Etzioni. New York: Holt.

———. 2001. "Processes of Legitimation: Recent Developments and New Directions." *Social Psychology Quarterly* 64(1):4–17.

Zelditch, Morris, and Anthony Floyd. 1998. "Consensus, Dissensus, and Justification." In *Power, Status, and Legitimacy*, edited by J. Berger and M. Zelditch, Jr. New Brunswick, NJ: Transaction.

Zelditch, Morris, Jr., and Henry A. Walker. 1984. "Legitimacy and the Stability of Authority." *Advances in Group Processes* 1:1-25, edited by E. J. Lawler. Greenwich, CT: JAI Press.

Zimbardo, Phillip G., and Michael R. Lieppe. 1991. *The Psychology of Attitude Change and Social Influence*. New York: McGraw-Hill.

Zucker, Lynn G. 1977. "Institutionalization and Cultural Persistence." *American Sociological Review* 42:726–43.

7

Comment: Social Influence in the Lab

Robert J. Bursik, Jr.

Some of the most heated debates throughout criminological history have involved the viability of alternative measurement and analytic strategies. While other fields have increasingly emphasized the benefits of methodological integration (typically referred to as "mixed model" approaches; see the essay of Miller and Gatta 2006), such efforts still are relatively rare in criminology and, in fact, some researchers bluntly dismiss the utility of particular models. David Weisburd (2005), for example, recently stated that "in practice there is no justification, given present knowledge, for (using non-experimental statistical approaches) in crime and justice" because of their questionable internal validity (p. 3).

Although I otherwise am a fan of David's work, such an ex cathedra position makes me very uncomfortable. Nevertheless, it has gained an increasing number of proponents over the last twenty-five years and this trend seems to be accelerating; I fully expected these two chapters to emphasize that same theme and, frankly, initially I was not looking forward to another rehashing of those arguments. Luckily, I read the introductory Horne and Lovaglia chapter before I began the review process and was pleasantly surprised by its explicit emphasis on methodological triangulation. These two pieces share that same orientation and, as such, they offer some provocative initial insights that would be extremely difficult to generate with traditional nonexperimental designs. Yet, while both chapters are provocative in this regard, I believe that the limited external validity imbedded in these two experimental designs significantly limits the substantive contributions that these studies could make to the kinds of future sophisticated neighborhood and peer group mixed models described by the authors.

Before proceeding further, I want to emphasize that my reservations are strictly methodological. A refreshing hallmark of both chapters is their theoretical cosmopolitanism, drawing convincingly from rarely considered social and behavioral science literatures and integrating the associated arguments seamlessly into mainstream criminological thought. Unfortunately, such broad, cross-disciplinary orientations are shockingly rare in much (but certainly not all) criminological work, causing Osgood (1998) to caution that criminology was in danger of becoming "isolated from the disciplines from which it sprang" (p.1). This tendency became especially frustrating to me when I served as editor of *Criminology* for, despite Jim Short's presidential theme of interdisciplinary integration at the 1997 meetings (the year before I assumed the editorship), a majority of the authors of our submissions seemed to have developed their conceptual arguments strictly on the basis of statements made by other criminologists. As such, many complicated concepts were presented almost as caricatures, without the richness or complexity of the original statements. I do not think that it is an accident that those recent papers and books with the greatest impacts have appreciated the interdisciplinary underpinnings of their approaches. For example, in my opinion, one of the primary reasons that the notion of "collective efficacy" caught the imagination of neighborhood criminologists was that Rob Sampson and his colleagues were fully aware of its grounding in the work of the psychologist Albert Bandura and familiar with the large body of educational research that had examined the concept long before it ever had been mentioned in criminological discourse. Horne and Hoffmann, and Younts, all are to be congratulated for introducing novel criminological considerations that will be essential to address in future studies, regardless of their designs.

Although I do not have major concerns about the Horne and Hoffmann experimental design itself (in fact I thought the operationalization of interdependence was quite clever), I do wish that more technical information had been provided, such as relative effect sizes, levels of significance, and so forth. In addition, I would have been more comfortable with a formal assurance that the subjects were randomly assigned to the test conditions; Horne (2004) notes that this was not the case for gender, but it did not affect the findings. Much more detail in these regards would have been very welcome.

Rather, my primary reservations are twofold. First, the experimental design fixes the norms, thereby precluding an examination of how norm enforcement and the development of metanorms are negotiated and evolve over time. A repeated measures approach might have been quite informative. Even more problematic is the material that begins with the Neighborhood Characteristics section in which the experimental findings are compared with "the empirical factors commonly used in social disorganization research." While they acknowledge the utility of survey approaches, they also argue that "we could also use additional lab experiments to explicitly examine not just the effects of abstract factors like costs and benefits, but the effects of particular concrete neighborhood characteristics." In Horne and Lovaglia's opening chapter, they note that a relatively simple deterrence experiment would require around five thousand respondents. How could we possibly design a laboratory study that would be financially, temporally, and administratively feasible that considered the much larger number of variables typically examined in social disorganization/ systemic/collective efficacy models? It certainly would be possible to restrict our attention to a limited number of neighborhoods, but that strategy already has been used successfully in contemporary ethnographic research (see, for example, Sullivan 1990). Thus, what we are left with is a proposal for the identification of new concepts or dynamics to be incorporated into standard nonexperimental studies. Regrettably, despite its intriguing theoretical framework, I think that the Horne and Hoffmann paper promises more than it delivers.

My concern about the Younts paper is far more mundane and certainly will (understandably) frustrate the author: I am skeptical about the degree to which the study design generated responses in which a great deal of faith can be placed. I have no basis for this criticism other than my long familiarity with college students and my own participation in many such experiments as an undergraduate. Students are not nearly as naïve as we often think, and most are aware that experiments are highly controlled exercises. Therefore, if as part of the training session, a member of the experimental team taught them how to cheat and encouraged them to do so, many of them immediately would be suspicious. That is not to say that these data are totally invalid; in fact, they generally replicate some of the central findings of the classic Whyte and Short and Strodtbeck studies. And some of the treatment manipulations are quite innovative. Nevertheless, I must confess that I am not yet convinced by this work.

REFERENCES

Horne, Christine. 2004. "Collective Benefits, Exchange Interests, and Norm Enforcement." *Social Forces* 82(3): 1037–62.

Miller, S. I., and J. L. Gatta. 2006. "The Use of Mixed Models and Designs in the Human Sciences: Problems and Prospects." *Quality & Quantity* 40:595–610.

Osgood, D. Wayne. 1998. "Interdisciplinary Integration: Building Criminology by Stealing from Our Friends." *The Criminologist* 23 (4):1, 3, 4, 41.

Sullivan, Mercer L. 1990. *Getting Paid: Youth Crime and Work in the Inner City.* Ithaca, NY: Cornell University Press.

Weisburd, David. 2005. "Editor's Introduction." *Journal of Experimental Criminology* 1:1–8.

III

Law

8

Prosecutorial Misconduct in Serious Cases: Theory and Design of a Laboratory Experiment

Can You Study a Legal System in a Laboratory?

Jeffrey W. Lucas, Corina Graif, and Michael J. Lovaglia

Morris Zelditch, Jr. published his classic paper, "Can You Really Study an Army in a Laboratory?" in 1969. In it, he explained how experimental research involving small groups of participants can inform understandings of interactions in groups both small and large. As Zelditch explained, this is achieved through designing experimental studies that meet the scope conditions and operationalize the key elements of well-established theories. Generalization of experimental findings then happens through theory. Zelditch's paper played a key role in spurring more than thirty-five years of experimental work on group processes that has contributed to understandings of how fundamental social processes play out in groups of any size. We now question the role that experiments can play in contributing to our knowledge base on the legal system. What can experimental studies with idiosyncratic samples and in artificial settings tell us about criminology and other aspects of the legal system?

We propose that experimental research can play a role in explaining prosecutorial misconduct in cases involving severe crimes. Legal scholars in recent years have begun to discuss prosecutorial misconduct as a serious issue confronting the legal system, one that may go relatively unchecked (Dunahoe 2005; Gershman 1992; Hime 2005; Johns 2005; Meares 1995; Schoenfeld 2005). Moreover, evidence indicates that misconduct becomes increasingly likely as crimes become more severe (Bedau and Radelet 1987). Investigating the relationship between crime severity and misconduct, however, presents challenges.

One approach to testing the relationship between crime severity and prosecutorial misconduct is to investigate misconduct among working prosecutors. This may take the form of analyzing case records or perhaps interviewing prosecuting attorneys. These approaches have significant limitations. Research taking the strategy of examining case records finds a relatively higher rate of overturned convictions for murder cases than for less severe cases, indicating that misconduct may be more likely in these cases. For example, although less than 5 percent of criminal convictions are for murders, about half of identified wrongful convictions are for murders. Interpreting this result is difficult, however, because more attention is focused on identifying wrongful convictions in murder cases than in less severe cases. In other words, it may be that there are no more wrongful convictions for murder than for other cases, but rather simply that more of these wrongful convictions are identified. Further, wrongful convictions and prosecutorial misconduct do not perfectly align.

Interviewing prosecuting attorneys also presents difficulties. One is that we might expect prosecutors who engage in misconduct to be less than forthcoming in interviews. Also, prosecutors especially committed to a conviction in a particular case may not define a behavior as misconduct that others, or even themselves under different circumstances, would define as such. Further, even if prosecutors were completely honest and entirely cognizant of misconduct, and if prosecutors indicated that they engaged in misconduct more often in trials involving more serious cases, determining cause and effect would be impossible due to the multiple complexities of the legal system. Perhaps more serious cases, for example, engender more misconduct not directly because the crimes are more severe but instead because the trials are longer and more complex and provide more opportunities for misconduct.

An alternative research approach is to experimentally test the relationship between crime severity and misconduct. Experiments assign different groups to different levels of an independent variable before a dependent variable is measured. An experiment on misconduct might randomly assign one group of student participants to act as prosecutors for a case involving a serious crime and another to act as prosecutors for a case involving a less serious crime. Participants in each group could then be given an opportunity to engage in misconduct. If participants assigned the more serious case are more likely to engage in misconduct, then we have evidence of a relationship between crime severity and misconduct.

Common sense and conventional logic tell us that such a study would reveal little about the behaviors of actual prosecutors working in real trials. Empirical investigations of any type in the social sciences always represent indirect efforts to measure social reality, and the goal of investigators is typically to use measures and design questions and settings that approximate reality as closely as possible. A survey researcher who cannot directly measure income, for example, will ask respondents to self-report their income levels. We generally accept these representations of income as accurate reflections of income. Similarly, ethnographic investigations will use researchers' observations of behaviors as indicators of behaviors themselves, indicators that we generally accept as accurate representations.

Drawing conclusions about the behaviors of actual working prosecutors from the experimental design described above, however, requires a much greater logical leap than concluding that self-reports of income represent income or that ethnographers' recordings of behavior reflect behaviors themselves. Conventional logic tells us that several elements of the experiment would limit what it could tell us about actual prosecutorial misconduct in the real legal system. One such element is that participants in the experiment would not be real working prosecutors, persons who have undergone significant training in the responsibilities associated with their jobs. Another is that the setting would not be one faced by real prosecutors: The trial would be shorter than an actual trial, there would not be a real defendant facing actual prison time, the "prosecutors" in the study would not be subject to the same costs and benefits associated with misconduct as real prosecutors, and so on.

An obvious approach to dealing with these problems, and one that follows the logic of other types of empirical investigations, would be to design the experimental setting to be as much as possible like an actual trial in the real legal system. One step the experimenter might take would be to select participants as much as possible like real working prosecutors, perhaps recruiting law students with ambitions to be prosecutors. The experimenter also might design a trial containing as many of the elements as possible that are faced by real prosecutors. This could include a trial that lasts several hours or days, training for the prosecutor in ethical conduct, a defendant, a jury, exhaustive legal procedures, significant benefits to the prosecutor for attaining a conviction, costs to the prosecutor for being caught in misconduct, and so on. With these steps, we might better be able to generalize the results of the experiment to misconduct among working prosecutors in real trials.

Such an approach to designing an experiment with implications for trials in natural settings would surely fail. It would fail because no matter how many steps a researcher took to make an experiment approximate a naturally occurring trial, numerous differences would necessarily remain. Each of these differences would exist as possible foils to any findings produced by the experiment. In other words, if participants prosecuting a more severe trial engaged in more misconduct than participants prosecuting a less severe trial, we would not be able to rule out the effect disappearing with the elimination of any or all of the differences between the experimental design and a naturally occurring trial.

THE COUNTERINTUITIVE LOGIC OF
EXPERIMENTAL INVESTIGATIONS

Because experiments are always approximations of natural settings, we can never rule out differences between the experimental setting and natural settings being responsible for effects found in experimental investigations. This is a significant problem if the goal of experiments is similar to other research investigations in attempting to construct settings and measures that approximate social reality as closely as possible. The logic of experimental investigations, however, is completely different. In essence, rather than attempting to design settings that approximate the natural world as closely as possible, experimentalists do just the opposite; they attempt to create conditions as unlike natural settings as possible.

An effective use of experiments to study the relationship between severity of crime and prosecutorial misconduct would be to draw from or develop a theory of why prosecutors may become more likely to engage in misconduct as crimes become more severe. If the elements of the theory could be recreated in an experimental laboratory, an experiment could then test the theory. Rather than attempting to *include* as many elements of trials in natural settings as possible, the experimenter would attempt to *exclude* all aspects of trials in natural settings not directly relevant to the theory.

The goal of the experimenter in this situation would not be to produce results that can be applied to trials in natural settings. Rather, the objective would be to find support for the theory. The experiment would be designed to test an *explanation*, not to establish an empirical generalization. Support for the theory would suggest a process that may or not play out when the many complexities of natural settings are introduced. In other words, experimental tests of theory can identify basic social processes that arise when the complexities of natural settings are controlled. Further research using other methods can identify whether elements of natural settings aggravate or mitigate those processes.

We developed a theory proposing that more serious cases would lead to greater perceptions of guilt, greater perceived importance of attaining a conviction, and more misconduct than less serious cases. We then designed an experiment to test that theory. The experiment produced results that well supported our theoretical propositions.

THEORETICAL DEVELOPMENT

Recent years have seen numerous incidents of procedural errors in the prosecution of serious crimes (Dunahoe 2005; Gershman 1992; Meares 1995). This has been evidenced by a high incidence of overturned convictions for rape and murder. One study, for example, found more erroneous convictions in capital murder cases than had been reported in published collections for all other kinds of cases (Bedau and Radelet 1987). Rattner (1988), in an overview of all known erroneous convictions, found that although homicides represent less than 2 percent of all criminal convictions, they represent 45 percent of known erroneous convictions.

These discoveries raise the question of whether serious criminal cases encourage prosecutorial misconduct (Gross 1996; Meares 1995). Prosecutors may face increased pressure to convict in trials involving serious crimes, and rewards for high conviction rates in serious cases obtained by prosecutors could lead to higher rates of misconduct in the prosecution of severe crimes. Moreover, if attaining a conviction is more important to prosecutors and there is a tendency to believe that defendants are guilty in serious cases, then prosecutors may be able to more easily justify their misconduct.

Research indicates that more severe crimes may be accompanied by greater belief in a defendant's guilt, irrespective of evidence tying the defendant to a crime (Bornstein 1998; Myers 1980). In a meta-analysis of research on the relationship between severity of outcomes and perception of responsibility to a possibly accountable individual, Robbennolt (2000) found significantly greater blame attributed to potential offenders of more severe crimes than of less severe crimes. In other words, as the consequences of an act become more severe, the responsibility attributed to a perceived perpetrator becomes greater. Other research has found that in cases with similar evidence of a person's guilt, the person is more likely to be considered guilty when the consequences are more severe (Howe 1991; Sanderson, Zanna, and Darly 2000).

The first proposition of our theory, then, is that more severe crime will be accompanied by stronger perceptions of a potential perpetrator's guilt. More specifically, we propose that when a crime is more severe, prosecutors will be more likely to believe that a suspect is guilty. Further, greater perceptions of a defendant's guilt may provide justification for misconduct.

Research on dishonest behavior finds that persons develop situation-specific attitudes on the relative appropriateness of behavior. In other words, ethical considerations of the situation mediate the relationship between one's potentially dishonest behavior and one's perceptions of that behavior (Birbeck and LaFree 1993; LaBeff, Clark, Haines, and Dieckoff 1990). An example in the legal system is "noble cause corruption," in which illegal acts violate the legal rights of citizens for moral considerations (Delattre 1989; Harrison 1999). Based on this research, it seems likely that perceptions of the immorality of misconduct among prosecutors will decrease as perceptions of the defendant's guilt increase. We thus further propose that prosecutors attaching higher perceptions of guilt to defendants in cases involving more serious crimes will make more likely and provide justification for misconduct.

Our goal is not to attempt to determine the prevalence of misconduct in the prosecution of crimes in natural settings. Such an effort would be beyond the goals of an experimental investigation. Moreover, the extensiveness of prosecutorial misconduct in criminal trials in the United States has been well documented in research using other investigative techniques (Harmon 2001; Lofquist 2001; Nidiry 1996; Radelet and Bedau 2001), and some argue that it is becoming more widespread (Gershman 2001; Johns 2005; Lawless and North 1984). Our goal is also not to determine whether prosecutorial misconduct is more likely for more severe crimes. Rather, we assume that it is, based on the accumulated evidence from research using other methods. Our goal is to understand the factors that produce misconduct in trials involving serious crimes, an important task (Meares 1995). The theory we develop and test proposes that perceptions of a defendant's guilt may be one such factor.

EXPERIMENTALLY INVESTIGATING MISCONDUCT

To test our theory, we employ an experimental methodology. Experimental studies of the legal system are uncommon. This is largely because empirical studies of the legal system are usually designed to test for the prevalence or likelihood of some phenomenon. Experiments are not well-suited to this purpose. Instead, experimental studies are designed to test theories that explain why established social phenomena might occur. Assuming that misconduct occurs more frequently in the prosecution of severe crimes, we use the scientific control possible in a laboratory experiment to test our theory with the potential to explain why more serious cases may generate more prosecutorial misconduct than minor ones.

Laboratory experiments do not capture the complexities of naturally occurring environments, and they are a valuable complement to studies in natural settings precisely because they control for those complexities. Basic social science experiments recreate only a limited number of theoretically relevant elements found in natural settings, controlling for extraneous factors that may mask fundamental processes, and thus increasing our understanding of fundamental social processes (Lucas 2003; Webster 2003; Zelditch 1969). An experimental test of our theory can create identical conditions for all participants except the severity of the crime that participants prosecute. Participants then can be assigned at random to prosecute either a more severe crime or a less severe one, controlling for individual differences among participants. Significantly greater misconduct among participants prosecuting the more severe crime would constitute strong evidence that severity of crime encourages prosecutorial misconduct.

An experiment that operationalizes only theoretically relevant elements can thus foreclose the many possible alternative explanations that studies of the legal system generate. An alternative plausible explanation for finding more errors in the prosecution of severe crimes, for example, is that more effort is spent trying to discover errors in serious cases. More media attention is focused on them and the legal system provides more checks to prevent the conviction of innocent defendants in cases where penalties are more serious (Pritchard 1986; Hoeffel 2005). For this reason, researchers might find more errors in the prosecution of serious cases even if errors actually occur just as frequently in minor ones (Gross 1996).

Laboratory research makes it possible to discover whether more serious cases are accompanied by increased belief in the defendant's guilt and whether that increased belief could help justify misconduct. If laboratory research supports the theory, then it can be used to guide future research to investigate conditions in naturally occurring settings that would exacerbate or mitigate the process found to increase prosecutorial misconduct in the laboratory. Thus, a laboratory experiment investigating prosecutorial misconduct will not provide direct evidence of the extent or frequency of misconduct by working prosecutors in criminal trials. It can, however, help us understand the conditions that encourage it. Research using other methods can then investigate the conditions faced by working prosecutors that may affect the occurrence of misconduct.

HYPOTHESES

We propose that more severe crimes will be accompanied by greater perceptions of guilt than will be less severe crimes. Research is consistent with this proposition in finding that in cases of identical law violations, perceivers are more likely to believe potential offenders are guilty when outcomes are more severe. An alternative explanation for these findings is that individuals are predisposed to believe a defendant for a more serious crime is guilty due to a belief that the defendant would not be charged for a serious offense unless there was overwhelming evidence of his or her guilt. Research on mock juries (for example, Freedman, Krismer, MacDonald, and Cunningham 1994), however, finds evidence against these sorts of predispositions. Nevertheless, we carefully constructed our experimental protocol so that participants in experimental conditions could see the process that led from the identification of the defendant as a suspect through his being charged with a crime. This process was identical across our experimental conditions. We predict that given identical evidence of a defendant's guilt, participants prosecuting a trial for a more serious crime will be more likely to believe the defendant is guilty than will participants prosecuting a less severe crime:

> *Hypothesis 1*: Participants prosecuting a murder will be more likely to believe the defendant is guilty than will participants prosecuting an assault.

We further propose that increased perceptions of guilt will increase the likelihood of misconduct as prosecutors attach greater importance to the attainment of a conviction. We thus predict that the personal importance of attaining a conviction will increase as severity of crime increases:

> *Hypothesis 2*: Participants prosecuting a murder will view the attainment of a conviction as more personally important than will participants prosecuting an assault.

We also propose that misconduct will become more likely as severity of crime increases. Our theoretical account indicates that higher perceptions of guilt and a higher perceived importance of attaining a conviction will provide justification for misconduct. This leads to the following prediction:

> *Hypothesis 3*: Participants prosecuting a murder will be more likely to engage in misconduct than will participants prosecuting an assault.

We created an experimental setting in which participants acted as prosecuting attorneys in contrived criminal trials involving either murders or assaults. We tested our hypotheses by comparing the behaviors and attitudes of individuals across the type of crime. Our hypotheses are predicated on an assumption that participants will view murders as more severe than assaults. If data support our hypotheses but participants do not view murders as more severe than assaults, then our theoretical propositions will not be supported. We thus measure participants' perceptions of severity of crime through a questionnaire item. Consistent with our theoretical account, we expect participants assigned murder trials to indicate higher perceptions of severity of crime than participants assigned assault trials.

CREATING THE OPPORTUNITY FOR
MISCONDUCT IN THE LABORATORY

We constructed an experimental study that allowed us to compare participants' misconduct when prosecuting a contrived case of severe crime (murder) with their misconduct when prosecuting a less severe crime (assault). The design also allowed measurement of participants' assessments of the defendant's guilt. Each study participant was randomly assigned the position of prosecuting a defendant for either murder or assault. Participants first constructed a case against the defendant. In constructing the case, participants had the opportunity to engage in misconduct to increase the likelihood of conviction. Participants then answered a number of questions about their behaviors as prosecutors and their perceptions of the defendant and the crime.

Methods

Participants in the study were undergraduate students at a large state university. Before each participant arrived for the study she or he was randomly assigned a criminal case, either murder or assault. In the murder condition, a victim died from injuries sustained during an attack. In the assault condition, the victim fully recovered from an attack. Aside from whether or not the victim died or fully recovered, the materials given to all participants were identical.

When arriving for the experiment, each participant was told that as part of the study, she or he would be acting as a prosecuting attorney, a defense attorney, or a judge in a mock criminal trial. The participant was then asked to draw one of three slips of paper from a hat to determine her or his role in the study. Although participants were led to believe that one slip of paper corresponded to the defense attorney role, one to the prosecuting attorney role, and one to the judge role, all slips of paper in fact contained the word *prosecutor*, and participants always acted as prosecuting attorneys in the study.

After learning their role in the study, participants read through a police report on the case and believed that the defense attorney and judge would do the same. The report followed a sequence of events beginning with an emergency call to a police department and concluding with criminal charges against a defendant. In reading the police report, participants learned that police officers traveled to the residence of an individual reported missing and found a ransacked home as well as a body inside the doorway. The police report notes that officers then called medical personnel. Depending on the participant's condition, emergency medical personnel either pronounced the individual deceased (murder condition) or the person fully recovered from his injuries in a matter of days (assault condition).

The police report further noted that fingerprints on the front door of the victim's home matched those of a convicted felon. Participants read that after this individual was interviewed he left the town and was arrested in another city. The police report ended with a description of an indictment against the individual for murder (murder condition) or assault (assault condition).

Participants then read a form titled "Facts Relevant to the Case." Participants again believed that both the judge and defense attorney in the case would read the same form. The form described multiple details of the case, most pointing to the defendant as the most likely suspect. Some materials, however, pointed to an alternative suspect as possibly guilty of the crime.

Participants then read a form specific to their duties in the trial. The form was titled "Your Job—Prosecutor" and explained the duties of the prosecuting attorney during the study. Participants read that prosecuting attorneys, defense attorneys, and judges would be completing the study at different times. Prosecuting attorneys and defense attorneys, they read, assembled cases to present to the judge. If they had been selected as judge, participants learned, they would have received materials put together by prosecuting and defense attorneys at earlier dates. Instructions stressed to participants that their goal in the study was not to attempt to determine who committed the crime against the victim, but only to present the case against the defendant to the best of their ability. They would do this by convincing the judge of the defendant's guilt.

Instructions also informed participants that they would be paid based on how well they presented the case against the defendant. Participants were told that they would receive $10 in payment for participating in the study regardless of the outcome of the trial, but that they would receive an additional $5 if the judge later returned a verdict of "guilty."

Participants were informed that as prosecuting attorneys, they would have special responsibilities in the case. Because the defendant had a court-appointed attorney, participants learned, the prosecution had more resources in collecting evidence than did the defense. Participants read that as prosecuting attorneys, they would have access to all police interviews. Participants also learned that they were obligated by law to turn over to the defense all materials that might have relevance to the guilt or innocence of the defendant. If the participant chose not to turn over any such materials, instructions noted, she or he would likely not be caught. Instructions stressed, however, that such actions were illegal and defined as misconduct. These actions happen to be misconduct in trials in the U.S. legal system. The Brady Rule requires prosecutors to give to defense attorneys summaries of interviews with witnesses that may be exculpatory to the defendant. Some argue that this rule has been laxly enforced (Kurcias 2000; Hoeffel 2005).

Participants then learned their specific duties in the trial. Instructions noted that participants would first read through interviews obtained by police officers. Their first task would be to put together a list of questions from the interviews that they wished to turn over to the defense. Their second task was to select ten interview questions that they thought would be most likely to convince the judge of the defendant's guilt. Participants were told that these questions would be turned over to the judge at a later date. Finally, participants were to write a one-page closing argument to be read by the judge.

Participants were then given a packet containing the interviews. Participants read six interviews with a total of sixty questions, each individually numbered. Information in the interviews generally pointed to the defendant being guilty of the crime. Four questions, however, identified the victim's wife as a potential suspect. In one question, for example, a neighbor identified the car of the victim's wife's boyfriend as having been in the victim's driveway on the day of the attack.

After reading through the interviews, participants completed their three duties. First, participants indicated pieces of relevant evidence that they wished to turn over to the defense attorney. To carry out this task, participants were given a form titled "Questions for Defense" that contained the identifying number of each interview question. Participants circled each question on the form that they wished to give to the defense attorney. Participants had the option of circling all, none, or any number of questions on this form. We determined misconduct by the number of the four questions pointing to the victim's wife as a suspect that participants chose not to turn over to the defense attorney. The participant's second and third duties in the study were not relevant to our hypotheses and were included only to decrease suspicion about the purposes of the list of questions for the defense.

After turning over questions to the defense, selecting questions for the judge, and writing their closing arguments, participants completed a post-study questionnaire. Items on the questionnaire included how much prison time the participant believed the perpetrator (whether the defendant or not) of the crime deserved, how personally important it was to the participant to attain a conviction in the case, how generally important the participant believed it was to convict the defendant, and how likely the participant believed it was that the defendant would be convicted. After participants answered these questions, the study was complete, and they were debriefed and paid.

FINDINGS

Participants in the study were eighty undergraduate students, forty in each of the two experimental conditions. Of these, fifty-four were female and twenty-six were male. Data from an additional seven participants were excluded from analyses. Four of these seven participants did not understand the study materials (three of these students were not native English speakers) and three of the seven did not believe that other participants in the study were acting as defense attorneys and judges.

Manipulation Check

We proposed that as severity of crime increased, participants would be more likely to believe that defendants were guilty and would become more likely to engage in misconduct. Our hypotheses predicted that murder trials would generate greater perceptions of guilt and higher misconduct than assault trials. In order for this hypothesis to accurately reflect our theory, participants must view murder as more severe than assault. To assess the severity with which participants viewed the crime, we asked each participant to rate the extent to which they saw the crime as severe, with 1 indicating very severe and 7 indicating not at all severe. The mean score for participants in the murder condition was 1.28 (SD = 0.85). The mean score in the assault condition was 3.03 (SD = 1.44). This difference is in the direction of participants viewing murders as more severe than assaults and is significant ($t = 6.62$, one-tailed p of difference in predicted direction < 0.001). We thus conclude that participants did perceive murder to be more severe than assault.

Hypothesis Tests

Our three hypotheses predicted that participants in the murder condition, compared to participants in the assault condition, would be more likely to believe the defendant was guilty, would attach greater personal importance to the attainment of a conviction, and would be more likely to engage in misconduct. We discuss findings on each hypothesis in turn.

Guilt Perceptions

Hypothesis 1 predicted that although participants in both conditions received identical evidence tying the defendant to the crime, participants in the murder condition would be more likely to view the defendant as guilty than would participants in the assault condition. We tested this hypothesis through a questionnaire item that asked participants to rate on a scale the extent to which they believed that the defendant was guilty (with 1 indicating definitely not guilty and 7 indicating definitely guilty). The mean score on the question for the murder condition was 5.25 (SD = 1.33) and for the assault condition was 4.40 (SD = 2.09). This difference is in the predicted direction and significant ($t = 2.17$, one-tailed $p = 0.017$), supporting Hypothesis 1. Participants in the murder condition were more likely to believe the defendant was guilty than were participants in the assault condition.

Personal Importance of Attaining a Conviction

We predicted with Hypothesis 2 that participants in the murder condition would view attaining a conviction as more important than would participants in the assault condition. A questionnaire item asked participants to indicate the extent to which they felt that attaining a conviction was personally important (with 1 indicating not at all important and 7 indicating very important). The mean answer on the scale for participants in the murder condition was 5.63 (SD = 1.61) and for the assault condition was 4.75 (SD = 1.94). This difference is in the direction of participants in the murder condition viewing conviction as more personally important and is significant ($t = 2.19$, one-tailed $p = 0.031$). This supports Hypothesis 2.

In addition to the question on personal importance of a conviction, we asked participants the extent to which they believed that attaining a conviction in the trial was generally important (with 1 indicating very important and 7 indicating not at all important). The mean score on the scale for participants in the murder condition was 2.70 (SD = 1.68) and in the assault condition was 2.83 (SD = 1.78). This difference is not significant ($t = 0.323$, two-tailed $p = 0.748$). This result does not bear on Hypothesis 2, which concerns the personal importance of a conviction as a potential motivating factor in misconduct, but it was unexpected. Participants in the murder condition expressed that attaining a conviction had significantly more personal importance but no more general importance than did participants in the assault condition.

Misconduct

Our third hypothesis predicted that participants in the murder condition would be more likely to engage in misconduct than would participants in the assault condition. We had a behavioral operationalization of misconduct, measuring it by the number of four questions pointing to an individual other than the defendant as a potential suspect that participants withheld from the defense. The mean number of the four questions withheld from the defense by participants in the murder condition was 2.15 (SD = 1.51) and in the assault condition was 1.50 (SD = 1.45). This difference is in the predicted direction and significant ($t = 1.96$, one-tailed $p = 0.027$), supporting Hypothesis 3. Because we only had four levels of misconduct, we also ran a non-parametric Mann-Whitney U-Test on the difference in items withheld. The U-Test also produced a significant result ($U = 609.00$, one-tailed $p = 0.03$). Participants in the murder condition were more likely to engage in misconduct than were participants in the assault condition.

In addition to our behavioral measure, a questionnaire item asked participants whether they had withheld relevant material from the defense. Participants were asked to rate (with 1 indicating that they did turn over all relevant information and 7 indicating that they did not turn over all relevant information) the extent to which they believed they had turned over all relevant facts to the defense. The mean score on the scale for participants in the murder condition was 2.70 (SD = 1.91) and for participants in the assault condition was 1.93 (SD = 1.31). This difference is in the direction of participants in the murder condition being more likely to withhold relevant information and is significant (t = 2.116, one-tailed p = 0.019). Thus, our behavioral and self-report measures were consistent in finding greater misconduct in the murder condition, and the self-report finding indicates that participants in the murder condition made conscious decisions to withhold exculpatory evidence.

We also had a questionnaire item that asked participants to indicate the extent to which they thought a guilty conviction in the case was likely (with 1 indicating very likely and 7 indicating not at all likely). Although we did not predict a difference on the item, we might expect participants in the murder condition to attach a higher likelihood to eventual conviction of the defendant because they withheld more relevant information from defense attorneys. The mean answer on this scale for participants in the murder condition was 2.40 (SD = 1.28) and for participants in the assault condition was 3.03 (SD = 1.58). This difference is in the direction of participants in the murder condition believing that conviction was more likely and approaches significance (t = 1.95, two-tailed p of a difference not predicted = 0.055).

Results on our third hypothesis demonstrate that participants in the murder condition were less likely to turn over relevant information to the defense than were participants in the assault condition. We also recorded the total number of all questions—potentially exculpatory or not—that participants turned over to the defense. Participants in the murder condition, on average, turned over 20.28 (SD = 12.80) questions while participants in the assault condition turned over an average of 21.40 (SD = 15.00) questions. This difference is not significant (t = 0.361, two-tailed p = 0.719). It appears that aside from differences in the four questions pointing to an alternative suspect, participants in the murder and assault conditions made similar decisions about questions to turn over to the defense.

CONCLUSION

We developed a theory with the potential to explain why prosecutorial misconduct becomes more likely as crimes become more severe. According to theory, the greater personal importance of attaining a conviction for prosecutors combines with a stronger perception of the guilt of defendants in severe cases, encouraging greater misconduct in the prosecution of severe crimes. Results of a controlled laboratory experiment support the propositions of that theory. We found that participants randomly assigned to prosecute a contrived case of murder attached greater personal importance to attaining a conviction, were more likely to believe defendants were guilty, and were more likely to engage in misconduct than participants randomly assigned to prosecute an assault.

The results of our study provided strong support for the theory, increasing our confidence in it. The results, however, tell us nothing directly about the prevalence of misconduct in naturally occurring trials or whether such misconduct becomes more likely as crimes become more severe. Instead, support for the theory suggests a basic process with the potential to increase misconduct in the prosecution of severe crimes, a process that may be aggravated or mitigated by the complex settings faced by working prosecutors.

Our research, then, discovered a process with the potential to increase misconduct in the prosecution of more severe crimes. That process may or may not produce more misconduct when working prosecutors handle more serious cases. One can argue that the legal system has safeguards in place to counteract the process or that the training of prosecutors mitigates its effects. The results of our study, however, shift the burden to showing how aspects of the legal system limit the processes that our findings suggest give rise to misconduct in the prosecution of severe crimes.

One factor that may limit the prevalence of misconduct in trials in natural settings is fear of reprisals for misconduct among prosecutors. In other words, fear of punishment may make misconduct less likely in cases involving severe crimes. The opposite effect also may occur, with the higher rewards and opportunities earned through obtaining convictions in serious cases increasing the pressure to engage in misconduct. The accumulated literature in fact suggests that prosecutors need fear few costs for engaging in misconduct (Chineson 1986; Dunahoe 2005; Gershman 1992; Johns 2005; Kurcias 2000; Meares 1995). Future research would be valuable in determining how the potential rewards and penalties for prosecutorial misconduct alter its prevalence.

Our research provides support for a theory proposing that presumptions of guilt and actions of misconduct will be greater for more serious crimes. Our experimental research suggests the need for research using different methods in order to determine how aspects of the legal system aggravate or mitigate the processes we find. As discussed, determining the extent to which severity of crime affects misconduct in natural settings is difficult. Support for our theory, however, provides a compelling reason to investigate misconduct among working prosecutors of serious crimes.

REFERENCES

Bedau, Hugo Adam, and Michael L. Radalet. 1987. "Miscarriages of Justice in Potentially Capital Cases." *Stanford Law Review* 40:21–179.

Birbeck, Christopher, and Gary LaFree. 1993. "The Situational Analysis of Crime and Deviance." *Annual Review of Sociology* 19:113–17.

Bornstein, Brian H. 1998. "From Compassion to Compensation: The Effect of Injury Severity on Mock Jurors' Liability Judgments." *Journal of Applied Social Psychology* 28:1477–502.

Chineson, Joel. 1986. "Do the Courts Encourage Prosecutorial Misconduct?" *Trial* June:78–81.

Delattre, Edwin. 1989. *Character and Cops*. Washington, DC: American Enterprise Institute.

Dunahoe, Alexandra White. 2005. "Revisiting the Cost-Benefit Calculus of the Misbehaving Prosecutor: Deterrence Economics and Transitory Prosecutors." *New York University Annual Survey of American Law* 61:45–110.

Freedman, Jonathan L., Kirsten Krismer, Jennifer E. MacDonald, and John A. Cunningham. 1994. "Severity of Penalty, Seriousness of the Charge, and Mock Jurors' Verdicts." *Law and Human Behavior* 18:189–202.

Gershman, Bennett L. 1992. "Tricks Prosecutors Play." *Trial*, April, 46–50.

———. 2001. *Prosecutorial Misconduct*, 2nd ed. St. Paul, MN: West Group.

Gross, Samuel R. 1996. "The Risks of Death: Why Erroneous Convictions are Common in Capital Cases." *Buffalo Law Review* 44:469–79.

Harmon, Talia Roitberg. 2001. "Predictors of Miscarriages of Justice in Capital Cases." *Justice Quarterly* 18:948–68.

Harrison, Bob. 1999. "Noble Cause Corruption and the Police Ethic." *FBI Law Enforcement Bulletin* 68:1–7.

Hime, Adam. 2005. "Life or Death Mistakes: Cultural Stereotyping, Capital Punishment, and Regional Race-Based Trends in Exoneration and Wrongful Execution." *University of Detroit Mercy Law Review* 82:181–218.

Hoeffel, Janet C. 2005. "Prosecutorial Discretion at the Core: The Good Prosecutor Meets Brady." *Penn State Law Review* 109:1133–54.

Howe, Edmund S. 1991. "Integration of Mitigation, Intention, and Outcome Damage Information by Students and Circuit Court Judges." *Journal of Applied Social Psychology* 21:875–95.

Johns, Margaret Z. 2005. "Reconsidering Absolute Prosecutorial Immunity." *Brigham Young Law Review* 1:53–154.

Kurcias, Lisa M. 2000. "Prosecutor's Duty to Disclose Exculpatory Evidence." *Fordham Law Review* 69:1205–29.

LaBeff, Emily E., Robert E. Clark, Valerie J. Haines, and George M. Dieckoff. 1990. "Situational Ethics and College Student Cheating." *Sociological Inquiry* 60:190–98.

Lawless, Joseph F., and Kenneth E. North. 1984. "Prosecutorial Misconduct: A Battleground in Criminal Law." *Trial* October: 26–29.

Lofquist, William S. 2001. "Whodunit? An Examination of the Production of Wrongful Convictions." In *Wrongly Convicted: Perspectives on Failed Justice*, edited by S. D. Westervelt and J. A. Humphrey. New Brunswick, NJ: Rutgers University Press.

Lucas, Jeffrey W. 2003. "Theory Testing, Generalization, and the Problem of External Validity." *Sociological Theory* 21: 236–53.

Meares, Tracey L. 1995. "Rewards for Good Behavior: Influencing Prosecutorial Discretion and Conduct with Financial Incentives." *Fordham Law Review* 64: 851–919.

Myers, Martha A. 1980. "Social Context and Attribution of Criminal Responsibility." *Social Psychology Quarterly* 43: 405–419.

Nidiry, Rosemary. 1996. "Restraining Adversarial Excess in Closing Argument." *Columbia Law Review* 96: 1299–1334.

Pritchard, David. 1986. "Homicide and Bargained Justice: The Agenda-Setting Effects of Crime News on Prosecutors." *Public Opinion Quarterly* 50: 143–59.

Radelet, Michael L., and Hugo Adam Bedau. 2001. "Erroneous Convictions and the Death Penalty." In *Wrongly Convicted: Perspectives on Failed Justice.*, edited by S.D. Westervelt and J.A. Humphrey. New Brunswick, NJ: Rutgers University Press.

Rattner, Arye. 1988. "Convicted but Innocent." *Law and Human Behavior* 12:283–94.

Robbennolt, Jennifer K. 2000. "Outcome Severity and Judgments of Responsibility: A Meta-Analytic Review." *Journal of Applied Social Psychology* 30:2575–2609.

Sanderson, Catherine A., Adam S. Zanna, and John M. Darly. 2000. "Making the Punishment Fit the Crime and the Criminal: Attributions of Dangerousness as a Mediator of Liability." *Journal of Applied Social Psychology* 30:1137–59.

Schoenfeld, Heather. 2005. "Violated Trust: Conceptualizing Prosecutorial Misconduct." *Journal of Contemporary Criminal Justice* 21:250–71.

Webster, Murray, Jr. 2003. "Laboratory Experiments." In *Encyclopedia of Measurement*, edited by K. Kempf-Leonard. New York: Academic Press.

Zelditch, Morris, Jr. 1969. "Can You Really Study an Army in a Laboratory?" In *A Sociological Reader on Complex Organizations*, edited by A. Etzioni. New York: Holt, Rinehart, and Winston.

9

Constructing Focal Points through Legal Expression: An Experimental Test

Richard H. McAdams and Janice Nadler

The social sciences contribute significantly to the study of legal compliance. Economics emphasizes that people obey law, to the extent they do, because legal sanctions raise the expected cost of noncompliance. Psychology and sociology emphasize that people obey law because and to the degree that they perceive it as authoritative and legitimate. In recent years, a number of theorists (for example, Cooter 1998; Garrett and Weingast 1993; Ginsburg and McAdams 2004; Hardin 1989; Hay and Shleifer 1998; McAdams 2000a, 2005; Posner 2000) have begun to explore a different although entirely complementary approach: that law sometimes induces compliance merely by its ability to make a particular behavior salient. Law tends to draw attention to the behavior it demands and, in certain situations, the fact that everyone's attention is focused on a particular behavior creates an incentive to engage in it. Specifically, when the parties involved have some incentive to "coordinate" their behavior, the law's articulation of a behavior will tend to create self-fulfilling expectations that it will occur. We call this "the focal point theory" of expressive law.

One reason that social science has generally ignored the focal point effect of law is that other compliance mechanisms are frequently more important. If legal compliance were not a significant matter, then we might not care much that we do not fully understand the reasons for compliance. We might be content to know that sanctions or legitimacy generate most of the compliance we observe without worrying about what generates *the rest*. But we assume that the issue of legal compliance is a matter of paramount concern, that policymakers wish to understand to the fullest degree possible how to predict and maximize the degree of compliance that law produces. If so, then it is important to understand and measure all mechanisms of compliance, including law's "focal effect"—the degree to which the mere salience of legal rules produces self-fulfilling expectations of the behavior the law demands. (For the same reason, we should be concerned about additional compliance theories that we do not explore here, such as expressive theories of a different sort, for example, Dharmapala and McAdams 2003; McAdams 2000b.)

The second reason that social science has failed to address the focal point theory is that it is exceedingly difficult to empirically test in the field. Much of the debate about compliance concerns the relative importance of legal sanctions versus legal legitimacy. It is possible in the field to obtain measures of the actual and perceived threat of legal sanctions as well as the perceived legitimacy of law or legal actors, so one can then separate the effect of the sanctions and legitimacy and therefore test the strength of the competing theories (for example, Tyler 1990). By contrast, in the field, one cannot easily disentangle the focal point effect from the sanctions or legitimacy effect. As we explain below, it is even possible that sanctions and legitimacy work in part by contributing to the law's ability to generate salience and therefore work in part through the focal effect. Experimentation is therefore strictly necessary, at least as a first step, for exploring the validity and power of this theory of compliance.

In this chapter, we proceed as follows. Section I explains the focal point theory and its particular relevance to criminal law. Section II explains the need for experimentation in measuring the focal effect and describes the existing literature. Section III describes one of our experiments. Section IV concludes.

THE FOCAL POINT THEORY AND
ITS RELEVANCE TO CRIMINAL LAW

In this section we discuss in some detail the focal point theory and its importance to criminal law.

The Theory

The theory we test arises out of the economic theory of strategic interaction— "game theory" (see, for example, Fudenburg and Tirole 1991)—which we present in informal terms. The focal point theory of expressive law relies on four basic claims: (1) that individuals' need for "coordination" is pervasive; (2) that where individuals need to coordinate among possible behaviors, any feature of the environment that causes them to commonly believe that one behavior is salient will tend to produce that behavior; and (3) that public third-party expression, by publicly endorsing a particular behavior, tends to make that behavior salient. If so, we then argue (4) that law is one form of third-party expression capable of making salient a behavior and thereby producing self-fulfilling expectations that it will occur. We here explain each point in turn.

The Need for Coordination is Pervasive

In our experience, many theorists understand the simplest version of a "co-ordination game" but overlook how commonly an element of coordination pervades social life. In the *pure* coordination game, two individuals each make some choice where each shares a desire to "match" or coordinate their choice with the other. For example, imagine two individuals are trying to find each other and must choose between going to place A and going to place B. Or two drivers in a new society must decide whether to drive on the left or drive on the right. In each case, each individual cares only about matching their outcomes—both choosing A or left or both choosing B or right. There is no other motive than this desire to coordinate.

If the need for coordination only existed in this pure form, it would not have much relevance to the world. But in more complex situations, where the motives of the individuals in some ways conflict, there may also be an element of coordination. In other words, the world does not consist of only (1) pure coordination situations and (2) situations of pure conflict, but also (3) mixed motive situations of conflict and coordination. For this reason, the need for coordination is socially pervasive (see Sugden 1986).

Many traffic situations illustrate this mix of conflict and coordination. For example, imagine two drivers approaching an intersection on perpendicular streets where each wishes to proceed first through the intersection; or two drivers traveling on the same road in opposite directions as they approach a one-lane bridge that each wishes to use first; or two drivers merging lanes where each wishes to get ahead of the other. In each case, there is an obvious element of conflict because each wants to proceed ahead of the other. But there is also a common interest in coordinating to avoid certain outcomes. Most obviously, of the possible outcomes, each regards a collision of their automobiles as the worst. For any but the most idiosyncratic driver, crashing is worse than letting the other proceed first. Each therefore has a common interest in coordinating to avoid a collision. It is also possible that the two drivers have a common interest in avoiding the outcome where both wait for the other to proceed. Not only does that waste time for each, but after they each realize that the other is also waiting, they must face the same situation again—deciding whether to proceed first or wait—which means they again risk the possibility of a collision. Thus, even though the drivers conflict over what is the best outcome, they still have a common interest in coordinating to avoid some outcomes—the collision for sure and possibly also the mutual wait.

In addition to traffic, many "disputes" have the same structure. For example, consider a dispute between two individuals who want to sit in a public space for a time where one wishes to smoke a cigarette and the other wishes not to be exposed to cigarette smoke. Or, two neighbors dispute the exact location of their property line and one may wish to plant a tree on the contested land while the other insists that no tree be planted. Or, some workers may seek to force concessions from an employer by a strike or work slow-down, while other workers insist on working at the normal pace. In each case, it is possible that these disputes involve "pure" zero-sum conflict and no element of coordination. Those who think of coordination as an exotic and rare feature of the world no doubt see disputes in this light—that each side wants to get its way and regards the worst outcome as giving in to the other.

But disputes will contain an element of coordination if there is *any outcome* the disputing parties *jointly regard* as the worst possible result. The outcome may be highly improbable, but if it exists, then the game is no longer one of pure conflict because the disputants share an interest in avoiding this bad result. The most pervasive reason is the potential for violence. However unlikely, illegal violence is always a background risk of disputing. Much of the violence that occurs in ostensibly ordered societies involves individuals engaged in "self-help" remedies against someone whom they regard as having infringed on their rights (see, for example, Black 1983; Nisbett and Cohen 1996; Merry 1981:175–86). So, if two sides in a protracted dispute each regard the outcome of violence as possible and the costs of violence as exceeding the costs of giving in to the other (which will be true if the costs of fighting are high relative to the value at stake), each may regard fighting as the worst possible outcome. This realization does not end the dispute because each still prefers the other to give in without a fight. But each retains an interest in coordinating to avoid the fight (even though each hopes to bluff the other into giving in by the threat of a fight). If so, then the situation is mixed motive because the conflict coexists with the mutual desire to coordinate to avoid violence. So an element of coordination exists in disputes between strangers over smoking, between neighbors over land, and between coworkers over a strike.

What is true of violence is true of many other negative consequences of disputing. People may regard, for example, a heated shouting match or an exchange of profane insults as being the worst possible outcome of a dispute. This may be particularly true between people who know each other socially—

such as the examples above involving neighbors and coworkers—because a heated exchange may terminate their relationship. Thus, where the risk of violence may be a particular concern in disputes with strangers (or individuals one knows to be violent), a social breach may be a particular concern in disputes with a social acquaintance. In the latter case too, the individuals may each regard the worst possible outcome not as giving in, but as enduring the costs of unresolved disputes. Thus, even when individuals prefer to get their way in some dispute, the element of coordination remains.

Salience Produces Coordination

In situations requiring an element of coordination, anything that makes *salient* one behavioral means of coordinating tends to produce self-fulfilling expectations that this behavior will result. Decades ago, Nobel Laureate Thomas Schelling (1960) first explained the significance of these "focal points" to solving coordination problems. The simplest examples involve pure coordination games. For example, suppose you ask two people to try to name the same positive whole number without communicating. Given the infinity of possible solutions, the odds of "matching" seem to be at or near zero, but in this situation most people select a number that seems to stand out from the rest—the number one. If you ask two people at what time of day they would try to meet each other during one day if they hadn't scheduled a particular time, there again are many logical possibilities, but there is a tendency to select noon. Schelling said that these were "focal points" because some feature of the particular solution not captured by the formal structure of the situation nonetheless draws the attention of the individuals. Other research confirms that individuals do not just thoughtlessly choose the salient solution, but reason about what is likely to be mutually understood as the salient solution (see Mehta, Starmer, and Sugden 1994).

Schelling asserts that what is true of the pure coordination game is also true of the mixed motive games involving conflict and coordination—that the salience of the outcome will tend to produce self-fulfilling expectations that this focal outcome will occur. We could imagine this point by introducing a slight degree of conflict in the above examples. Suppose that two individuals are told they will receive a significant monetary payoff if they "match" in naming a positive whole number (or time of day), and zero if they fail to match. But suppose that each is told that one individual—Player A—will receive $100 if they match on an odd number and $99 if they match on an even number, while Player B will receive $100 for an even numbered match and $99 for an odd numbered match. The conflict here is trivial compared to the coordination, so we should not expect it to matter. For the positive whole number, Player B will name the most salient number—one—and accept $99 rather than name a nonfocal even number and risk getting nothing. For the time of day, Player A will name the salient time—noon—and accept $99 rather than name a nonfocal odd number and risk getting nothing. And although the size of the focal point effect is a contingent and empirical matter, there is no reason a priori to think that it disappears entirely as the magnitude of the conflict grows. So, even if an individual gets $100 from one kind of match and only $10 from another, he may expect the other to play the salient solution and therefore prefer to play it himself, getting $10 rather than nothing.

We can say the same about the actual mixed motive games discussed above. Just as two drivers in the pure coordination situation who must choose whether to drive on the left or right will tend to select whatever they believe is the mutually salient behavior, two drivers in the mixed motive situations described above—such as two drivers merging into a single lane—will tend to choose the behavior that they regard as mutually salient. Each driver would like to proceed ahead of the other, but each wants to avoid a collision. If one solution is focal—for example, the driver on the right proceeds first—then even the driver on the left, disadvantaged by that solution, will prefer it to the collision. Expecting the focal solution, the driver on the left will slow down and let the driver on the right merge first.

According to the theory, the same point should apply to a dispute, if it involves a mixed motive situation. If the two disputants wish to avoid the cost of a fight or social breach, then the existence of a focal solution to the dispute will create self-fulfilling expectations that the individuals will choose it. For example, Schelling mentions "precedent" as one obvious reason that a particular solution is focal—it is the solution everyone knows was used in the past. If the context is a place and time in which nonsmokers have always in the past deferred to smokers, then that is the salient solution. It is possible, of course, that the nonsmoker in this sense has internalized a norm of deference to smokers, but Schelling's point does not depend on that. Even if we imagine that the nonsmoker is a visitor from a culture with very different customs, if he is aware of the past behavior in this culture, and if the smoker knows he is aware of (or merely assumes he is, not knowing he is a visitor), then the influence remains. The influence will be most powerful if the two individuals have what game theorists call "common knowledge" of the same past precedent (and no other precedent), meaning not only that each knows the local custom, but each knows that the other knows, each knows that the other knows the other knows, and so on. Because the nonsmoker knows that the salient outcome is for him to defer and because he wishes to avoid possible violence or social breach, he defers.

Third-party Expression Produces Salience

Precedent is not the only thing that makes a particular solution salient. Schelling contended that third-party expression can make a solution focal and thereby influence behavior. In a sense, the third party "constructs" a focal point merely by words or acts that draw attention to a particular outcome. Most obviously, a third party can recommend or demand that the individuals coordinate in a particular way, and thereby create self-fulfilling expectations that the recommended or demanded behavior will occur.

In the pure coordination game, the influence of a third party seems obvious. As an example, Schelling proposes that two individuals are accidentally separated from each other in a department store. Relocating each other is a coordination problem; they each share the common desire to go to the same place as the other. Although they will probably find each other eventually, they may waste a lot of time doing so. Schelling then imagines that the department store owner has posted prominent signs through the store stating something like "Lost parties should reunite at the fountain on the first floor." If the individuals know each other to be literate, it is easy to imagine that this third-party expression influences the behavior of the individuals. If the sign is (or even might be) common knowledge, then it seems to give each individual a reason to look for the other at the recommended place. Interestingly, this is not a theory captured by the dominant economic concern with sanctions because the department store is not threatening to sanction anyone who fails to follow its advice. Nor is the importance of salience captured by theories of authority or legitimacy. Even if the individuals do not perceive the department store owner as a legitimate authority figure, or even if they are in the store precisely to protest its illegitimacy (for example, for its polices involving labor or the environment), the salience of the recommended meeting place gives the individuals a reason to go there.

But can third parties construct focal points in mixed games involving conflict as well as coordination? Certainly Schelling thought so, and he gave a compelling example in the traffic context. Suppose that the traffic light fails at some busy intersection and a bystander—not a police officer—steps into the intersection to direct traffic. Schelling conjectured that his hand signals would influence the drivers' behavior. As two drivers approach from different streets, each prefers to proceed ahead of the other, although each regards the worst outcome as a collision. If the drivers can both see (and see that the other sees; in short, have common knowledge of that) the bystander motioning one driver to stop and the other to proceed, then the driver who is told to stop will now have much more reason to fear that the other driver will proceed. Given that expectation, his best response is to stop, which is to comply with the third party's expression. Again, the third party appears to wield behavioral influence even without possessing legitimate authority and without threatening sanctions. Certainly, those two elements would likely increase the degree of compliance with the bystander's signals, but we should *not* predict the complete absence of compliance even if the bystander lacks any legitimate authority or sanctioning ability.

Law is a Form of Third-party Expression for Constructing Focal Points

Legal rules are human expressions. Whether the source is a group of legislators, a judge or group of judges, an executive official or an administrative agency, a party announcing a legal rule expresses how to resolve certain conflicts. The law is therefore a form of "third-party expression." If the situation the law addresses includes an element of coordination, if the law is sufficiently clear and public, and if there are no other competing focal points, the state's public declaration of a legal rule should influence behavior by providing a focal point.

These conditions do not always hold: Law may address situations of pure conflict, where there is not even the slightest element of coordination. Even if there is an element of coordination, the publicity of the law often depends largely on media coverage, which does not always exist. Law cannot create a focal point if the content of the law is generally unknown. Even if publicized, the content of the law is often unclear, especially to nonlawyers. Law cannot align expectations unless it is sufficiently clear that most individuals have the same interpretation of it. Finally, even if the law enjoys clarity, it may face strong competition from other factors that make a particular outcome salient. Most commonly, the law might attempt to change an existing norm that, as precedent for past behavior, continues to make salient the behavior that adheres to the norm.

Nevertheless, the necessary conditions sometimes do hold. Indeed, we might see law as being the third-party expression in which these conditions are most likely to hold. First, law addresses disputes, which, as we explain above, often contain an element of coordination (because each side often regards the worst outcome as some form of destructive conflict). Second, there is often great publicity to legal rules either from media coverage of the enactment of a new statute or from direct government advertising of a new rule (by public service announcements or the posting of signs). Third, although many laws are opaque, some are fairly simple, for example, the right-of-way goes to the driver on the right or no smoking in restaurants.

The last point is the most complex. Law often does compete with other focal points, such as existing norms. Law often fails to achieve compliance in these situations. But the focal point effect remains causally significant for two reasons. One is that the law often operates where expectations are not fully settled. Perhaps past behavior is not so homogeneous as to provide a focal point for future behavior. For example, if women enter a new workplace, there might be some instances of hostility that go unchallenged and some that provoke a response (for example, a complaint to a supervisor, a shouting match, violence). In this context, a new law articulating a prohibition on harassment could influence expectations in a way that diminishes harassment.

The other reason that salience matters is that law usually does carry with it the power of sanctions and legitimacy. If the other conditions hold, when we observe law change behavior, we have reason to believe that the focal effect plays some role in that change. The process should be additive, so that the force of law is greatest when it combines the effects of sanctions, legitimacy, and salience. Given how rarely the law achieves perfect compliance, any influence should have some effect. Or, it is possible that instead of being additive, there are multiple equilibria of high and low compliance with law. If so, sanctions or legitimacy might be sufficient to destabilize the existing norm but, by themselves, not quite sufficient to tip the behavior into a new equilibrium. In some cases, the focal point might make the difference between a return to the initial equilibrium (noncompliance) and reaching the tipping point where behavior shifts to a new equilibrium (compliance).

The Importance of Focal Points to Criminal Law

The focal point theory of expressive law matters in several ways to criminal law. Most simply, there may be some criminal laws that achieve compliance, at least in part, via salience. Whenever the conditions identified above hold—a situation with an element of coordination, a clear, well-known legal rule, and the absence of some other stronger focal point—we would expect that the focal point effect contributes to compliance.

To illustrate, consider our traffic examples. Traffic may seem prosaic, yet considering that automobile accidents cause 43,000 deaths per year in the United States (NHTSA Report 2006) and over a million worldwide (WHO Report 2004), compliance with the rules of the road is a serious matter. Traffic is quintessentially a matter of coordination, where drivers would most prefer that everyone yield to them but rank yielding to others as better than the collision that occurs where neither yields. And there is every reason to think that the government exploits the focal point effect for its traffic rules because (1) those rules are relatively clear and (2) the government publicizes them by requiring driver's tests and by the posting of traffic signs. Thus, without denying the effect of sanctions and legitimacy, we conjecture that the focal effect is a significant cause of the compliance with traffic laws, which is substantial despite obvious examples of violations (such as speeding). When a driver approaching a busy intersection observes a sign or traffic light indicating "stop" or "yield," she has a strong reason to comply independent of sanctions and legitimacy. Even if she has no fear of or respect for law, she fears an accident. Knowing that others expect her to comply, and that miscoordination entails a serious risk of collision, her best choice is to comply.

The focal point effect will also matter for laws that regulate externalities between individuals in face-to-face interactions. Suppose one person is engaging or about to engage in some activity that does or will cause a nearby individual to incur costs. There is frequently some positive (if low) probability that the resulting conflict will escalate to physical or verbal altercation. For example, a conflict may arise between two individuals who want to occupy the same public space—a park, bus, bus stop, or mall waiting area— where one wants to smoke a cigarette and the other wants to avoid exposure to cigarette smoke, one wants to play music or talk on a cell phone and the other wants quiet for reading or napping, or one wants to let his dog off leash and the other wants to be free from worry about contact with the dog. In each of these cases, each party wants the other to defer to her wishes, but they may jointly regard an altercation as the worst outcome. If so, then anything that influences their expectations of what the other will do—how far she will push the issue—will influence their behavior. Here the law can influence the expectations, among other ways, merely by making salient one behavioral outcome. Where a sign states that a local ordinance bans smoking or cell phone use in the area, or requires dogs to be leashed, each party may be more likely to believe that the party preferring that outcome will be less likely to back down, which gives the other party a greater incentive to back down, thus producing compliance. On the other hand, if a dispute arises in another area that is left unregulated, we would expect the opposite.

What is true of strangers can be true of acquaintances. Two neighbors may conflict over an externality one imposes on the other, as for example, loud noise. Again, if the neighbors regard the worst outcome to be a physical or verbal altercation, or even just the sacrifice of their social relationship, then the criminal law may influence behavior via salience. If the noise ordinance is clear and well known, then it may create expectations that the party objecting to the noise will not give in when the party making the noise is violating the ordinance.

The focal point theory could also matter to criminal law indirectly because noncompliance with civil law can lead to crime. A significant number of assaults and property damage occurs as one individual to a civil dispute seeks to punish the other. These are low-level vigilantes who take the law into their own hands precisely because the stakes are sufficiently low that neither side is likely to bother involving the police or courts. Imagine two neighbors dispute the precise location of their property line, or who owns the branches of a tree overhanging the property line, or whether one property owner has an obligation to block water runoff or not to block light onto the property of another. In each case, as with the public space examples, the continued conflict here risks a physical altercation—which is to say a crime. Further, because they know each other, the dispute might escalate in additional ways, such as sabotage, for example, one neighbor responding to the other side's refusal to give in by engaging in vandalism or theft. The result may be a spiral of low-level crime. One solution is not just better criminal law enforcement, but better enforcement of the property law rules that underlie the initial dispute. The focal point effect can contribute to this enforcement by making salient one particular resolution of the dispute, for example, by creating an official record of the property boundary and by stating a clear rule for ownership of tree branches and obligations regarding water runoff and access to light. Even though the disputes may be too small for either side to resort to the courts, a clear and well-known legal rule may create self-fulfilling expectations that the party the law sides against will give in to the party the law favors. Thus, the focal point effect may indirectly decrease crime by resolving disputes that lead to crime.

THE NEED FOR EXPERIMENTATION TO
TEST THE FOCAL POINT THEORY

In the real world, law is usually associated with sanctions and imbued with some level of legitimacy. Because of this, it is difficult to determine whether law can influence behavior through means independent of sanctions and legitimacy. Indeed, testing the focal point theory in the real world is difficult to imagine, because of the nearly constant presence of sanctions and legitimacy. One could imagine trying to compare a situation involving coordination, where law could potentially influence behavior by creating a focal point, to a situation not involving coordination, where law could not create a focal point. But there are many difficulties with such a comparison. One law could be endowed with more legitimacy than another for complex historical, social, or political reasons. Similarly, one law might have a stronger deterrent effect than the other, for reasons relating to perceptions about the magnitude of punishment and perceptions about the likelihood of detection. In short, the complex nature of a real world context makes it difficult to generate empirical evidence supporting the idea that law influences behavior expressively by facilitating coordination, independent of sanctions and legitimacy.

Fortunately, experimental methods provide a useful means of examining the influence of legal expression on behavior in coordination situations. In an experiment, we can construct a coordination situation involving conflict, and then hold constant the effects of sanctions and legitimacy. We can then create a focal point by highlighting one equilibrium, and observe whether making one equilibrium focal influences decisions. We argue that anything that makes a particular behavior salient can push behavior in that direction whenever the parties benefit by coordinating. The law is one of many possible sources of focal points. In the section that follows, we describe a laboratory experiment that tests the claim that making a particular behavior salient can induce that behavior in coordination situations, even when the parties' preferences conflict. In the experiment, we demonstrate this in the context of a stylized "Hawk-Dove" game, where the focal point is created by having a random spinner or a person generate a message.

The existing experimental literature provides results that are suggestive of the focal point theory but do not adequately verify its claims. Various experiments demonstrate that third-party expression can influence behavior in certain coordination situations (see Bohnet and Cooter 2001; Brandts and Holt 1992; Brandts and MacLeod 1995; Chaudhuri and Graziano 2003; Croson and Marks 2001; Schotter and Sopher 2003; Tyran and Feld 2002; Van Huyck et al. 1992; Wilson and Rhodes 1997). Yet these experiments typically involve pure coordination games or other situations devoid of conflict, which makes them poor models for judging the focal effect of law in resolving disputes. Even when they do involve conflict, as in Schotter and Sopher (2003), the level of conflict is extremely mild, not the sort of rigorous test we propose below for determining the focal power of legal expression.

In addition, existing experiments fail to isolate the different dimensions of legal expression; indeed, only two experiments even aim to model the expression provided by law. One is Bohnet and Cooter (2001), which put subjects in a situation where all prefer the same outcome, thus, without conflict of the sort law usually addresses. Bohnet and Cooter introduce law in one condition by describing to subjects a "punishment" for certain action. Given the normative dimensions of a term like *punishment,* especially when the source is the experimenter, there is a significant risk that the subjects may comply because they are deferring to legitimate authority rather than coordinating around a constructed focal point. Tyran and Feld (2002) appear to introduce conflict in the public goods game they use, although it remains unclear whether the game involves an element of coordination the theory says is necessary for a focal point effect (given that the game appears to have only one equilibrium). Tyran and Feld introduce law by having the subjects vote for particular rules, which may also create a perceived legitimacy to the resulting rule. Thus, they fail to isolate any focal effect. For additional discussion of the existing literature, see McAdams and Nadler (2005:98–103).

EXPERIMENT: GENERATING COMPLIANCE BY COORDINATING AROUND A THIRD-PARTY MESSAGE (MCADAMS AND NADLER 2005)

We began by examining whether any third-party expression (as opposed to law specifically) can help coordinate behavior in a mixed motive situation where players have conflicting preferences about the preferred equilibrium, and where both players have a shared interest in coordinating to avoid a non-equilibrium outcome. One real world instantiation of this situation is the example of a four-way intersection with a broken traffic light. Each car at the intersection prefers to proceed and for the car approaching from the other road to wait; at the same time, everyone prefers waiting rather than proceeding simultaneously and crashing. Recall Schelling's claim that a bystander who steps into the intersection and begins directing traffic might find that drivers actually comply with her hand signals directing who should wait and who should proceed. The reason for this is that by making a particular equilibrium focal (for example, car heading north proceeds; car heading west waits), each driver might now have a more definite expectation of the other driver's intentions. Specifically, because the bystander is situated so that both drivers can see her, and because both drivers know that the other driver can see her, each driver might infer that the other driver is likely to obey her signal. Thus, the driver heading north might infer that the other driver will obey the bystander's signal to wait and the driver heading north thus will proceed. Likewise, the driver heading west might infer that the other driver will obey the bystander's signal to proceed and thus the driver heading west will wait. Note that because the bystander is just an ordinary citizen who happened by, her directions are not backed by sanctions and not imbued with the legitimacy of law. In this sense, this thought experiment suggests that *any* third-party message can create a focal point to help coordinate players who have conflicting preferences.

To convert this thought experiment into a laboratory experiment, we asked undergraduate students to play the Hawk-Dove game illustrated in figure 9.1. Notice that the structure of this game is very much like the bystander in the intersection example. There are two players, called Row Player and Column Player. Each player must choose between Strategy 1 (which we refer to as "Dove" outside the experiment) and Strategy 2 (which we refer to as "Hawk" outside the experiment). Choices are made simultaneously, without knowing what the other player's choice will be. These strategies are analogous to each driver deciding to wait (Dove) or to proceed (Hawk). Each player receives a payoff that is determined by the combination of both players' simultaneous choice. (Row Player's payoffs are located on the lower left of each box, in italics.) So, if Row Player chooses Hawk and Column Player (simultaneously) chooses Hawk, each player receives a payoff of $-$1$. If both players choose Dove, then both receive a payoff of $1. There are two equilibria in this game—these are outcomes that satisfy the Nash criterion that neither player would benefit by unilaterally switching strategies. For example, if Row Player chose Hawk and Column Player chose Dove, then Row Player would receive $2 and Column Player would receive $0. From Row's perspective, given that Column Player will choose Dove, Row cannot do any better than choosing Hawk (because switching to Dove would mean receiving $1 rather than $2). At the same time, from Column's perspective, given that Row Player will choose Hawk, Column cannot to any better than choosing Dove (because switching to Hawk would mean receiving $-$1$ rather than $0). So, Row-Hawk, Column-Dove is an equilibrium outcome. This is also true of Row-Dove, Column-Hawk.

This game is parallel to the intersection example in that the Hawk-Hawk outcome is akin to both drivers proceeding simultaneously and crashing. The Dove-Dove outcome is akin to both players waiting, and then starting the game all over again. In order to get to their destination, drivers must coordinate on choosing either Dove-Hawk or Hawk-Dove. We hypothesized that players who did not have the benefit of a focal point would have a difficult time coordinating. At the same time, we hypothesized that any message that modeled the bystander in the intersection should create a focal point that helps players coordinate on a single equilibrium.

We also wondered about the legitimacy of the third party who delivers the message. Specifically, we thought that if we increased the legitimacy of the

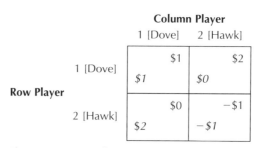

Figure 9.1.   A Hawk-Dove game. The labels Hawk and Dove appear here for illustrative purposes only—participants did not view these labels.

third-party message, compliance with the message might increase as well. To do this, we tested two different kinds of third parties that generated messages that highlighted a single equilibrium. The first message source we tested was a spinner that randomly pointed to one of the two equilibria. That is, the spinner pointed to "Row-Hawk, Column-Dove" or "Row-Dove, Column-Hawk."[1] Notice two features about this source: it is not human, and its messages are selected in an overtly random manner. The second type of message source we tested was a human being who wrote down a recommendation on the blackboard. The human being was actually one of the participants who showed up for the experiment.[2] We hypothesized that the random spinner would generate less compliance, while the human (designated the "leader") would generate the most compliance.[3]

Participants came into the laboratory and played the Hawk-Dove game against another anonymous participant. Their task was to choose between Dove and Hawk; of course, we did not label the choices this way during the experiment—the participants were told to choose "Strategy 1" or "Strategy 2." At the same time, their anonymous counterpart would simultaneously (and silently) make their own choice. Participants were told in advance that they would be paid according to the outcome resulting from their own and their counterpart's selection. Thus, players would lose $1 if both they and their counterpart selected Hawk. They would earn $2 if they selected Hawk and their counterpart selected Dove, and so on.[4]

In the absence of a coordinating device (like a bystander or a traffic signal) it is difficult to decide what to do in this game. One could decide to play Dove to "play it safe." If the counterpart does the same, then each earns $1. Of course, if one anticipates that the other person will play Dove it makes sense, instead, to play Hawk and earn $2. But if the counterpart expects you to "play it safe" and play Dove, then they might try to play Hawk; if you played Hawk as planned then both would end up playing Hawk and both would lose $2. The best choice here depends entirely on one's expectation of what the counterpart will do; but in the absence of a coordinating device or a focal point, it is difficult if not impossible to know what the counterpart will do.

When a third party sends a message highlighting one equilibrium, there now may be a reason to choose one strategy over another. So, in the spinner condition, prior to making a decision, players saw a spinner point to one of two possible equilibria: "Row Player Hawk / Column Player Dove" or "Row Player Dove / Column Player Hawk."[5] Each player had already been informed that they were randomly assigned to be the Row or Column player. Now the spinner was randomly selecting a strategy and highlighting it. We were careful to ensure that the players understood that they were not bound—by the rules of the experiment, the experimenter's expectation, or anything else—to play the strategy highlighted by the spinner. Instead they were merely told, "If you wish, you may consider the result of the spin in your decision, in whatever manner you choose. You are also entirely free to ignore it." Unlike in the control condition, in the spinner condition participants had some reason to anticipate their counterpart's choice. That is, if a player thought that the counterpart was considering complying with the recommendation of the spinner, then the player would be better off complying with the spinner also. Our results show that players were, in fact, influenced by the spinner. Players complied with the spinner—that is, played Hawk if the spinner recommended Hawk and played Dove if the spinner recommended Dove—65 percent of the time. This is significantly greater than the 50 percent compliance rate expected if the spinner had no influence on decisions.

Next we tested the hypothesis that having a person send a message would be even more effective than a spinner in making one equilibrium salient and increasing the likelihood that players will try to coordinate. The person who announced the recommended strategy was designated to be the leader. We found that players complied with the recommendations of the leaders 75 percent of the time, which was significantly greater than the 65 percent compliance rate from the random spinner. Receiving a message delivered by a random spinner increased the probability of choosing the focal strategy by 13 percent, compared to receiving no message. Receiving a message delivered by a leader increased the probability of choosing the focal strategy by 24 percent, compared to no message.

After the game, we asked players to rate how fair it was for their counterpart to disregard the message and choose a different strategy. We found that fairness judgments depended on which strategy was focal; when the message recommended Dove for the counterpart, but the counterpart ignored the message and played Hawk, this was perceived as considerably less fair than when the reverse occurred. It appears that playing Dove is perceived as basically fair regardless of the message, but playing Hawk is perceived as fair only when authorized by the message.

Overall, we see from this experiment that a third-party message can indeed influence behavior when players need to coordinate among multiple equilibria, but where their preferences conflict. In the game we tested, each player would prefer to play Hawk, but if both players choose Hawk, both are worse off. There is a need in this situation to coordinate on who will play Hawk and who will play Dove.[6] In the absence of any reason to focus on one equilibrium rather than the other, it is difficult for players to coordinate on either of them, because one player prefers one equilibrium and the other player prefers the other equilibrium. The danger is that if both players insist on their preferred strategy of Hawk, both end up worse off. And, in the absence of any ability to communicate, coordination is difficult indeed.

The presence of a third-party message helps to solve this problem, by focusing attention on one of the two equilibria. By having a message that makes a single equilibrium salient, players are more likely to choose that equilibrium than if there was no message. The third-party message created a focal point, which helped people to focus their attention on one strategy, and to think about which strategy the counterpart is likely to choose. It is notable that even in the most minimal expressive condition we tested—an overtly random mechanical device—the message influenced behavior. When the third-party message was delivered by a human being designated as the leader, the focal point effect was stronger than when the third-party message was delivered by a device that randomly highlighted an outcome. Like law, the leader's message was a product of conscious human intention. This additional element of expression contributed to the effectiveness of the message and its ability to create a focal point.

Notice that the Hawk-Dove game provides a particularly strong test of the focal point theory. This is because it is tempting to defect after one's less preferred equilibrium has been recommended. Before the fact, it is easy for everyone to agree that coordinating on one equilibrium is better than not coordinating at all. So in principle, it is easy, before the fact, for everyone to agree that they will all follow the recommendation of the spinner (or leader, as the case may be). But after the spinner (or leader) highlights one equilibrium, one player will be quite happy with this choice (the one slated to receive $2) and one will be less happy with this choice (the one slated to receive $0). For the "disfavored" player, the best thing that could happen would be for the counterpart to get cold feet and *not* follow the third party's recommendation to play Hawk. Then the "disfavored" player could take a chance and play Hawk, hoping that their own favored equilibrium outcome will result. In this way, the Hawk-Dove game represents a strong test of the focal point theory, because after the focal point is selected, half the players have an incentive to disregard the focal point. It is in some sense surprising, then, that something as arbitrary as a spinner influenced behavior in this situation involving significant conflict.

The postgame questions about fairness may shed some light on why third-party expression influenced behavior here. Recall that ex ante, it is in everyone's interest to agree to follow the spinner (or leader) in order to avoid the Hawk-Hawk outcome. Recognizing this as the best method for ensuring the best joint outcome, any ex post deviation from the recommendation of the spinner (or leader) was seen as unfair, especially any deviation that produced a Hawk-Hawk outcome. Therefore, selecting Hawk when the message recommended selecting Dove is an action that was perceived by most people as unfair. Players may have been motivated to avoid an action that others would perceive as unfair, and this may partially explain compliance with a message that recommended Dove. In situations involving coordination, the law may receive deference because it produces an arbitrary way to coordinate strategies and avoid a mutually disastrous outcome. In these situations, apart from moral obligations and threatened sanctions, people may obey law because they feel obligated to choose the most salient outcome.

At the same time, playing Dove contrary to a message that recommends Hawk was not perceived as unfair. This might be because the player choosing Dove contrary to a Hawk recommendation is attempting to produce a Dove-Dove outcome; in the particular game that we tested, such an outcome is equally as efficient as the two equilibria, and also has the attraction of distributing equal outcomes to each player. At the same time, the question remains about why the message nonetheless influenced behavior equally for both Hawk and Dove recommendations. One reason might be that players who receive a recommendation to play Hawk are more confident that their counterpart will defer and play Dove when the message is present, compared to when there is no message.

CONCLUSION

Just as the spinner in the laboratory pointed to an outcome, legal expression in the real world also points to an outcome. The results of our experiment suggest that among the many ways that law influences behavior, merely pointing to an outcome is one. The experiment did not invoke legal expression specifically. This avoidance of any reference to law conferred distinct advantages for maintaining experimental controls. Avoiding law assured that our results were not confounded with other ways that law influences behavior, such as via deterrence or legitimacy. Specifically, in the experiment we partitioned out the effect of sanctions simply by imposing no penalty or change in payoffs as a result of failure to comply with the third-party expression. Similarly, we partitioned out the effect of perceived legitimacy of the law by simply not invoking law or legal processes at all in the third-party expression. The results provide direct evidence for the ability of any third-party message to create a focal point; at the same time, the evidence that law can function as a third-party message in this situation is indirect.

In future experiments, we seek to show more explicitly that the third-party expression tested in the experiment actually models what law does in the real world. So, instead of using starkly presented normal form games, we plan to present participants with a vignette more closely modeling a real world situation. Instead of the third-party message being delivered by a spinner or leader, in future experiments law will serve as the third party delivering the message. To accomplish this, we will present participants with a vignette involving a dispute. We will examine the effect of law first in a situation where there is conflict but where there is no coordination problem that law can solve. We hypothesize that this effect would be magnified in a similar situation involving a coordination game in which law can serve as a focal point.

Law influences behavior in many ways. We believe the attention paid to legal sanctions and legitimacy, and the debate over their relative importance, obscures the causal significance of other mechanisms for compliance. In particular, in what we argue are common situations involving an element of coordination, legal expression influences behavior by constructing a focal point. By publicly announcing a state of affairs (for example, "No Smoking Here" or "The disputed property belongs to A"), law can make one of the multiple equilibria salient and create self-fulfilling expectations that this outcome will occur. It is, however, difficult to disentangle the focal power of law from its sanctions and legitimacy. We have therefore begun to test that theoretical claim with experiments that make it possible to isolate the law's focal effect. As predicted, mere expression pointing to a particular outcome influences behavior even when the subjects conflict over which outcome is best. In the experiment, we found that even an explicitly random mechanical device could cause behavior merely by pointing to it. In sum, the experiments allow us to isolate the focal effect of third-party expression and we find evidence that this effect by itself influences behavior.

NOTES

1. In the experiment, the terms *Hawk* and *Dove* were never mentioned. Instead, strategies were simply labeled "1" and "2." We use the former labels here for ease of understanding.

2. The leader was selected in one of two ways: either in an overtly random manner by drawing a numbered ticket from a box, or else on the basis of a quiz testing knowledge about current political events. Results did not differ significantly between these two types of leaders, so we do not discuss them further.

3. The leaders wrote a message on the blackboard suggesting one equilibrium. Although it appeared to the participants that the leaders chose the messages themselves, we secretly directed the leaders to select a particular equilibrium. The reason for this was to yoke the particular equilibria selected by the leaders to the very same equilibria

already selected in the spinner condition, to ensure identical timing of recommendations across all conditions.

4. Players played about nine rounds of the game. In each round the counterpart was anonymous; players were told ahead of time that they would not play against any person more than once. There were no discernable changes in patterns of play across rounds.

5. Recall that in the experiment we never used the terms *Hawk* or *Dove.* Instead we used the terms "Strategy 1" or "Strategy 2." We use the more colorful labels here for ease of understanding.

6. Of course, both could play Dove. But any player who anticipates the counterpart choosing Dove would be better off switching to Hawk.

REFERENCES

Black, Donald. 1983. "Crime as Social Control." *American Sociological Review* 48:34–45.

Bohnet, Iris, and Robert D. Cooter. 2001. "Expressive Law: Framing of Equilibrium Selection?" Unpublished manuscript.

Brandts, Jordi, and Charles A. Holt. 1992. "An Experimental Test of Equilibrium Dominance in Signaling Games." *American Economic Review* 82:1350–65.

Brandts, Jordi, and W. Bentley MacLeod. 1995. "Equilibrium Selection in Experimental Games with Recommended Play." *Games and Economic Behavior* 11:36–63.

Chaudhuri Ananish, and Sara Graziano. 2003. "Evolution of Conventions in an Experimental Public Goods Game with Private and Public Knowledge of Advice." Unpublished manuscript.

Cooter, Robert. 1998. "Expressive Law and Economics." *Journal of Legal Studies* 27:585–608.

Croson, Rachel, and Melanie Marks. 2001. "The Effect of Recommended Contributions in the Voluntary Provision of Public Goods." *Economic Inquiry* 39:238–49.

Dharmapala, Dhammika, and Richard H. McAdams. 2003. "The Condorcet Jury Theorem and the Expressive Function of Law: A Theory of Informative Law." *American Law and Economics Review* 5:1–31.

Fudenberg, Drew, and Jean Tirole. 1991. *Game Theory.* Cambridge, MA: MIT Press.

Garrett, Geoffrey, and Barry Weingast. 1993. "Ideas, Interests, and Institutions: Constructing the European Community's Internal Market." In *Ideas and Foreign Policy: Beliefs, Institutions, and Political Change*, edited by J. Goldstein and R. O. Keohane. Ithaca, NY: Cornell University Press.

Ginsburg, Tom, and Richard H. McAdams. 2004. "Adjudicating in Anarchy: An Expressive Theory of International Dispute Resolution." *William and Mary Law Review* 45:1229–339.

Hardin, Russell. 1989. "Why a Constitution?" In *The Federalist Papers and the New Institutionalism*, edited by B. Grofman and D. Wittman. New York: Agathon Press.

Hay, Jonathan R., and Andrei Shleifer. 1998. "Private Enforcement of Public Laws: A Theory of Legal Reform." *American Economic Review* 88:398–403.

McAdams, Richard H. 2000a. "A Focal Point Theory of Expressive Law." *Virginia Law Review* 86:1649–729.

——. 2000b. "An Attitudinal Theory of Expressive Law." *Oregon Law Review* 79:339–390.

——. 2005. "The Expressive Power of Adjudication." *University of Illinois Law Review* 2005:1043–121.

McAdams, Richard, and Janice Nadler. 2005. "Testing the Focal Point Theory of Legal Compliance: The Effect of Third Party Expression in an Experimental Hawk/Dove Game." *Journal of Empirical Legal Studies* 2:87–123.

——. 2007. "Coordinating in the Shadow of the Law: Two Contextualized Tests of the Focal Point Theory of Legal Compliance," unpublished working paper.

Mehta, Judith, Chris Starmer, and Robert Sugden. 1994. "The Nature of Salience: An Experimental Investigation of Pure Coordination Games." *American Economic Review* 84:658–73.

Merry, Sally E. 1981. *Urban Danger: Life in a Neighborhood of Strangers.* Philadelphia, PA: Temple University Press.

NHTSA Report. 2006. National Highway Safety Administration 2005 Projections: Overall Statistics, last accessed 6/25/06 at www-nrd.nhtsa.dot.gov/pdf/nrd-30/NCSA/PPT/2006/810583/pages/5.htm.

Nisbett, Richard E., and Dov Cohen. 1996. *Culture of Honor: The Psychology of Violence in the South.* Boulder, CO: Westview Press.

Posner, Eric A. 2000. *Law and Social Norms.* Cambridge, MA: Harvard University Press.

Schelling, Thomas C. 1960. *The Strategy of Conflict.* Cambridge, MA: Harvard University Press.

Schotter, Andrew, and Barry Sopher. 2003. "Social Learning and Coordination Conventions in Intergenerational Games: An Experimental Study." *Journal of Political Economy* 111:498–529.

Sugden, Robert. 1986. *The Economics of Rights, Cooperation and Welfare.* Oxford, UK: Basil Blackwell.

Tyran, Jean-Robert, and Lars. P. Feld. 2002. "Why People Obey the Law: Experimental Evidence from the Provisions of Public Goods." Unpublished manuscript.

Van Huyck, John B., Ann B. Gillette, and Raymond C. Battalio. 1992. "Credible Assignments in Coordination Games." *Games and Economic Behavior* 4:606–26.

WHO Report. 2004. World Health Organization Report on Road Traffic Injuries, last accessed 6/25/06 at http://www.who.int/world-health-day/2004/en/traffic_facts_en.pdf.

Wilson, Rick K., and Carl M. Rhodes. 1997. "Leadership and Credibility in N-Person Coordination Games." *Journal of Conflict Resolution* 41:767–91.

10

Comment: Exploring the Limits of Law

Lisa J. McIntyre

In 1964 the philosopher of science Abraham Kaplan introduced us to what he called *the law of the instrument:* "Give a small boy a hammer, and he will find that everything he encounters needs pounding." This law explains the fact that a scientist will formulate problems in a way

> which requires for their solution just those techniques in which he himself is especially skilled. To select candidates for training as pilots, one psychologist will conduct depth interviews, another will employ projective tests, a third will apply statistical techniques to questionnaire data, while a fourth will regard the problem as a 'practical' one beyond the capacity of a science which cannot yet fully predict the performance of a rat in a maze. And standing apart from them all may be yet another psychologist laboring in remote majesty—as the rest see him—on a mathematical model of human learning. (Kaplan 1964:28)

The tendency for researchers to be method-driven is understandable. It takes time to gain expertise in any particular research strategy and, anyway, some of us just find beauty in a well-crafted questionnaire while others can think of no more interesting way to spend one's afternoons than devising devilishly clever computer simulations. And perhaps this is as it should be because, as Kaplan points out, the law of the instrument "is by no means wholly pernicious in its working. What else is a man to do when he has an idea . . . but to ride it as hard as he can, and leave it [to] others to hold it back within proper limits" (p. 29).

Social scientists widely accept the fact that it is only through carefully controlled experiments that we can hope to assess causal relations accurately. It has even been said that the experiment is "the sole source of truth" (Poincaré 1913). But many object to the experiment because its strength is also its weakness.

"Control" means separating the variables that interest us from the usual contamination of social life. Yet, real social interaction is always contaminated by a multitude of factors. What can be the relevance of data discovered from contrived circumstances? The chapters in this volume offer convincing evidence that both criminology and legal studies can benefit from research that takes advantage of what Lucas, Graif, and Lovaglia (this volume) call the *counterintuitive logic of experimental investigations*—studying social phenomenon in "conditions as unlike natural settings as possible" in order to test a theory.

For example, in "Constructing Focal Points Through Legal Expression: An Experimental Test," McAdams and Nadler (this volume) hypothesize that the mere presence of a legal rule will influence people's behavior even when no legal sanctions are threatened. The law can do this, they suggest, by acting as a *focal point* around which people can coordinate their actions.

It is generally accepted that certain kinds of law actually are welcomed by people inasmuch as law can make it easier to coordinate, for example, business activities and make the pursuit of profit more predictable (see, for example, Friedman 2005). But the general acceptance of this notion has been based more on logic than careful evidence. Surely uniform laws regulating banks in different jurisdictions, or the uses of commercial paper have made life more predictable for business people, but would those laws have worked so effectively had they not been accompanied by a threat of sanction for those who violated them?

McAdams and Nadler designed their experiment in such a way as to tease out the effects of a focal point in guiding behavior in the absence of sanctions. They used a version of the "Hawk-Dove" game. Originally drawn from studies of animal behavior (Smith and Price 1973), this sort of game involves two players who must individually decide to follow one of two strategies in their competition: "Hawk"—to act aggressively, or "Dove"—to withdraw from danger. What distinguishes the Hawk/Dove situation from other games is that the players' choices are constrained by the fact that while playing Hawk against a Dove offers a great payoff, playing Hawk against a Hawk will result in the worst possible outcome. A familiar example of a Hawk/Dove game is the game of Chicken played by some very unwise drivers who each drive toward one another hoping the other driver will veer off. In other words, the Hawk/Dove game is such that if both players act aggressively, disaster will result.

McAdams and Nadler's experiment creates a similar dynamic—absent the risk of bodily injury. In the game each player must choose one of two strategies: Hawk (pursue one's interests at the expense of the other player) or Dove ("play it safe"). For a particular player, the best outcome is to play Hawk against a competitor who chooses to play Dove. As these researchers operationalize the possible outcome, a Hawk who plays against a Dove wins $2.

The worst outcome is to play Hawk against a competitor who also chooses Hawk (each player loses $2). If each player chooses Dove, each wins $1. As the authors point out, "the best choice here depends entirely on one's expectation of what the counterpart will do." But, they also note that the game is difficult when there are no clues to how the opponents will act.

McAdams and Nadler introduce a focal point into the game—a spinner that randomly selects a strategy for the players. Players were made to understand "that they were not bound—by the rules of the experiment, the experimenter's expectation, or anything else—to play the strategy highlighted by the spinner. Instead they were merely told 'If you wish, you may consider the result of the spin in your decision, in whatever manner you choose. You are also entirely free to ignore it'" (p. 152).

The results were significant—"Players complied with the spinner—that is, played Hawk if the spinner recommended Hawk and played Dove if the spinner recommended Dove—65 percent of the time. This is significantly greater than the 50 percent compliance rate expected if the spinner had no influence on decisions." In other words, the presence of a focal point known to both players seemed to affect players' choices in ways that were different from chance.

McAdams and Nadler then looked at the rate of compliance when, instead of a random spinner, the suggested strategy/focal point was announced by an individual designated as a "leader." They "found that players complied with the recommendations of the leaders 75 percent of the time, which was significantly greater than the 65 percent compliance rate from the random spinner." Their hypothesis is that leaders gained more compliance than the inanimate spinner because "like law, the leader's message was a product of conscious human intention."

After the experiment, the researchers debriefed players by asking about their reactions to players who had deviated from the spinner's or the leader's suggested strategy. Participants suggested that players who deviated from the suggested strategy in order to gain an advantage (for example, chose to play Hawk when the spinner or leader had proposed they play Dove) were seen as playing unfairly: "Players may have been motivated to avoid an action that others would perceive as unfair, and this may partially explain compliance with a message that recommended Dove" (p. 150). From this, they conclude that "In situations involving coordination, the law may receive deference because it produces an arbitrary way to coordinate strategies and avoid a mutually disastrous outcome. In these situations, apart from moral obligations and threatened sanctions, people may obey law because they feel obligated to choose the most salient outcome" (p. 151).

In "Can You Study a Legal System in a Laboratory?" Lucas, Graif, and Lovaglia tackled the problem of prosecutorial misconduct. More specifically, they tested the hypothesis that the probability for such misconduct varies with the seriousness of the alleged crime. The experimental design was elegant: Participants were randomly assigned to "prosecute" either an assault or murder case. The facts of the two cases were identical, save that in the case of the assault the victim lived while in the case of the murder the victim died.

We know that prosecutorial misconduct has been found more frequently in serious cases, although as Lucas, Graif, and Lovaglia admit, we don't know whether such misconduct is more likely to occur in serious cases or whether it is found because higher stakes bring more scrutiny (after the fact, at least). Lucas, Graif, and Lovaglia's experiment suggests, however, that the urge to misbehave in prosecuting a criminal case might well increase as the severity of the alleged offense increases.

More specifically, they found that prosecutors in the murder case were more likely to believe in the guilt of the defendant, had more personal investment in convicting the defendant, and were more likely to knowingly violate the law in pursuing the conviction than prosecutors in assault cases.[1]

The idea that it is more important to obtain a conviction for a serious crime than for a minor crime is hardly a novel one in our society. In fact, the principle is implicit in the organization of courts in most jurisdictions: Less experienced lawyers are allowed to learn their craft in misdemeanor and juvenile courts where the stakes are considered to be relatively low. However, when it comes to more serious offenses only the experienced lawyers are allowed to prosecute.

The juxtaposition of these two chapters led me to consider Lucas, Graif, and Lovaglia's findings about prosecutorial misconduct in light of McAdams and Nadler's observations about law's ability to influence people's decision making.

If ever law has a role to play as a focal point, it ought to be in the criminal courts. And yet many of the naïve prosecutors studied by Lucas, Graif, and Lovaglia chose to not just ignore but violate law in order to win their cases. Violations were more frequent when these prosecutors felt as if they had a personal investment in the outcome and it seems that they were more likely to be personally invested in the more serious cases. Thus, prosecutorial misconduct was more likely to occur in the more serious cases. This finding is more than a little alarming given that the consequences for the accused in murder cases can be much more severe than in cases of assault. This is a finding worthy of being taken note of by those who oversee prosecutors, especially given that it is likely that attorneys prosecuting more serious offenses, because of their seniority and experience, are apt to receive less supervision. Moreover, if this tendency exists among those who prosecute, it may well be that the urge to convict in serious cases may taint the objectivity of judges and jurors. This possibility makes it all the more important that we understand what other factors affect choices to violate the law by prosecutors.[2]

Horne and Lovaglia suggest that "good research" is research that "solves important problems." In and of itself, no experiment is likely to solve an important problem; nor can any survey or observation. Horne and Lovaglia correctly observe that, "researchers in law and criminology have a toolbox of methods at their disposal." While I am not optimistic that any amount of evidence will compel individual researchers to rummage around in their tool box to pull out something different, I am persuaded that the search for solutions would be facilitated by more talk among researchers pursuing different approaches, including different methodological approaches to the problem.

NOTES

1. Parenthetically, one wonders whether the variable being measured is "severity of crime" or an expression of society's repugnance for murder—with apologies to Justice Brennan's point, "death is different" *(Furman v Georgia,* 408 U.S. 238 [1972]). It would be interesting to see a test of this theory when the different offenses were merely quantitatively different rather than, as I suspect they are, qualitatively different.

2. Paradoxically, defense lawyers also seem to become more heavily invested in the course of defending clients accused of the most serious crimes. I've explored the ways in which this occurs elsewhere (McIntyre 1987).

REFERENCES

Donninger, Christian. 1986. "Is It Always Efficient to Be Nice?" In *Paradoxical Effects of Social Behavior: Essays in Honor of Anatol Rapoport*, edited by A. Dickman and P. Mitter. Heidelberg: Physica Verlag.

Friedman, Lawrence M. 2005. *The History of American Law,* 3rd ed. New York: Touchstone.

Kaplan, Abraham. 1964. *The Conduct of Inquiry: Methodology for Behavioral Sciences.* Scranton, PA: Chandler Publishing Company.

Mauer, Stephen B., and Albert W. Tucker. 1983. "An Interview with Albert W. Tucker." *The Two-Year College Mathematics Journal* 13:210–24.

McIntyre, Lisa J. 1987. *The Public Defender: The Practices of Law in the Shadows of Repute.* Chicago: University of Chicago Press.

Poincaré, Henri. [1913] 1982. *The Foundations of Science.* Washington, DC: University Press of America.

Smith, John Maynard, and George Price. 1973. "The Logic of Animal Conflict." *Nature* 246:15–18.

IV

CONCLUDING REMARKS

11

Whither Experiments in Crime, Deviance, and Law?

Christine Horne and Michael J. Lovaglia

Experimental methods can contribute to knowledge gain in criminology and law. In this volume, the experimental research and the comments of noted researchers working with other methods highlight existing progress and suggest avenues of further advance. Studying crime, deviance, and law entails enormous challenges in developing good measures, disentangling causal relations, and identifying causal mechanisms. Research in natural settings is vital to provide basic knowledge and will continue to be important. But while that research has produced evidence regarding the importance of particular variables, it has been less successful in specifying causal relations and the mechanisms responsible for observed correlations (Sampson 2000). Because laboratory experiments can efficiently develop causal theories, they can complement the knowledge gained through field experiments and other methods.

More laboratory research alone cannot produce a spurt of knowledge growth in the field. Also needed is increased communication among theorists and researchers using different methods. As social research increases in volume and sophistication, individual researchers become more specialized. Successful research areas branch off as subfields that produce subfields of their own. Research methods become ever more rigorous and technical. Because of those technical demands, fewer researchers will work in more than one research area or with more than one research method. Increased specialization in all sciences continues despite constant promotion of interdisciplinary research. Ironically, the result of successful interdisciplinary research is a new specialty area. Sciences progress rapidly when researchers using a variety of methods appreciate the work of colleagues using other methods and use that work to inform their own (Szmatka and Lovaglia 1996). In this volume, the interplay of experimental research and comments by researchers using traditional methods suggests areas where understanding across methodologies will help to develop knowledge in law and criminology.

EXPERIMENTER BIAS

Rather than increasing understanding, are experimenters doomed to create experimental settings that confirm their preferred theory? To the extent that researcher bias is a problem, what can be done to protect against it?

Neutralizing the biases of individual researchers is perhaps the greatest achievement of science. Researcher bias is as big a threat to valid results for experimenters as it is to all other researchers. The myth that individual scientists manage to be objective has been dismantled during the last fifty years as the behavior of scientists themselves has been studied more scientifically (Barnes 1974). Given the control afforded by a laboratory, experimenter bias might be even more of a problem than for researchers with less control over the conditions of their research. Science's answer to researcher bias is the same for all methods. More research by diverse researchers with different biases eventually weeds out invalid results. The system is messy, as famous scientific scandals have shown, but remarkably effective as demonstrated by stunning solutions to difficult research problems.

Galison (1987) explains the difficulty for individual researchers. If an experiment provides convincing results that the theory being tested is correct, then the researcher ends the experiment and publishes. If results do not support the theory, then the researcher has a number of questions to answer. Was the experimental setting an adequate test of the theory? If no, then design a better one and continue experimenting. Was the theory inadequate to explain the phenomenon? If no, then further develop the theory and continuing experimenting. Are the results, although unexpected and inconclusive, sufficiently interesting to help other researchers progress? If so, then end the experiment and publish despite the criticism that will follow, while designing a new experiment to clarify understanding. The decision to end an experiment is always subjectively taken by the researcher. The result is that experimenters, as much or more than other researchers, publish results that support their theories. How might criminology incorporate programs of experimentation to neutralize the inevitable bias of individual researchers?

Consider Gottfredson and Hirschi's general theory of crime. The studies in this volume find modest support for the theory. Fetchenhauer, Simon, and Fetchenhauer find that the correlation between self-control and cheating is positive, but it is only marginally significant. They also find, however, that in the immediate reward condition, as predicted, the correlation between self-control and cheating is statistically significant.

Kalkhoff and Willer find that self-control reduces cheating when there is no chance of being punished. That is, when punishment is uncertain, people with low self-control are more likely to cheat than individuals with high self-control. This finding is consistent with the theoretical prediction that people with low self-control are more likely to engage in deviance. But self-control has no correlation with cheating in conditions where punishment is certain. That is, the threat of a future punishment *did* deter low self-control individuals just as it did high self-control individuals. This finding seems inconsistent with Gottfredson and Hirschi's (1990) expectation that people with low self-control are less "governed by the restraints imposed by the consequences of acts" (p. xv).

How might researchers respond to these results? Hirschi (this volume) has two criticisms. First, the findings could be due to the tendency of experimentalists to design studies that confirm their own biases. What about the design of the two studies could have reduced the likelihood that they would support Hirschi's theory? By asking that question, we have begun the interplay of theoretical development and experimentation that characterizes rapidly advancing sciences.

Thinking about the experimental design, a likely possibility comes to mind. Many basic social science experiments use college undergraduates as participants. Whether the participant pool impacts the results is a theoretical question. What about the choice of participants could have interacted with the variables in the experiment, reducing support for Hirschi's theory? Undergraduates at a top university are characterized by a high degree of self-control relative to their noncollege peers. Because college students might be different than typical criminals in ways relevant to theoretically important variables, the experiments' results may not reflect the processes that engender crime outside the laboratory.

Given that the results of well-designed experiments seem to question the predictions of a theory supported by research using other methods, what should we do? All results from any method are evidence, no more and no less. Evidence can be weighed and interpreted to increase understanding. Rather than dismiss inconvenient results, a rapidly progressing discipline investigates. Hirschi's theory has many supporters. How might they design an experiment that would provide a better test? If use of college student subjects is theoretically problematic, researchers could design a similar experiment but use different kinds of participants, perhaps recruiting them in shopping malls or sports events. With more diverse participants, a wider range of self-control will be observed, presumably giving the theory a greater chance for support. A rapidly progressing field would do such an experiment quickly.

Hirschi's second criticism suggests that the experimenters in this volume misunderstood the theory. This is likely, as no one understands a theory as well as its creator. Experimental results are most compelling tests of theories when theorists, experimenters, and the scientific audience agree *in advance* that a particular research design will decide a theoretical question. If the designs of current experiments are inadequate to test Hirschi's theory, then what would be an adequate design? Thinking about an ideal experimental design is an excellent way for theorists to refine their theories. Communicating those ideas to experimenters would increase the rate of progress in the field.

At a general level, the cure for experimenter error and bias is the same as it is for those using other methods—competition among researchers. A researcher cannot forever get away with research that confirms their invalid theories when others are producing contradictory results. When different researchers with different biases ask the same questions, they may come up with different answers. As they test their theories—and try to disprove those of their competitors—beliefs are challenged. Researchers strive to explain others's findings that appear to undermine their theories. As they do so, theories are refined and improved. Knowledge grows.

THE ARTIFICIAL AND THE CONCRETE

Experiments create artificial settings. This artificiality gives experimental results their power to convince because most extraneous causes for observed results can be ruled out (Lovaglia 2003). Some settings appear less similar to a relevant natural setting than others. McAdams and Nadler (this volume), for example, present an abstract theory that treats law as a producer of focal points. They test their theory by having subjects play an abstract game. The game looks very different from anything we might encounter in a legal context. Lucas, Graif, and Lovaglia (this volume), by contrast, start with a more concrete issue—prosecutorial misconduct in serious cases. Their experimental setting to some extent mimics the real world. Younts's experiment on justifications of deviance falls somewhere between the two. In designing an experiment, researchers create settings that incorporate relevant variables from the theory being tested, while trying to exclude as many other variables as possible.

The artificiality of experiments creates opportunities and challenges. One set of challenges has to do with how participants perceive the experimental setting. Bursik (this volume) points out that college students are not naive experimental subjects. In this day and age, students who have learned about Milgram and Asch are aware that what an experiment appears to be about may not be what it is about at all. Students may try to figure out what is really going on. They may be suspicious. This may be particularly true for experiments that attempt to create situations that feel more "real." That is, the more that an experiment relies on a "cover story," the more opportunity there is for the subject to disbelieve that story. To the extent that this problem exists, it may or may not invalidate the experimental results. In weighing the evidence from an experiment, the theorist asks how a participant's suspicion might alter her responses.

For example, if as Bursik (this volume) suggests, students in Younts's study were suspicious, we might expect that suspicion to affect overall levels of cheating instruction across the experiment. Thus the effect of suspicion would be similar in all experimental conditions. The theorist then thinks about how participants' suspicions might differ in one experimental condition compared to another. Those ideas can then be used to develop better experiments and as a bonus may lead to new theoretical ideas. Communication among theorists and researcher improves both theoretical development and research design.

Participant suspicion may be less a problem than most researchers realize. Just as survey researchers have tools to assess validity issues such as respondents wanting to present themselves in a desirable light, so too do experimenters have tools for assessing the credibility of their experimental setting. They pre-test the experiment, asking participants for their impressions while they participate. Experimenters administer questionnaires to participants at the end of the experiment to determine their degree of suspicion and the effects it may have had on their responses. Experimenters also debrief participants after an experiment asking for their impressions of and feelings about their experience. A trained experimenter knows quite accurately the level of participant suspicion, often surprisingly low. Further, the Internet has made life easier for experimenters. As the Internet has become an important part of people's lives, they consider their interactions via computer increasingly real.

COMPLEXITY AND SIMPLICITY

Is it possible to study something as complex as crime in the lab? As Bursik (this volume) points out, crime research typically considers a large number of independent variables. Is it feasible to design an experiment that would include all the variables that crime researchers typically include? The answer, as Bursik indicates, is no. The problem of complexity is shared by a number of scientific disciplines. Think of the complexity of life forms that over-whelmed biologists prior to Darwin.

Fortunately, a rapidly advancing discipline need not include all those variables in every study. One of the reasons that researchers include so many variables in statistical analyses is that they are controlling for the effects of some variables so that the effects of other more theoretically relevant variables can be assessed. Along with statistical control, experiments provide an additional form of control. Experiments use design and random assignment of participants to experimental conditions to control for unobserved variables. Thus experiments can focus on a few theoretically relevant variables having controlled for much possible variation without having to assess each of those additional variables.

But aren't some of those other variables relevant to a valid theory? Undoubtedly, and those variables that are identified in studies conducted in natural settings become the basis for developing theories. Experimenters then test the causal impact of different variables in a number of studies in the lab. Experimental results are used to further refine valid theories that can, in turn, be applied in naturally occurring settings. Progress accelerates.

In other words, experiments tend to start simple—identifying key factors and testing their effects, and then adding complexity. Through this process, experimental research programs cumulate knowledge. Other methods start with more complexity—incorporating all the factors that might matter. Each approach can inform the other.

The implication is that experimenters do not need to include all of the independent variables that crime researchers typically incorporate. Instead, they can focus specifically on those that are theoretically relevant, or those that will be most useful for helping us disentangle particular causal mechanisms of interest. In other words, while ethnographers might restrict themselves to a limited number of neighborhoods (Bursik, this volume), experimenters restrict themselves to a limited number of potentially causal factors.

Suppose, for example, that we wanted to look at the effects of neighborhood racial composition on people's perceptions of whether others would support their control efforts, and whether expectations of such support would affect their sanctioning behavior (Horne, this volume). Suppose also that existing research has found a correlation between informal control and the racial makeup of neighborhoods in American cities. In these cities, race is confounded with other factors. It is therefore very difficult to determine why it is correlated with crime. To investigate the underlying mechanisms, we could create an experimental setting in which people were randomly assigned to groups with varying racial compositions. We could see whether people in majority white groups had different perceptions of support for sanctioning than those in majority black groups, and if these perceptions, in turn, affected sanctioning.

If the theory is supported, then we would have more confidence that people's expectations regarding others' support for sanctioning matters for producing informal control, and that such perceptions vary with racial composition. Thus we would have evidence of a mechanism that could account for neighborhood racial composition on informal control. If the evidence is inconsistent with the theory, then we would need to think again. We would need to develop new ideas and new experimental designs to help us account for observed correlations between race and informal control.

In other words, we could conduct experiments strategically—focusing on distinguishing mechanisms in a way that we cannot do effectively using other methods. A research team including researchers with expertise in surveys, ethnographic methods, and lab experiments might be able to design a series of studies taking advantage of the strengths of the different methods to fill in gaps that a single method would leave. As McIntyre (this volume) points out, researchers tend to be fond of their methods. Szmatka and Lovaglia (1996) showed how protective researchers can be of their methodological turf. Researchers are invested in their methods. Therefore, we would not expect a single researcher to be able to use more than one method; but a team of researchers could. More generally, a discipline that appreciates many kinds of evidence will weigh all of it and use it to progress.

CONCLUSION

Researchers recognizing the value of experimental design have advocated increased use of field experiments. Field experiments are a useful tool, as are surveys, ethnographies, and other traditional methods. Moreover, field experiments are the best way to assess the value of new policies related to crime and law. A system that produced a constant stream of field experiments to test the effectiveness of legal innovations could produce social progress similar to the way the system of clinical trials has spurred medical progress.

Research in criminology, deviance, and law would progress more rapidly if, along with systematic field experiments, a number of laboratory research programs grew up as well. Historically, scholars interested in crime and deviance have used lab experiments (Steffensmeier and Terry 1975). Among criminologists, such experiments fell out of fashion for a time—even as researchers in other social science disciplines embraced them and forged ahead. The value of experiments has not changed. Further, technology is rapidly increasing our ability to conduct good experiments while bringing down their cost.

Lab experiments are thought to be high on internal validity and low on external validity (Farrington, this volume). Survey methods may be the reverse (see Bursik's quote of Weisburd 2005, this volume). (It is interesting to note that Campbell's original discussion of internal and external validity concerns threats to validity when using methods *other* than well-controlled laboratory experiments.) When researchers appreciate the results of different methods with different strengths, it offsets the weaknesses associated with any one method.

Both theory and existing findings regarding patterns of correlations in natural settings might provide guidance toward the most pressing questions. If criminologists observe correlations, but cannot disentangle the causal mechanisms responsible for those correlations, experiments can help to do so. As in so many other scientific disciplines, increased communication across disciplinary and methodological divides, as well as coordination among theorists and practitioners of various methods, can accelerate understanding and innovation in criminology, deviance, and law.

REFERENCES

Barnes, Barry. 1974. *Scientific Knowledge and Sociological Theory*. London: Routledge and Kegan Paul.

Galison, Peter L. 1987. *How Experiments End*. Chicago: University of Chicago Press.

Gottfredson, Michael R., and Travis Hirschi. 1990. *A General Theory of Crime*. Stanford, CA: Stanford University Press.

Lovaglia, Michael J. 2003. "From Summer Camps to Glass Ceilings: The Power of Experiments." *Contexts* 2(4):42–49.

Sampson, Robert J. 2000. "Whither the Sociological Study of Crime." *Annual Review of Sociology* 26: 711–14.

Szmatka, Jacek, and Michael Lovaglia. 1996. "The Significance of Method." *Sociological Perspectives* 39(3):393–415.

Steffensmeier, Darrell J., and Robert M. Terry. 1975. *Examining Deviance Experimentally*. Port Washington, NY: Alfred Publishing.

12

Criminology as an Experimental Science

David P. Farrington

I am delighted to welcome this volume because of its contribution to the development of criminology as an experimental science. Key features of the scientific method include statements backed up by evidence, quantitative data, systematic observation, valid and reliable measurement, controlled experiments, falsifiable theories, testing causal hypotheses, and replication of empirical results. Criminology has not yet progressed very far along the road toward becoming an experimental science.

Ideally, criminological theories should be tested and refined in a program of experimental research in which each experiment builds on and extends the previous one. Loose ends from one experiment should generate testable hypotheses for the next one. I was trained as an experimental psychologist, and my Ph.D. thesis (Farrington 1969) describes twelve laboratory experiments on human learning, trying to compare and contrast continuous and discontinuous theories. To a considerable extent, each experiment was trying to resolve issues raised in a previous one, in a cumulative research program. A program of cumulative experimental research, testing theories, would be highly desirable in criminology.

This volume describes some very interesting laboratory experiments. Several of the authors raise the issue of external validity: to what extent can the behavior of students in a laboratory be generalized to behavior in real life? This has been a key issue in experimental social psychology for many years:

> Ideally, research should be high in both internal and external validity. It should be able to demonstrate unambiguously, by isolating and manipulating the variables of interest and controlling others, either experimentally or statistically, that changes in one variable produce changes in another. Traditionally, social

175

psychology research has been high in internal validity because of the use of the experimental method and the random allocation of subjects to conditions. However, in addition, results obtained in one research setting, with certain subjects and certain operational definitions of variables, should be generalizable to other settings. Social psychology has been less concerned in the past with external validity, and especially with generalization to real life, although there are signs that journals are increasingly taking this into account in evaluating manuscripts for publication. . . . External validity is even more important in applied social psychology than in social psychology in general. If the external validity of a research project is low, how far can the results be applied? (Farrington 1980:184)

There is a long history of research, often using hypothetical scenarios, in which people have been asked whether they think they would commit crimes. Pioneering studies were conducted by Horne (1970), Jackson (1970, 1979), and West, Gunn, and Chernicky (1975), for example. However, apparently the first investigation of the external validity of such verbal statements about offending in relation to real-life offending was conducted by Farrington, Knapp, Erickson, and Knight (1980). They asked youths about their stealing in hypothetical situations and also gave them an opportunity to steal (in a coin-sorting task). Surprisingly, they found that the youths who actually stole were not significantly more likely to say that they would steal in a hypothetical situation. However, this comparison was based on small numbers (twenty-five youths).

Doubts about the validity of verbal statements about stealing in hypothetical situations led me to embark upon a program of field experiments on stealing between 1975 and 1978 (Farrington 1979; Farrington and Kidd 1977; Farrington and Knight 1979, 1980a, 1980b). These kinds of studies can be traced back to the pioneering work of Hartshorne and May (1928), who devised a variety of methods of measuring cheating, lying, and stealing by children, in school, in athletic contests, and in party games. However, Hartshorne and May did not carry out any experiments. *Unobstrusive Measures* (Webb, Campbell, Schwartz, and Sechrest 1966) was another important milestone study.

Pioneering field experiments on real offending behavior (as opposed to cheating and lying) were published by Feldman (1968) and by Hornstein, Fisch, and Holmes (1968). Feldman pretended to pick up money in the street and offered it to members of the public, asking if they had dropped it. The unsuspecting participants therefore had an opportunity to claim the money dishonestly. He also gave cashiers and store clerks too much money when buying items, again giving them an opportunity to claim money dishonestly. Hornstein and his colleagues left a wallet containing cash in an envelope in the street for members of the public to pick up (see also Hornstein 1970;

Tucker, Hornstein, Holloway, and Sole 1977). This provided an opportunity for people to steal the cash.

I used these methods in England in the 1970s. In the Farrington and Kidd (1977) study, the experimenter walked past a member of the public in the street, pretended to pick up a coin, and then ran after the person, offering the coin and asking whether he or she had dropped it. The person then had the opportunity to claim the coin dishonestly. In later experiments, Farrington and Knight (1979, 1980b) left stamped, addressed, apparently lost, unsealed letters on the street, each containing a handwritten note and also (except for control conditions) a sum of money. The experimenter, who was blind to the condition of each letter, observed the personal characteristics and behavior of each person who picked up the letter. Each person could honestly mail the letter and money to the intended recipient or could steal the money.

We found that behavior after picking up the letter predicted stealing. Almost all of the participants were observed to take out the note and read it. Those who then walked along holding the letter were likely to return it, whereas those who put the letter in a pocket or handbag were likely to steal it. This suggested that the decision to steal was made immediately. The prevalence of stealing varied remarkably, from about 20 percent to 80 percent in different conditions. This suggested that, depending on the experimental conditions, almost everyone would steal or almost no one would steal.

Just as most of the experiments in this volume were designed to test ideas of deterrence, our experiments were inspired by subjective expected utility theories (Farrington 1979; Farrington and Knight 1980a). We found that stealing increased with the amount of money that could be stolen, decreased when the apparent victim was an impoverished old lady (high cost) compared with an affluent young man (low cost), and decreased when the probability of detection was greater (with a postal order compared to cash). We also found that younger people were more likely to steal than older ones, although in most cases (except when there was a large amount of money) there were few gender differences in stealing.

Criminologists should attempt to carry out more experiments to investigate theories of offending, using a realistic measure of offending as the dependent variable. The most feasible dependent variables are probably stealing and vandalism; it is hard to imagine conducting an experiment with real violence as the dependent variable, although verbal aggression might possibly be studied. Experiments on traffic offenses such as worn tires (Buikhuisen 1974) and turning against a red light (Sigelman and Sigelman 1976) have been conducted.

There have been field experiments on stealing since 1980, both using the lost letter technique (for example, Gabor and Barker 1989) and using overpayment techiques (for example, Bersoff 1999; Gabor, Strean, Singh and Varis 1986). I have not kept up with the literature, but my impression is that such experiments decreased in prevalence as ethical standards became tougher. One of the reasons I gave up these kinds of experiments was ethical concerns; for example, I had an article rejected because of reviewers' concerns that participants in our experiments were never debriefed. Another reason I gave up was because I could not obtain funding; for example, the Home Office was concerned about possible adverse publicity (about encouraging crimes) if it provided money to be stolen, and also that people who successfully stole when provided with the opportunity to do so might as a result embark upon a life of crime (!). My application for funding probably came at a bad time, since the Home Office was then abandoning randomized experiments on correctional treatment in favor of situational crime prevention, but that is another story (Farrington 2003).

There is now a great deal of interest by criminologists in conducting experiments, as evidenced by the foundation of the *Academy of Experimental Criminology* and by the establishment of the *Journal of Experimental Criminology*. However, most criminological experiments have studied policing, early prevention, corrections, courts, or community treatment (Farrington and Welsh 2005, 2006). There is surely a need for experiments that test theories of offending. This volume on laboratory experiments presents some important examples, and I hope that it will stimulate criminologists to carry out more laboratory—and field—experiments, so that we can finally get serious about the idea of criminology as an experimental science.

REFERENCES

Bersoff, D. M. 1999. "Why Good People Sometimes Do Bad Things: Motivated Reasoning and Unethical Behavior." *Personality and Social Psychology Bulletin* 25:28–39.

Buikhuisen, W. 1974. "General Deterrence: Research and Theory." *Abstracts in Criminology and Penology* 14:285–98.

Farrington, D. P. 1969. Continuity and Discontinuity in Verbal Learning. Unpublished Ph.D. thesis, Psychological Laboratory, Cambridge University.

———. 1979. "Experiments on Deviance with Special Reference to Dishonesty." In *Advances in Experimental Social Psychology*, vol. 12, edited by L. Berkowitz. New York: Academic Press.

———. 1980. "External Validity: A Problem for Social Psychology." In *Advances in Applied Social Psychology*, vol. 1, edited by R. F. Kidd and M. J. Saks. Hillsdale, NJ: Lawrence Erlbaum.

———. 2003. "British Randomized Experiments on Crime and Justice." *Annals of the American Academy of Political and Social Science* 589:150–67.

Farrington, D. P., and R. F. Kidd. 1977. "Is Financial Dishonesty a Rational Decision?" *British Journal of Social and Clinical Psychology* 16:139–46.

Farrington, D. P., W. S. Knapp, B. E. Erickson, and B. J. Knight. 1980. "Words and Deeds in the Study of Stealing." *Journal of Adolescence* 3:35–49.

Farrington, D. P., and B. J. Knight. 1979. "Two Non-Reactive Field Experiments on Stealing from a 'Lost' Letter." *British Journal of Social and Clinical Psychology* 18:277–84.

———. 1980a. "Four Studies of Stealing as a Risky Decision." In *New Directions in Psycholegal Research*, edited by P. D. Lipsitt and B. D. Sales. New York: van Nostrand Reinhold.

———. 1980b. "Stealing from a 'Lost' Letter: Effects of Victim Characteristics." *Criminal Justice and Behavior* 7:423–36.

Farrington, D. P., and B. C. Welsh. 2005. "Randomized Experiments in Criminology: What Have We Learned in the Last Two Decades?" *Journal of Experimental Criminology* 1:9–38.

———. 2006. "A Half-Century of Randomized Experiments on Crime and Justice." In *Crime and Justice*, vol. 34, edited by M. Tonry. Chicago: University of Chicago Press.

Feldman, R. E. 1968. "Response to Compatriot and Foreigner who Seek Assistance." *Journal of Personality and Social Psychology* 10:202–14.

Gabor, T., and T. Barker. 1989. "Probing the Public's Honesty: A Field Experiment Using the 'Lost Letter' Technique." *Deviant Behavior* 10:387–99.

Gabor, T., J. Strean, G. Singh, and D. Varis. 1986. "Public Deviance: An Experimental Study." *Canadian Journal of Criminology* 28:17–29.

Hartshorne, H., and M. A. May. 1928. *Studies in Deceit.* New York: Macmillan.

Horne, W. C. 1970. "Group Influence on Ethical Risk Taking." *Journal of Social Psychology* 80:237–38.

Hornstein, H. A. 1970. "The Influence of Social Models on Helping." In *Altruism and Helping Behavior,* edited by L. Macauley and L. Berkowitz. New York: Academic Press.

Hornstein, H. A., B. Fisch, and M. Holmes. 1968. "Influence of a Model's Feeling about His Behavior and His Relevance as a Comparison Other on Observer's Helping Behavior." *Journal of Personality and Social Psychology* 10:222–26.

Jackson, M. S. 1970. "The Motives of Children who Yield in Temptation to Steal Situations." *Australian and New Zealand Journal of Criminology* 3:231–37.

———. 1979. "The Perceived Behavior of Parents by Children in Moral Dilemmas." *Australian and New Zealand Journal of Criminology* 12:17–23.

Sigelman, C. K., and L. Sigelman. 1976. "Authority and Conformity: Violation of a Traffic Regulation." *Journal of Social Psychology* 100:35–43.

Tucker, L., H. A. Hornstein, S. Holloway, and K. Sole. 1977. "The Effects of Temptation and Information about a Stranger on Helping." *Personality and Social Psychology Bulletin* 3:416–20.

Webb, E. J., D. T. Campbell, R. D. Schwartz, and L. Sechrest. 1966. *Unobtrusive Measures: Nonreactive Research in the Social Sciences.* Chicago: Rand McNally.

West, S. G., S. P. Gunn, and P. Chernicky. 1975. "Ubiquitous Watergate: An Attributional Analysis." *Journal of Personality and Social Psychology* 32:55–65.

13

Thinking Experimentally

Christopher Uggen

Taken together, the chapters in this volume articulate a clear and convincing scientific rationale for experimental studies in law and criminology. If the reader will indulge a more personal perspective, however, I would like to relate my own story of "researcher meets experiments, researcher loses experiments, and researcher rediscovers experiments."

RESEARCHER MEETS EXPERIMENTS

As a wide-eyed new graduate student at the University of Wisconsin, I was fortunate to experience the sort of thrilling *gedankenblitz* of realization and understanding that I thought only great scientists could experience. In contrast to Archimedes, who famously shouted "Eureka!" from his bathtub, I was simply taking notes one day during a particularly engaging lecture by Chuck Halaby in a research methods class. I made no great discovery myself that day, but I neverthcless emerged from the assigned material on causal inference with a new perspective on social science that I have yet to shake. Then, as now, I found myself extremely skeptical of observational approaches to the study of crime, law, and deviance, and enthralled with the potential of experimental research in this area.

The shift in orientation was instant and dramatic. I knew almost nothing about lab experimentation but had learned about policy interventions and field experiments while working in social services prior to graduate school. In social services, we tend to consider social interventions as a means to serve the public good. Of course, one cannot determine whether such interventions are serving the public good or the "public bad" without conducting a rigorous analysis of their effects, so I took a keen interest in methods to determine "what works."

Upon entering graduate school, I dutifully studied survey research, panel designs, and statistical techniques such as covariate adjustment, but I was quick to jump ship when confronted with a powerful logical and statistical critique of nonexperimental methods. Upon embracing experimental methods and reasoning, I had both a legitimate license to manipulate or intervene in the world, which appealed to my inner social worker, and a powerful means to judge the success or failure of such interventions. As a sociological criminologist in training, I could not help but think of Cesare Lombroso's great moment of discovery, reported in his address to the Sixth Congress of Criminal Anthropology in 1906:

> In 1870 I was carrying on for several months researches in the prisons and asylums of Pavia upon cadavers and living persons, in order to determine upon substantial differences between the insane and criminals, without succeeding very well. Suddenly, the morning of a gloomy day in December, I found in the skull of a brigand a very long series of atavistic anomalies, above all an enormous middle occipital fossa and a hypertrophy of the vermis analogous to those that are found in inferior vertebrates. At the sight of these strange anomalies, as a large plain appears under an inflamed horizon, the problem of the nature and of the origin of the criminal seemed to me resolved. (See Parmelee 1912:25)

In my case, however, the "skull of the brigand" turned out to be Paul Holland's (1986) exposition of the Rubin/Holland causal model. With the appearance of a few simple equations and a short dictum in capitalized letters, as on a large plain under an inflamed horizon, the problem of the nature of causal inference seemed to me resolved: *No Causation Without Manipulation* (Holland 1986:959). I left the lecture resolved to devote my own researches to experiments, or at least to think experimentally whenever designing a project.

The Rubin/Holland model is attractive, in part, because it directs researchers to seek the effects of causes rather than the causes of effects. Much social research, including most of my own work, seeks to trace or reconstruct the causes of observed effects. Indeed, the disciplinary field of "criminology" is largely organized around a single dependent variable. We observe the effect—conditions of crime and noncrime—in an observational sample, and then make heroic statistical efforts to disentangle the myriad forces that give rise to it. Rubin (1974) and Holland (1986) make a convincing case that it is much more sensible for a researcher to actively manipulate a cause and then to observe its effects—to *do* something and watch what happens. In doing so, researchers can compare the effects of the cause they subject to treatment (t) with the counterfactual case in which some other cause or a control condition is applied (c).

Irving Piliavin and I offered an extended application of the model to the study of criminal desistance (Uggen and Piliavin 1998). For Rubin and Holland, the fundamental problem of causal inference is that it is impossible to observe the effects of both cause t and cause c on the same person or unit. That is, we simply cannot observe the counterfactual condition in standard observational studies. For example, if a parolee is unemployed upon release from prison and commits a new crime within a month, we cannot tell whether she would have recidivated had she secured employment.

If we could assume *unit-homogeneity*, we could measure the causal effect as the difference in recidivism rates between an employed and an unemployed parolee. But, of course, unemployed parolees are not identical to employed parolees. Alternatively, we could assume *temporal stability* and compare the criminal activity of the *same* parolee during periods of employment and unemployment. But, of course, a spell of unemployment in the first few weeks of freedom could be far more consequential than unemployment after two years of law-abiding behavior in the community.

This is why we typically try to estimate an *average* causal effect based on the expected value of the difference over everybody in a population. In this case, that would mean deviating the average number of crimes among employed parolees from the average number of crimes among unemployed parolees. This replaces the impossible-to-observe effect of employment on a person with the possible-to-estimate average effect of employment over a population. But this approach breaks down in practice because it relies on an untenable assumption regarding *mean independence*: that the average number of crimes for the employed and unemployed groups are independent of the selection mechanism that determines whether we observe treatment t (employment) or treatment c (unemployment) for a given person.

Under what conditions would the assumption of mean independence hold? If the selection mechanism is random assignment to jobs, this is a reasonable assumption. If the mechanism is one of self-selection, we are likely to encounter big omitted variable problems. In particular, working is likely to be associated with factors such as ambition or self-control that can be extremely difficult to name and measure.

Criminological research is particularly vulnerable to violations of mean independence because the processes guiding selection into levels of our independent variables are so poorly understood. Without control over the assignment of treatments, we must assume *"strong ignorability"*: that we can safely ignore the selection process into each variable of causal interest. Such an assumption would require fine-grained data on selection process into work as well as theory and data on all other factors related to both employment and recidivism.

The case of prisoner reentry might offer a best-case scenario for applying experimental methods in the field. The state has a legitimate and expansive license to intervene in the lives of former prisoners, so random assignment to strong but benign treatments such as employment is well within their purview. While treatments such as marriage are less amenable to intervention, random assignment to family support *programs* or supervision conditions is certainly feasible. While experiments on self-control, social control, and legal systems may be best administered in the sort of laboratory settings described in this volume, experimental methods remain criminally underutilized in criminal justice settings.

RESEARCHER LOSES EXPERIMENTS

Given their obvious advantages, why do so few criminologists and legal scholars employ experimental techniques? This volume of original research, along with the new studies appearing in the *Journal of Experimental Criminology,* speaks to a resurgence of interest in the application of experimental methods. An earlier collection of experimental studies on deviance (Steffensmeier and Terry 1975) reprinted powerful work that truly reoriented thinking on some central issues in the field: the Stanford prison experiments (Haney, Banks, and Zimbardo 1973), Stanley Milgram's (1965) classic laboratory experiments on obedience to authority, Schwartz and Skolnick's (1962) field experiments on legal stigma, and quasi-experiments such as H. Laurence Ross and colleagues' (1970) analysis of the British "Breathalyser" crackdown. More recent reviews (Farrington and Welsh 2005) show a significant increase in the number of randomized experiments in criminology, albeit from a low base rate. According to Farrington and Welsh, there were thirty-five experimental studies during the period from 1957 to 1981 and eighty-three during the period from 1982 to 2004.

Apart from the raw numbers, field experiments have yielded some of the most provocative and influential recent articles published in the criminology, criminal justice, and law and society literatures. Lawrence Sherman and Richard Berk's (1984) mandatory arrest experiment for domestic violence cases, Devah Pager's audit study of the effects of race and criminal records on employment decisions (2003), and David Olds and colleagues' powerful (1998) study of the long-term effects of nurse home visits on delinquency surely rank among the most important and useful articles published in criminology in recent decades.

Nevertheless, I confess that my personal resolve has weakened since graduate school and—despite my professed commitment—I have conducted precious few experiments in the intervening years. Unless young scholars receive graduate training in a lab-based research shop and retain access to similar facilities as assistant professors, they can have an exceedingly difficult time getting an experimental research agenda off the ground. Outside the lab, the difficulties are equally daunting for those doing field experiments. The experimental data that I analyzed for my dissertation, for example, cost in excess of $100 million dollars (Uggen 2000; Hollister et al. 1984). A commitment to experimental thinking, however, has nevertheless served me well, whether studying criminology, the sociology of law, or deviance more generally. Jeff Manza and I adopted a simple counterfactual approach in estimating the political consequences of laws that bar convicted felons from voting, asking whether election outcomes would have differed had the disenfranchised been permitted to vote (Uggen and Manza 2002). In criminology, when Melissa Thompson and I (2003) tried to estimate the unique contribution of heroin and cocaine use to illegal earnings, we employed a model of within-person change to address the unit homogeneity problem, albeit not the temporal stability assumption inherent in most observational studies. While it seems unreasonable to randomly administer heroin and cocaine to research subjects, lab experiments such as those presented in the chapters by Fetchenhauer, Simon, and Fetchenhauer and by Kalkhoff and Willer can certainly help elucidate the mechanisms—economic versus sensation-seeking, for example—thought to link substance use and criminal activity.

With regard to the sociology of law, similar logics may be applied in the study of legal consciousness or mobilization (Ewick and Silbey 1998). In trying to understand why some targets of discrimination or harassment remain silent and others come forward, one cannot randomly assign an experience such as severe discrimination (Edelman et al. 1999) or sexual harassment (Blackstone and Uggen 2003) in the field. While statistical selectivity techniques may be employed to mimic the logic of an experiment, however, the lab-based work on legal systems and compliance in this volume offers a tremendously promising approach in understanding legal environments and the individual and social determinants of consciousness and mobilization (Vidmar and Schuller 1987).

With regard to deviance, lab experiments on stigma offer tremendous promise in elucidating the strong effects observed in audit studies (Pager 2003; Pager and Quillian 2005), public opinion polls (for example, Manza et al. 2004), and surveys (Steffensmeier and Kramer 1980) that incorporate experimental designs. In addition to its scientific contribution, such lab work surely has the potential to facilitate the reentry and reintegration of millions of former felons in the United States.

RESEARCHER REDISCOVERS EXPERIMENTS

When students have difficulty identifying an appropriate method for their work, I often ask them what sorts of evidence they find most convincing. Most of them make some reference to experiments in their answer, but few then go on to conduct experiments in the field or in the lab. I too have long been convinced that experiments provide the most persuasive evidence on the social science questions that I consider most important. Yet, I too have rarely employed such methods for reasons of expedience and expertise.

The laboratory experiments reported in this volume constructively engage some of the most compelling theories and questions in the study of crime, law, and deviance. As is the case for many other criminologists, I may be late to the party. Nevertheless, I attempt to incorporate experimental design and thinking into every new project, making a halting but inexorable return to the Rubin/Holland model that so inspired me upon my first encounter with the dictum of "no causation without manipulation." In fact, my recent projects have involved small-scale survey experiments, the design of a networked experimental computer lab, and a large-scale experimental audit study in Minneapolis. In my view, advancement in crime, law, and deviance research hinges upon its engagement with experiments in the field and in the lab. Properly conducted, such work can serve a public criminology mission as well, creating the knowledge that makes for a safer and more just society.

REFERENCES

Blackstone, Amy, and Christopher Uggen. 2003. "'If I didn't like something, I'd tell them': Making Sense of Responses to Sexual Harassment." Paper presented at the annual meetings of the Law and Society Association. Pittsburgh, PA.

Edelman, Lauren B., Christopher Uggen, and Howard S. Erlanger. 1999. "The Endogeneity of Legal Regulation: Grievance Procedures as Rational Myth." *American Journal of Sociology* 105:406–54.

Ewick, Patricia, and Susan S. Silbey. 1998. *The Common Place of Law.* Chicago: University of Chicago Press.

Farrington, David P., and Brandon C. Welsh. 2005. "Randomized Experiments in Criminology: What Have We Learned in the Last Two Decades?" *Journal of Experimental Criminology* 1:9–38.

Haney, Craig, Curtis Banks, and Philip Zimbardo. 1973. "Interpersonal Dynamics in a Simulated Prison." *International Journal of Criminology and Penology* 1:69–97.

Holland, Paul W. 1986. "Statistics and Causal Inference." *Journal of the American Statistical Association* 81:945–60.

Hollister, Robinson G. Jr., Peter Kemper, and Rebecca A. Maynard. 1984. *The National Supported Work Demonstration.* Madison: University of Wisconsin Press.

Manza, Jeff, Clem Brooks, and Christopher Uggen. 2004. "Public Attitudes toward Felon Disenfranchisement in the United States." *Public Opinion Quarterly* 68:276–87.

Milgram, Stanley. 1965. "Some Conditions of Obedience and Disobedience to Authority." *Human Relations* 18:57–75.

Olds, David L., Charles R. Henderson, Jr., Robert Cole, John Eckenrode, Harriet Kitzman, Dennis Luckey, Lisa Pettitt, Kimberly Sidora, Pamela Morris, and Jane Powers. 1998. "Long-Term Effects of Nurse Home Visitation on Children's Criminal and Antisocial Behavior: 15-Year Follow-Up of a Randomized Controlled Trial." *Journal of the American Medical Association* 280:1238–44.

Pager, Devah. 2003. "The Mark of a Criminal Record." *American Journal of Sociology* 108:937–75.

Pager, Devah, and Lincoln Quillian. 2005. "Walking the Talk? What Employers Say versus What They Do." *American Sociological Review* 70:355–80.

Parmelee, Maurice. 1912. *The Principles of Anthropology and Sociology in Their Relations to Criminal Procedure.* New York: Macmillan.

Ross, H. Laurence, Donald T. Campell, and Gene V. Glass. 1970. "Determining the Effects of a Legal Reform: The British 'Breathalyser' Crackdown of 1967." *American Behavioral Scientist* 13:493–509.

Rubin, Donald B. 1974. "Estimating Causal Effects of Treatments in Randomized and Nonrandomized Studies." *Journal of Educational Psychology* 66:688–701.

Schwartz, Richard D., and Jerome H. Skolnick. 1962. "Two Studies of Legal Stigma." *Social Problems* 10:133–38.

Sherman, Lawrence W., and Richard A. Berk. 1984. "The Specific Deterrent Effects of Arrest for Domestic Assault." *American Sociological Review* 49:261–72.

Steffensmeier, Darrell J., and John H. Kramer. 1980. "The Differential Impact of Criminal Stigmatization on Male and Female Felons." *Sex Roles* 6:1–8.

Steffensmeier, Darrell J., and Robert M. Terry. 1975. *Examining Deviance Experimentally.* Port Washington, NY: Alfred Publishing.

Uggen, Christopher. 2000. "Work as a Turning Point in the Life Course of Criminals: A Duration Model of Age, Employment, and Recidivism." *American Sociological Review* 65:529–46.

Uggen, Christopher, and Jeff Manza. 2002. "Democratic Contraction? Political Consequences of Felon Disenfranchisement in the United States." *American Sociological Review* 67:777–803.

Uggen, Christopher, and Irving Piliavin. 1998. "Asymmetrical Causation and Criminal Desistance." *Journal of Criminal Law and Criminology* 88:1399–1422.

Uggen, Christopher, and Melissa Thompson. 2003. "The Socioeconomic Determinants of Ill-gotten Gains: Within-Person Changes in Drug Use and Illegal Earnings." *American Journal of Sociology* 109:146–85.

Vidmar, Neil, and Regina A. Schuller. 1987. "Individual Differences and the Pursuit of Legal Rights: A Preliminary Inquiry." *Law and Human Behavior* 11:299–317.

Index

Contributors

Robert J. Bursik, Jr. is Curators Professor of criminology and criminal justice at the University of Missouri, St. Louis. Prior to that, he was a research scientist at the Institute for Juvenile Research in Chicago (1978–1983) and then came through the professorial ranks in the Department of Sociology at the University of Oklahoma (1983–1996). He is a fellow and former vice president of the American Society of Criminology, a former editor of *Criminology* (1998–2003), the president of the Crime, Law, and Deviance Section of the American Sociological Association, and president-elect of the American Society of Criminology.

David P. Farrington is professor of psychological criminology at the Institute of Criminology, Cambridge University, and adjunct professor of psychiatry at Western Psychiatric Institute and Clinic, University of Pittsburgh. He is former president of the American Society of Criminology and the Academy of Experimental Criminology. His major research interest is in developmental criminology.

Detlef Fetchenhauer is professor of economic and social psychology at the University of Cologne (Germany) and part-time lecturer at the University of Groningen (The Netherlands). His research interests include evolutionary psychology and prosocial and antisocial behavior.

Felix Fetchenhauer is a research assistant at the University of Cologne. He is interested in self-insight and self-control.

Corina Graif is a Ph.D. candidate in sociology at Harvard University. She studies crime and delinquency and methodological aspects of measuring diversity, social capital, ecological systems, and spatial interdependencies.

Travis Hirschi is Regents Professor Emeritus, University of Arizona. He is author of *Causes of Delinquency* and coauthor (with Michal Gottfredson) of *A General Theory of Crime*.

John Hoffmann is professor of sociology at Brigham Young University. His research interests include delinquency theory, sociology of religion, and visual studies.

Christine Horne is an associate professor in the Department of Sociology at Washington State University. She is interested in the emergence and enforcement of social norms. Her research develops theoretical understanding, tests theoretical predictions in experimental settings, and applies theoretical insights to explain naturally occurring norms. Her work has appeared in a variety of outlets including *Social Forces*, *European Sociological Review*, and *Social Psychology Quarterly*. She is coeditor of *Theories of Social Order*.

Will Kalkhoff is assistant professor of sociology at Kent State University. His research interests include developing and testing structural social psychological theories, biosociology, experimental methods, and deviant behavior. He is currently working on developing a biosocial explanation of affect and social exchange (with Shane R. Thye) and on testing a theoretical integration of status characteristics theory and social influence network theory (with Noah E. Friedkin and Eugene C. Johnsen).

Michael J. Lovaglia, professor of sociology at the University of Iowa, investigates power and status and how fundamental group processes can be applied to problems in areas such as educational achievement, leadership, and crime. His latest articles on leadership diversity have appeared in *Advances in Group Processes*. See also "Misconduct in the Prosecution of Severe Crimes: An Experimental Study" in *Social Psychology Quarterly* 69:97–107. Rowman & Littlefield has published the second edition of his book, *Knowing People: The Personal Use of Social Psychology*.

Jeffrey W. Lucas is associate professor of sociology at the University of Maryland. His research, which is primarily experimental, focuses on the basic nature of fundamental social processes, particularly status, power, and leadership.

Richard H. McAdams is Bernard D. Meltzer Professor at the University of Chicago Law School.

Lisa J. McIntyre is associate professor in the department of sociology at Washington State University. Her previous works include *Law in the Sociological Enterprise* and *The Public Defender: The Practice of Law in the Shadows of Repute*.

Janice Nadler is a research fellow at the American Bar Foundation and professor of law at Northwestern University School of Law. Her research lies at the intersection of law and psychology and focuses on compliance with the law, perceptions of justice, and negotiation.

James F. Short, Jr. is professor emeritus of sociology at Washington State University. He is a former president of the American Sociological Association and the American Society of Criminology and former editor of the *American Sociological Review*.

Joseph Simon is an independent marketing consultant. His main interests are self-control, consumer preferences, and perceptions of foods and beverages.

Christopher Uggen is Distinguished McKnight Professor and Chair of the University of Minnesota Sociology Department. He studies crime, law, and deviance, especially how former prisoners manage to put their lives back together. With Jeff Manza, he is the author of *Locked Out: Felon Disenfranchisement and American Democracy* (2006). His other research, teaching, and advising interests include crime and drug use, discrimination and inequality, and sexual harassment.

Robb Willer is assistant professor of sociology at the University of California, Berkeley. Recently his research has focused on how reputation and status motivate and reward prosocial behavior, the dynamics of unpopular norms, and masculine overcompensation.

C. Wesley Younts is assistant professor of sociology at the University of Connecticut. He is conducting several experimental studies in the recently established Group Process Research Lab in the sociology department at the University of Connecticut, including studies on the effects of interdependence, group cohesion, and social validation on deviant behavior and the transmission of deviance norms.